T0309547

BASIC SIMPLE TYPE THEORY

Cambridge Tracts in Theoretical Computer Science

Editorial Board

S. Abramsky, *Department of Computing Science, Edinburgh University*
P. H. Aczel, *Department of Computer Science, University of Manchester*
J. W. de Bakker, *Centrum voor Wiskunde en Informatica, Amsterdam*
J. A. Goguen, *Programming Research Group, University of Oxford*
Y. Gurevich, *Department of Electrical Engineering and Computer Science, University of Michigan*
J. V. Tucker, *Department of Mathematics and Computer Science, University College of Swansea*

Titles in the series

1. G. Chaitin *Algorithmic Information Theory*
2. L. C. Paulson *Logic and Computation*
3. M. Spivey *Understanding Z*
4. G. Revesz *Lambda Calculus, Combinators and Functional Programming*
5. A. Ramsay *Formal Methods in Artificial Intelligence*
6. S. Vickers *Topology via Logic*
7. J.-Y. Girard, Y. Lafont & P. Taylor *Proofs and Types*
8. J. Clifford *Formal Semantics & Pragmatics for Natural Language Processing*
9. M. Winslett *Updating Logical Databases*
10. K. McEvoy & J. V. Tucker (eds) *Theoretical Foundations of VLSI Design*
11. T. H. Tse *A Unifying Framework for Stuctured Analysis and Design Models*
12. G. Brewka *Nonmonotonic Reasoning*
14. S. G. Hoggar *Mathematics for Computer Graphics*
15. S. Dasgupta *Design Theory and Computer Science*
17. J. C. M. Baeten (ed) *Applications of Process Algebra*
18. J. C. M. Baeten & W. P. Weijland *Process Algebra*
19. M. Manzano *Extensions of First Order Logic*
21. D. A. Wolfram *The Clausal Theory of Types*
22. V. Stoltenberg-Hansen, I. Lindström & E. Griffor *Mathematical Theory of Domains*
23. E.-R. Olderog *Nets, Terms and Formulas*
26. P. D. Mosses *Action Semantics*
27. W. H. Hesselink *Programs, Recursion and Unbounded Choice*
28. P. Padawitz *Deductive and Declarative Programming*
29. P. Gärdenfors (ed) *Belief Revision*
30. M. Anthony & N. Biggs *Computational Learning Theory*
31. T. F. Melham *Higher Order Logic and Hardware Verification*
32. R. L. Carpenter *The Logic of Typed Feature Structures*
33. E. G. Manes *Predicate Transformer Semantics*
34. F. Nielson & H. R. Nielson *Two Level Functional Languages*
35. L. Feijs & H. Jonkers *Formal Specification and Design*
36. S. Mauw & G. J. Veltink (eds) *Algebraic Specification of Communication Protocols*
37. V. Stavridou *Formal Methods in Circuit Design*
38. N. Shankar *Metamathematics, Machines and Gödel's Proof*
39. J. B. Paris *The Uncertain Reasoner's Companion*
40. J. Desel & J. Esparza *Free Choice Petri Nets*
41. J.-J. Ch. Meyer & W. van der Hoek *Epistemic Logic for AI and Computer Science*
42. J. R. Hindley *Basic Simple Type Theory*

BASIC SIMPLE TYPE THEORY

J. Roger Hindley
University of Wales, Swansea

CAMBRIDGE
UNIVERSITY PRESS

PUBLISHED BY THE PRESS SYNDICATE OF THE UNIVERSITY OF CAMBRIDGE
The Pitt Building, Trumpington Street, Cambridge CB2 1RP, United Kingdom

CAMBRIDGE UNIVERSITY PRESS
The Edinburgh Building, Cambridge CB2 2RU, United Kingdom
40 West 20th Street, New York, NY 10011-4211, USA
10 Stamford Road, Oakleigh, Melbourne 3166, Australia

© Cambridge University Press 1997

This book is in copyright. Subject to statutory exception
and to the provisions of relevant collective licensing agreements,
no reproduction of any part may take place without
the written permission of Cambridge University Press.

First published 1997

Typeset in 10/13 point Times

A catalogue record for this book is available from the British Library

Library of Congress Cataloguing in Publication data

Hindley, J. Roger.
Basic simple type theory / J. Roger Hindley.
p. cm. – (Cambridge tracts in theoretical computer science ; 42)
Includes bibliographical references and index.
ISBN 0 521 46518 4
1. Programming languages (Electronic computers) 2. Type theory.
I. Title. II. Series.
QA76.7.H55 1996
005.13–dc20 95-9058 CIP

ISBN 0 521 46518 4 hardback

Transferred to digital printing 2002

To Carol

Contents

Introduction

This book is not about type theories in general but about one very neat and special system called "TA" for "type-assignment". Its types contain type-variables and arrows but nothing else, and its terms are built by λ-abstraction and application from term-variables and nothing else. Its expressive power is close to that of the system called *simple type theory* that originated with Alonzo Church.

TA is polymorphic in the sense that a term can have more than one type, indeed an infinite number of types. On the other hand the system has no $\forall$-types and hence it is weaker than the strong polymorphic theories in current use in logic and programming. However, it lies at the core of nearly every one of them and its properties are so distinctive and even enjoyable that I believe the system is worth isolating and studying on its own. That is the aim of this book. In it I hope to try to pass on to the reader the pleasure the system's properties have given me.

TA is also an excellent training ground for learning the techniques of type-theory as a whole. Its methods and algorithms are not trivial but the main lines of most of them become clear once the basic concepts have been understood. Many ideas that are complicated and tedious to formulate for stronger type-theories, and many complex techniques for analysing structures in these theories, appear in TA in a very clean and neat stripped-down form. This book will take advantage of this neatness to introduce some of the most important type-theoretic techniques with particular emphasis on explaining why things happen the way they do.

Thus the reader who learns the basic techniques of type-theory from TA will acquire a very good foundation for the study of other type-systems.

Type theories in general date back to the philosopher Bertrand Russell and beyond.[1] They were used in the early 1900's for the very specific purpose of getting round the paradoxes that had shaken the foundations of mathematics at that time, but their use was later widened until they came to be part of the logicians' standard bag of technical tools, especially in proof-theory. (Their use in combinatory logic dates back to Curry 1934 and in λ-calculus to Church 1940.) However, they remained a relatively specialist tool until around the 1970's.

About that time the need for stronger programming languages brought type-theories to the attention of computer scientists, and several of the new languages developed in the 1970's and 80's were built on a type-theory base. These languages

[1] See for example Russell 1903 Appendix B and the comments in Gandy 1977 and Church 1976.

have proved themselves in many applications and have now become well established in the research community (and are even becoming known outside it!). The chief example is ML, developed at Edinburgh University by the group led by Robin Milner, but others include HOL (Cambridge University), Miranda (Regd trademark, Research Software Ltd.) and Nuprl (Cornell University).

The system TA is, with slight modifications, a common part of all of these. Indeed, in its early days it was studied mainly as a prelude to studies of stronger systems and this is the way it was treated in Curry and Feys 1958.[1] But from the 1960's onward it gradually became clear that TA was not as trivial as it had at first seemed and was worth isolating and studying in its own right. Natural questions about TA turned out to be much harder to answer than expected. Their answers are not completed even today, but from them have come some very interesting techniques that have had applications elsewhere, such as type-checking algorithms and filter λ-models.

In fact more is now known about TA than can fit into a book of reasonable length. The present book will therefore be very selective. Although covering all the main basic properties of TA it will focus on the following three algorithms. The first is well known but the other two are scarcely known at all and their consequences are still not nearly fully understood, though they were first discovered well over fifteen years ago.

(1) *Type-checking or principal-type algorithm.* This algorithm is the core of the type-checking algorithm used in ML. It takes a λ-term and decides whether a type can be assigned to it and, if so, outputs the most general such type (the *principal type* of the term). The method behind the algorithm was sketched in Curry and Feys 1958 and versions of the algorithm itself have appeared in Morris 1968, Curry 1969, Hindley 1969 and Milner 1978.

(2) *Converse principal-type algorithm.* This algorithm takes a closed λ-term M and any type τ which can be assigned to M, and outputs a closed λ-term M^* such that τ is the principal type of M^*. Via the formulae-as-types correspondence with propositional logic it leads to a completeness proof for a variant of the Resolution rule called the *rule of condensed detachment* in a system of implicational logic. In fact several converse principal-type algorithms are known, each producing an M^* with slightly different properties and giving completeness for a slightly different logic. (Hindley 1969, Meyer and Bunder 1988, Mints and Tammet 1991.)

(3) *Inhabitant-counting algorithm.* A *normal inhabitant* of a type τ is a closed λ-term M in β-normal form to which τ can be assigned. The counting-algorithm takes a type τ and outputs the number of its normal inhabitants $(0, 1, 2, \ldots$ or infinity, modulo changes of bound variables), and then lists these one by one; in particular it decides in a finite time whether this list will be infinite or not. It is like the known algorithm for deciding whether a regular language is infinite but with extra procedures to deal with bound variables. It is also like known algorithms for deciding provability in Intuitionist propositional logic but with extra procedures

[1] Barendregt 1992 is a good survey of type-theories which shows the relations between TA_λ and others; see especially §3.1 where TA_λ is called *λ→-Curry*. Other modern introductions to type theories in general are Andrews 1986, Girard et al. 1989, Krivine 1990, Mitchell 1990 and 1996, Constable 1991, Gallier 1993, Nerode and Odifreddi 199-, Scedrov 1990.

added to do the counting. It originated in Ben-Yelles 1979 though part of the proof that it works is due to Hirokawa 1993c.

Each of the above algorithms will be presented in full with a proof of correctness included.

Acknowledgements

I am very grateful to all who have helped in producing this book, especially the following.

For invitations to give the lecture-courses from which this book has (very slowly) developed: Institut d' Informatique, Université de Tizi-Ouzou, Algeria (1988), and the U.K. Science and Engineering Research Council's "Logic for I.T." Initiative (1990).

For a period of reduced teaching duties without which the book would not have been possible: my colleagues in the Mathematics Department, University of Wales Swansea.

For finance and accommodation which facilitated some of the meetings and discussions involved: the European Community's "Esprit" Basic Research Actions 3230 and 7232, the Australian Research Grants Scheme, and the Mathematics Department of the University of Wollongong.

For useful criticisms, discussions, and helpful suggestions: Yohji Akama, Choukri-Bey Ben-Yelles, Martin Bunder, Naim Çağman, Felice Cardone, Mariangiola Dezani-Ciancaglini, Roy Dyckhoff, Fritz Henglein, Sachio Hirokawa, Hans Leiss, Mohamed Mezghiche, Seref Mirasyedioglu, Gordon Plotkin, Adrian Rezus, Jon Seldin, Masako Takahashi, Anne Troelstra, Werner Wolff, Marek Zaionc and anonymous referees. (Any errors remaining in the work are my own responsibility, however.)

For perseverance: the staff of Cambridge University Press, especially David Tranah.

And last but not least, for a healthy combination of support and cynicism, my wife Carol.

Notes on the text

Chapter 1 contains a very short summary of all the basic facts about λ-calculus needed in this book, though the reader is assumed to have met λ-calculus before. Further information can be found in standard text-books; for example (in English) Barendregt 1984, Curry and Feys 1958, Hindley and Seldin 1986, Révész 1988, Hankin 1994, or (in French or English) Krivine 1990, or (in Japanese) Takahashi 1991.

Chapter 9 at the end of the book collects together some technical details that are needed in the correctness-proofs of the main algorithms: readers who prefer to omit these proofs can omit this chapter too.

Some exercises are provided in the text. Answers to starred ones are at the end of the book.

Throughout this book "HS 86" refers to Hindley and Seldin 1986.

1

The type-free λ-calculus

The λ-calculus is a family of prototype programming languages invented by a logician, Alonzo Church, in the 1930's. Their main feature is that they are *higher-order*; that is, they give a systematic notation for operators whose input and output values may be other operators. Also they are *functional*, that is they are based on the notion of *function* or *operator* and include notation for function-application and abstraction.

This book will be about the simplest of these languages, the *pure* λ-calculus, in which λ-terms are formed by application and abstraction from variables only. No atomic constants will be allowed.

1A λ-terms and their structure

1A1 Definition (λ-terms) An infinite sequence of ***term-variables*** is assumed to be given. Then linguistic expressions called ***λ-terms*** are defined thus:

(i) each term-variable is a λ-term, called an ***atom*** or ***atomic term***;
(ii) if M and N are λ-terms then (MN) is a λ-term called an ***application***;
(iii) if x is a term-variable and M is a λ-term then $(\lambda x \cdot M)$ is a λ-term called an ***abstract*** or a ***λ-abstract***.

A ***composite*** λ-term is a λ-term that is not an atom.

1A1.1 *Notation* *Term-variables* are denoted by "u", "v", "w", "x", "y", "z", with or without number-subscripts. Distinct letters denote distinct variables unless otherwise stated.

Arbitrary λ-terms are denoted by "L", "M", "N", "P", "Q", "R", "S", "T", with or without number-subscripts. For "*λ-term*" we shall usually say just "*term*".

Syntactic identity: "$M \equiv N$" will mean that M is the same expression as N (if M and N are terms or other expressions). But for identity of numbers, sets, etc. we shall say "=" as usual.

Parentheses and repeated λ's will often be omitted in such a way that, for example,

$$\lambda xyz \cdot M \equiv (\lambda x \cdot (\lambda y \cdot (\lambda z \cdot M))), \quad MNPQ \equiv (((MN)P)Q).$$

(The rule for restoring parentheses omitted from $MNPQ$ is called *association to the left*.)

1A2 Definition The ***length***, $|M|$, of a λ-term M is the number of occurrences of variables in M; in detail, define

$$|x| = 1, \quad |MN| = |M| + |N|, \quad |\lambda x \cdot M| = 1 + |M|.$$

1A2.1 *Example* $|(\lambda x \cdot yx)(\lambda z \cdot x)| = 5$.

1A3 Definition (Subterms) The ***subterms*** of a term M are defined by induction on $|M|$ as follows:

(i) an atom is a subterm of itself;
(ii) if $M \equiv \lambda x \cdot P$, its subterms are M and all subterms of P;
(iii) if $M \equiv P_1 P_2$, its subterms are all the subterms of P_1, all those of P_2, and M itself.

1A3.1 *Example* If $M \equiv (\lambda x \cdot yx)(\lambda z \cdot x(yx))$ its subterms are x, y, yx, $\lambda x \cdot yx$, $x(yx)$, $\lambda z \cdot x(yx)$ and M itself. (But not z.)

1A4 Notation (Occurrences, components) A subterm of a term M may have more than one occurrence in M; for example the term

$$(\lambda x \cdot yx)(\lambda z \cdot x(yx))$$

contains two occurrences of yx and three of x. The precise definition of "occurrence" is written out in 9A2, but the reader who already has a good intuitive idea of the occurrence-concept will go a long way without needing to look at this definition.

In this book occurrences will be underlined to distinguish them from subterms; for example we may say

"Let $\underline{P}$ be any occurrence of P in M".

An occurrence of λx will be called an ***abstractor***, and the occurrence of x in it will be called a ***binding occurrence of*** x.

All the occurrences of terms in M, other than binding occurrences of variables, will be called ***components of*** M.

1A5 Definition (Body, scope, covering abstractors) Let $\underline{\lambda x \cdot P}$ be a component of a term M. The displayed component $\underline{P}$ is called the ***body of*** $\underline{\lambda x \cdot P}$ or the ***scope of the abstractor*** $\underline{\lambda x}$.

The ***covering abstractors*** of a component $\underline{R}$ of M are the abstractors in M whose scopes contain $\underline{R}$.

1A6 Definition (Free, bound) A non-binding variable-occurrence $\underline{x}$ in a term M is said to be ***bound in*** M iff it is in the scope of an occurrence of λx in M, otherwise it is ***free in*** M.

A variable x is said to be ***bound in*** M iff M contains an occurrence of λx; and x is said to be ***free in*** M iff M contains a free occurrence of x. The set of all variables free in M is called

$$FV(M).$$

1A6.1 *Warning* Two distinct concepts have been defined here, free/bound occurrences and free/bound variables. A variable x may be both free and bound in M, for example if $M \equiv x(\lambda x \cdot x)$, but a particular occurrence of x in M cannot be both free and bound.

Also note that x is said to be bound in $\lambda x \cdot y$ even though its only occurrence there is a binding one.

1A7 Definition (Substitution) Define $[N/x]M$ to be the result of substituting N for each free occurrence of x in M and making any changes of bound variables needed to prevent variables free in N from becoming bound in $[N/x]M$. More precisely, define for all N, x, P, Q and all $y \not\equiv x$

(i) $[N/x]x \equiv N$,
(ii) $[N/x]y \equiv y$,
(iii) $[N/x](P,Q) \equiv (([N/x]P)([N/x]Q))$,
(iv) $[N/x](\lambda x \cdot P) \equiv \lambda x \cdot P$,
(v) $[N/x](\lambda y \cdot P) \equiv \lambda y \cdot P$ *if* $x \notin FV(P)$,
(vi) $[N/x](\lambda y \cdot P) \equiv \lambda y \cdot [N/x]P$ *if* $x \in FV(P)$ *and* $y \notin FV(N)$,
(vii) $[N/x](\lambda y \cdot P) \equiv \lambda z \cdot [N/x][z/y]P$ *if* $x \in FV(P)$ *and* $y \in FV(N)$.

(In (vii) z is the first variable in the sequence given in 1A1 which does not occur free in NP.)

1A7.1 *Notation* (Simultaneous substitution) For any $N_1, \ldots, N_n$ and any distinct $x_1, \ldots, x_n$, the result of simultaneously substituting N_1 for x_1, N_2 for $x_2, \ldots$ in M, and changing bound variables to avoid clashes, is defined similarly to $[N/x]M$. (For a neat definition see Stoughton 1988 §2.) It is called

$$[N_1/x_1, \ldots, N_n/x_n]M.$$

1A8 Definition (Changing bound variables, α-conversion) Let $y \notin FV(M)$; then we say

$$(\alpha) \qquad \lambda x \cdot M \equiv_\alpha \lambda y \cdot [y/x]M,$$

and the act of replacing an occurrence of $\lambda x \cdot M$ in a term by $\lambda y \cdot [y/x]M$ is called a ***change of bound variables***. If P changes to Q by a finite (perhaps empty) series of changes of bound variables we say P ***α-converts to*** Q or

$$P \equiv_\alpha Q.$$

1A8.1 *Note* Some basic lemmas about α-conversion and substitution are given in HS 86 §1B. Two simple properties that will be needed here are

(i) $P \equiv_\alpha Q \implies |P| = |Q|$,
(ii) $P \equiv_\alpha Q \implies FV(P) = FV(Q)$.

1A9 Definition A term M ***has a bound-variable clash*** iff M contains an abstractor $\underline{\lambda x}$ and a (free, bound or binding) occurrence of x that is not in its scope.

Examples of terms with bound-variable clashes are

$$x(\lambda x\cdot N),\quad \lambda x\cdot\lambda y\cdot\lambda x\cdot N,\quad (\lambda x\cdot P)(\lambda x\cdot Q).$$

We shall be mainly interested in terms *without* such clashes.

1A9.1 *Lemma* *Every term can be α-converted to a term without bound-variable clashes.*

Proof By the lemmas in HS 86 §1B. □

1A10 Definition (Closed terms) A ***closed term*** or ***combinator*** is a term in which no variable occurs free.

1A10.1 *Example* The following closed terms will be used in examples and results throughout this book.

$$\begin{array}{lll}
\mathbf{B} \equiv \lambda xyz\cdot x(yz), & \mathbf{B}' \equiv \lambda xyz\cdot y(xz), & \\
\mathbf{C} \equiv \lambda xyz\cdot xzy, & \mathbf{I} \equiv \lambda x\cdot x, & \\
\mathbf{K} \equiv \lambda xy\cdot x, & \mathbf{S} \equiv \lambda xyz\cdot xz(yz), & \\
\mathbf{W} \equiv \lambda xy\cdot xyy, & \mathbf{Y} \equiv \lambda x\cdot(\lambda y\cdot x(yy))(\lambda y\cdot x(yy)), & \\
\bar{0} \equiv \lambda xy\cdot y, & \bar{1} \equiv \lambda xy\cdot xy, & \\
\bar{n} \equiv \lambda xy\cdot x^n y \equiv \lambda xy\cdot x(x(\ldots(xy)\ldots)) & (n\ x\text{'s applied to } y)\ . &
\end{array}$$

(**Y** is Curry's ***fixed-point combinator***, see HS 86 Ch.3 §3B for background; the terms $\bar{n}$ are the ***Church numerals*** for $n = 0, 1, 2, \ldots$, see HS 86 Def. 4.2.)

1B β-reduction and β-normal forms

This section outlines the definition and main properties of the term-rewriting procedure called β-reduction. Further details can be found in many other books, for example HS 86 Chs. 1–6 and Barendregt 1984 Chs. 3 and 11–14.

1B1 Definition (β-contraction) A ***β-redex*** is any term $(\lambda x\cdot M)N$; its ***contractum*** is $[N/x]M$ and its ***re-write rule*** is

$$(\lambda x\cdot M)N \rhd_{1\beta} [N/x]M.$$

Iff P contains a β-redex-occurrence $\underline{R} \equiv \underline{(\lambda x\cdot M)N}$ and Q is the result of replacing this by $[N/x]M$, we say P ***β-contracts to*** Q $(P \rhd_{1\beta} Q)$ and we call the triple $\langle P, \underline{R}, Q\rangle$ a ***β-contraction of*** P.

1B1.1 *Lemma* $P \rhd_{1\beta} Q \implies FV(P) \supseteq FV(Q)$.

1B2 Definition (β-reduction) A ***β-reduction*** of a term P is a finite or infinite sequence of β-contractions with form

(i) $$\langle P_1, \underline{R}_1, Q_1\rangle,\quad \langle P_2, \underline{R}_2, Q_2\rangle,\ \ldots$$

where $P_1 \equiv_\alpha P$ and $Q_i \equiv_\alpha P_{i+1}$ for $i = 1, 2, \ldots$. (The empty sequence is allowed.) We say a finite reduction is ***from*** P ***to*** Q iff either it has $n \geq 1$ contractions and $Q_n \equiv_\alpha Q$

or it is empty and $P \equiv_\alpha Q$. A reduction from P to Q is said to ***terminate*** or ***end*** at Q. Iff there is a reduction from P to Q we say P ***β-reduces to*** Q, or

$$P \triangleright_\beta Q.$$

Note that α-conversions are allowed in a β-reduction.

1B3 Definition The ***length*** of a β-reduction is the number of its β-contractions (finite or ∞). A reduction with ***maximal length*** is one that continues as long as there are redexes to contract (i.e. one that either is infinite or ends at a term containing no redexes).

1B4 Definition (β-conversion) Iff we can change P to Q by a finite sequence of β-reductions and reversed β-reductions, we say P ***β-converts to*** Q, or P ***is β-equal to*** Q, or

$$P =_\beta Q.$$

A reversed β-reduction is called a ***β-expansion***.

1B4.1 *Exercise* For every term F let $X_F \equiv \mathbf{Y}F$ where $\mathbf{Y}$ is the fixed-point combinator defined in 1A10.1; show that

$$FX_F =_\beta X_F.$$

1B5 Church-Rosser Theorem for β (i) *If $M \triangleright_\beta P$ and $M \triangleright_\beta Q$ (see Fig. 1B5a) then there exists T such that*

$$P \triangleright_\beta T, \quad Q \triangleright_\beta T.$$

(ii) *If $P =_\beta Q$ (see Fig. 1B5b) then there exists T such that*

$$P \triangleright_\beta T, \quad Q \triangleright_\beta T.$$

Proof of 1B5 (i) See HS 86 Appendix 1 or Barendregt 1984 §3.2. (ii) This is deduced from (i) as suggested in Fig. 1B5b. □

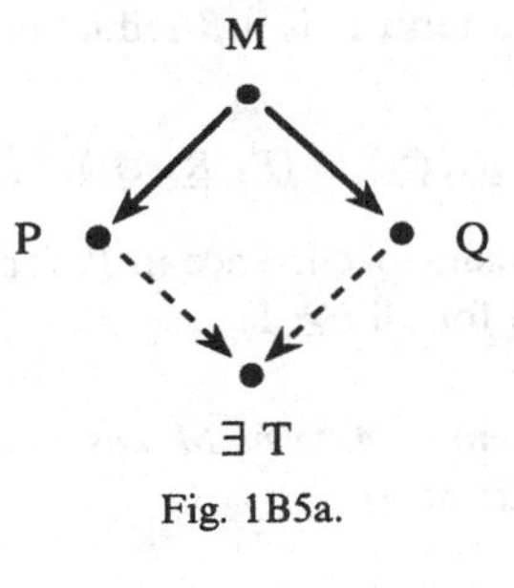

Fig. 1B5a.

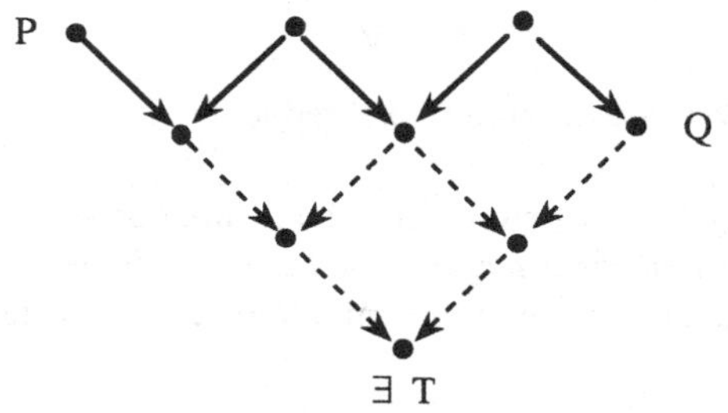

Fig. 1B5b.

1B6 Definition (β-normal forms) A ***β-normal form*** is a term that contains no β-redexes. The class of all β-nf's is called ***β-nf***. We say a term M ***has β-nf*** N iff

$$M \triangleright_\beta N \text{ and } N \in \beta\text{-}nf.$$

1B6.1 *Note* Roughly speaking, a reduction can be thought of as a computation and a β-nf as its result. One main aim when designing a type-theory is to give it the property that every computation can be pursued to a result if the operator wishes, i.e. that every term with a type has a β-nf. This gives normal forms even more significance in a type-theory than they already have in a type-free theory.

(Terms in general do not necessarily have β-nf's of course. The simplest term without one is $(\lambda x \cdot xx)(\lambda x \cdot xx)$.)

1B7 NF-Uniqueness Lemma *Modulo α-conversion, a term M has at most one β-nf.*

Proof An easy application of the Church-Rosser theorem. □

1B7.1 *Notation* If M has a β-nf it will be called $M_{*\beta}$.

1B8 Definition (Leftmost reductions) The ***leftmost β-redex-occurrence*** in a term P is the β-redex-occurrence whose leftmost parenthesis is to the left of all the parentheses in all the other β-redex-occurrences in P.

The leftmost β-reduction of a term P is a β-reduction of P with maximal length, say

$$\langle P_1, \underline{R}_1, Q_1 \rangle, \quad \langle P_2, \underline{R}_2, Q_2 \rangle, \ \ldots,$$

such that $\underline{R}_i$ is the leftmost β-redex-occurrence in P_i for all $i \geq 1$ (and P_1 α-converts to P and P_{i+1} α-converts to Q_i for all $i \geq 1$).

1B9 Leftmost-reduction Theorem *A term M has a β-nf $M_{*\beta}$ iff the leftmost β-reduction of M is finite and ends at $M_{*\beta}$.*

Proof See Curry and Feys 1958 §4E Cor. 1.1. (In fact this result is an immediate corollary of a slightly deeper result called the *standardization theorem*; for the latter see Curry and Feys 1958 §4E Thm. 1 or Barendregt 1984 Thm. 11.4.7, or the particularly clear proof in Mitschke 1979 Thm. 7.) □

1B9.1 *Example* The leftmost reduction of the fixed-point combinator **Y** in 1A10.1 is easily seen to be infinite, so **Y** has no β-nf.

1B9.2 *Note* (Seeking β-normal forms) The leftmost reduction of a term M is completely determined by M, so by 1B9 it gives an algorithm for seeking $M_{*\beta}$: if $M_{*\beta}$ exists the leftmost reduction of M will end at $M_{*\beta}$, and if not, this reduction will be infinite. Of course this algorithm does not decide in finite time whether M has a β-nf; and in fact this cannot be done, as the set of terms with normal forms is not recursive. (See e.g. HS 86 Cor 5.6.2 or Barendregt 1984 Thm. 6.6.5.)

1B10 Lemma (Structure of a β-normal form) *Every β-nf N can be expressed uniquely in the form*

(i) $$N \equiv \lambda x_1 \ldots x_m \cdot y N_1 \ldots N_n \qquad (m \geq 0, n \geq 0),$$

where $N_1, \ldots, N_n$ are β-nf's. And if N is closed then $y \in \{x_1, \ldots, x_m\}$.

Proof Easy induction on $|N|$. Note the uniqueness. □

1B10.1 *Note* The following special cases of 1B10 are worth mention:

$m = n = 0$:	$N \equiv y$		(an atom);
$m = 0, n \geq 1$:	$N \equiv yN_1 \ldots N_n$		(an application);
$m \geq 1$:	$N \equiv \lambda x_1 \ldots x_m \cdot P$		(an abstract);
$m \geq 1, n = 0$:	$N \equiv \lambda x_1 \ldots x_m \cdot y$		(called an ***abstracted atom***).

1B10.2 *Exercise* Prove that β-nf is the smallest class of terms satisfying (i) and (ii) below:

(i) all variables are in β-nf;
(ii) for all $m, n \geq 0$ with $m + n \geq 1$, and all $x_1, \ldots, x_m, y$,

$$N_1, \ldots, N_n \in \beta\text{-}nf \quad \Longrightarrow \quad \lambda x_1 \ldots x_m \cdot y N_1 \ldots N_n \in \beta\text{-}nf.$$

1C η- and βη-reductions

This section sketches the most basic properties of η- and $\beta\eta$-reductions. For more details see HS 86 Ch. 7 and Barendregt 1984 §15.1.

1C1 Definition (η-reduction, η-conversion) An ***η-redex*** is any term $\lambda x \cdot Mx$ with $x \notin FV(M)$; its re-write rule is

$$\lambda x \cdot Mx \rhd_{1\eta} M.$$

Its ***contractum*** is M. The definitions of ***η-contracts***, ***η-reduces*** ($\rhd_\eta$), ***η-converts*** ($=_\eta$), etc. are like those of the corresponding β-concepts in 1B.

1C2 Lemma *All η-reductions are finite; in fact an η-reduction $P \rhd_\eta Q$ must have length $\leq |P|/2$.*

Proof Each η-contraction reduces $|P|$ to $|P|-2$. □

1C3 Definition The ***η-family*** $\{P\}_\eta$ of a term P is the set of all terms Q such that $P \rhd_\eta Q$.

1C3.1 *Note* By 1C2, $\{P\}_\eta$ is finite.

1C4 Church-Rosser Theorem for η *If $P =_\eta Q$ then there exists T such that*

$$P \rhd_\eta T, \qquad Q \rhd_\eta T.$$

Proof Straightforward. (Barendregt 1984 Lemma 3.3.7.) □

1C5 Definition (βη-reduction, βη-conversion) A ***βη-redex*** is any β- or η-redex. The definitions of ***βη-contracts, βη-reduces*** ($\rhd_{\beta\eta}$), ***βη-converts*** ($=_{\beta\eta}$) are like those of the corresponding β-concepts in 1B.

1C5.1 *Lemma* $\quad P \rhd_{\beta\eta} Q \quad \Longrightarrow \quad FV(P) \supseteq FV(Q).$

1C5.2 *Note* A βη-reduction may have α-steps as well as β and η. The following theorem says that all its η-steps can be postponed to the end of the reduction.

1C6 η-Postponement Theorem *If $M \rhd_{\beta\eta} N$ then there exists a term P such that*

$$M \rhd_\beta P \rhd_\eta N.$$

Proof Nederpelt 1973 Thm. 7.28 or Barendregt 1984 Cor. 15.1.6. □

1C7 Commuting Lemma *If $M \rhd_\beta P$ and $M \rhd_\eta Q$ (see Fig. 1C7a) then there exists a term T such that*

$$P \rhd_\eta T, \qquad Q \rhd_\beta T.$$

Proof Barendregt 1984 Lemma 3.3.8. □

1C7.1 *Corollary* *If $M \rhd_{\beta\eta} P$ and $M \rhd_\beta Q$ then there exists a term T such that*

$$P \rhd_\beta T, \qquad Q \rhd_{\beta\eta} T.$$

Proof By 1B5, 1C4 and 1C7. □

1C8 Church-Rosser Theorem for βη (i) *If $M \rhd_{\beta\eta} P$ and $M \rhd_{\beta\eta} Q$ then there exists T such that*

$$P \rhd_{\beta\eta} T, \qquad Q \rhd_{\beta\eta} T.$$

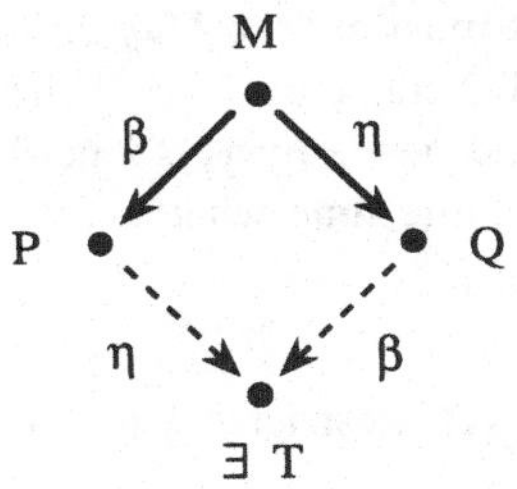

Fig. 1C7a.

(ii) *If* $P =_{\beta\eta} Q$ *then there exists* T *such that*

$$P \rhd_{\beta\eta} T, \qquad Q \rhd_{\beta\eta} T.$$

Proof (i) From 1B5, 1C4, 1C6, 1C7. (ii) From (i) as in Fig. 1B5b. □

1C9 Definition ($\beta\eta$- and η-normal forms) A ***$\beta\eta$-normal form ($\beta\eta$-nf)*** is a term without $\beta\eta$-redexes. The class of all $\beta\eta$-nf's is called ***$\beta\eta$-nf***. We say M ***has $\beta\eta$-nf*** N iff

$$M \rhd_{\beta\eta} N, \qquad N \in \beta\eta\text{-}nf.$$

Similarly we define ***η-normal form, η-nf,*** and M ***has η-nf*** N.

1C9.1 *Notation* The $\beta\eta$-nf and η-nf of a term M are unique modulo $\equiv_\alpha$ by the Church-Rosser theorems for $\beta\eta$ and η; they will be called

$$M_{*\beta\eta}, \qquad M_{*\eta}.$$

1C9.2 *Lemma* (i) *An η-reduction of a β-nf cannot create new β-redexes; more precisely*

$$M \in \beta\text{-}nf \text{ and } M \rhd_\eta N \quad \Longrightarrow \quad N \in \beta\text{-}nf.$$

(ii) *For every* M, $M_{*\beta\eta}$ *is the η-nf of* $M_{*\beta}$; *i.e.* $M_{*\beta\eta} \equiv (M_{*\beta})_{*\eta}$.

Proof (i) It is easy to check all possible cases. (ii) By 1C2, $M_{*\beta}$ has an η-nf $(M_{*\beta})_{*\eta}$, and this is a $\beta\eta$-nf by (i). □

1C9.3 *Corollary* *If N is a β-nf then all the members of its η-family are β-nf's and exactly one of them is a $\beta\eta$-nf, namely* $N_{*\eta}$.

1C9.4 *Lemma* *A term has a $\beta\eta$-nf iff it has a β-nf.*

Proof For "only if", see Curry et al. 1972 §11E Lemma 13.1 or Barendregt 1984 Cor. 15.1.5. For "if", see 1C9.2. (By the way, do not confuse the present lemma with a claim that a term is *in* β-nf iff it is *in* $\beta\eta$-nf, which is of course false!) □

1C9.5 *Note* (Seeking $\beta\eta$-normal-forms) To seek for $M_{*\beta\eta}$, reduce M by its leftmost β-reduction. If this is finite, it must end at $M_{*\beta}$ and then the leftmost η-reduction will reach an η-nf in $\leq |M_{*\beta}|/2$ steps, by 1C2. If the leftmost β-reduction of M is infinite, $M_{*\beta}$ does not exist and hence by 1C9.4 neither does $M_{*\beta\eta}$. Of course this procedure does not decide in finite time whether $M_{*\beta\eta}$ exists; see the comment in 1B9.2.

1D Restricted λ-terms

The following restricted classes of λ-terms will play a role later in the correspondence between type-assignment and propositional logic.

1D1 Definition (λI-terms) A λ-term P is called a ***λI-term*** iff, for each subterm with form $\lambda x \cdot M$ in P, x occurs free in M at least once.

1D1.1 *Note* The λI-terms are the terms that were originally studied by Church. They have the property that if a λI-term has a normal form, so have all its subterms (Church 1941 §7, Thm. 7 XXXII). Church restricted his system to λI-terms because he regarded terms without normal forms as meaningless and preferred that meaningful terms did not have meaningless subterms. The λI-terms are discussed in detail in Barendregt 1984 Ch. 9.

The standard example of a non-λI-term is $\mathbf{K} \equiv \lambda xy \cdot x \equiv \lambda x \cdot (\lambda y \cdot x)$.

1D1.2 *Notation* Sometimes unrestricted λ-terms are called ***λK-terms***, and the unrestricted λ-calculus the ***λK-calculus***, to contrast with λI-terms and to emphasise the absence of restriction.

1D2 Definition (BCKλ-terms) A ***BCKλ-term*** is a λ-term P such that

(i) *for each subterm* $\lambda x \cdot M$ *of* P, x *occurs free in* M *at most once,*
(ii) *each free variable of* P *has just one occurrence free in* P.

1D2.1 *Examples* Of the terms in the list in 1A10.1 the following are BCKλ-terms:

$$\mathbf{B} \equiv \lambda xyz \cdot x(yz), \qquad \mathbf{B}' \equiv \lambda xyz \cdot y(xz), \qquad \mathbf{C} \equiv \lambda xyz \cdot xzy,$$
$$\mathbf{I} \equiv \lambda x \cdot x, \qquad \mathbf{K} \equiv \lambda xy \cdot x, \qquad \bar{n} \equiv \lambda xy \cdot x^n y \ (n = 0 \text{ or } 1).$$

And the following are not:

$$\mathbf{S} \equiv \lambda xyz \cdot xz(yz), \qquad \mathbf{W} \equiv \lambda xy \cdot xyy,$$
$$\mathbf{Y} \equiv \lambda x \cdot (\lambda y \cdot x(yy))(\lambda y \cdot x(yy)), \qquad \bar{n} \equiv \lambda xy \cdot x^n y \ (n \geq 2).$$

1D2.2 *Lemma The class of all BCKλ-terms is closed under abstraction, i.e. if* M *is a BCKλ-term then so is* $\lambda x \cdot M$ *for every variable* x.

Proof By 1D2(ii), x occurs free at most once in M. □

1D2.3 *Notes* (i) In contrast to the above lemma the class of all λI-terms is only closed under abstractions $\lambda x \cdot M$ such that x occurs free in M.

(ii) The BCKλ-terms are so called because the closed terms in this class correspond to combinations of three combinators called "**B**", "**C**" and "**K**" in combinatory logic (see 9F for details). They have also sometimes been called *linear λ-terms* but this name is nowadays usually applied to the following class.

1D3 Definition (BCIλ-terms) A ***BCIλ-term*** or ***linear λ-term*** is a λ-term P such that

(i) *for each subterm* $\lambda x{\cdot}M$ *of* P, x *occurs free in* M *exactly once,*
(ii) *each free variable of* P *has just one occurrence free in* P.

Clearly every BCIλ-term is a BCKλ-term, but the BCKλ-term **K** is not a BCIλ-term; in fact a term is a BCIλ-term iff it is both a λI-term and a BCKλ-term. The closed BCIλ-terms correspond to combinations of the combinators called **B**, **C** and **I** in combinatory logic; details are in 9F.

1D4 Lemma *Each of the three classes (λI-terms, BCKλ-terms and BCIλ-terms) is closed under βη-reduction, i.e. every term obtained by βη-reducing a member of the class is also in the class.*

Proof Straightforward. □

1D5 Definition A β-contraction $(\lambda x{\cdot}M)N \rhd_{1\beta} [N/x]M$ is said to ***cancel*** N iff x does not occur free in M; it is said to ***duplicate*** N iff x has at least two free occurrences in M.

A β-reduction is ***non-duplicating*** iff none of its contractions duplicates; it is ***non-cancelling*** iff none cancels.

1D6 Lemma *Every β-reduction of a λI-term is non-cancelling; every one of a BCKλ-term is non-duplicating, and every one of a BCIλ-term is both.*

2

Assigning types to terms

The topic of this book is one of the simplest current type-theories. It was called TA in the Introduction but in fact it comes in two forms, TA_C for combinatory logic and TA_λ for λ-calculus. Since most readers probably know λ-calculus better than combinatory logic, only TA_λ will be described here. (The reader who wishes to see an outline of TA_C can find one in HS 86 Ch.14; most of its properties are parallel to those of TA_λ.)

The present chapter consists of a definition and description of TA_λ. It is close to the treatment in HS 86 Ch. 15 but differs in some technical details.

2A The system TA_λ

2A1 Definition (Types) An infinite sequence of ***type-variables*** is assumed to be given, distinct from the term-variables. ***Types*** are linguistic expressions defined thus:

(i) each type-variable is a type (called an ***atom***);
(ii) if σ and τ are types then $(\sigma \to \tau)$ is a type (called a ***composite type***).

2A1.1 *Notation* ***Type-variables*** are denoted by "a", "b", "c", "d", "e", "f", "g", with or without number-subscripts, and distinct letters denote distinct variables unless otherwise stated.

Arbitrary types are denoted by lower-case Greek letters except "λ".

Parentheses will often (but not always) be omitted from types, and the reader should restore omitted ones in such a way that, for example,

$$\rho \to \sigma \to \tau \quad \equiv \quad (\rho \to (\sigma \to \tau)).$$

This restoration rule is called ***association to the right.***[1]

2A1.2 ***Informal interpretation*** To interpret types we think of each type-variable as a set and $\sigma \to \tau$ as a set of functions from σ into τ. The precise nature of this set of functions (all functions, all functions definable in some given system, etc.) will depend on the particular interpretation we may have in mind.

[1] It is the opposite of the rule for terms! The reason originates in the fact that terms follow the common notation convention in which an operator's input is written on the right, but in a type $\sigma \to \tau$ the type of the input is on the left of that of the output.

2A2 Definition The total number of occurrences of type-variables in a type τ will be called $|\tau|$ or the ***length*** of τ; more precisely, define

$$|a| \equiv 1, \qquad |\rho \to \sigma| \equiv |\rho| + |\sigma|.$$

The number of distinct type-variables occurring in τ will be called

$$\|\tau\|$$

and the set of all these variables will be called

$$Vars(\tau).$$

2A2.1 *Example* If $\tau \equiv (a \to b \to c) \to (a \to b) \to a \to c$, then

$$|\tau| = 7, \qquad \|\tau\| = 3, \qquad Vars(\tau) = \{a, b, c\}.$$

The structure of an arbitrary type is analysed in detail in 9D–E. The lemmas there will be used in some later chapters but not in this one.

2A3 Discussion (The Church and Curry approaches) In current use there are two main ways of introducing types into λ-calculus, one attributable to Alonzo Church and the other to Haskell Curry.

The former goes back to a type-system introduced in Church 1940. In it, the definition of "λ-term" is restricted by giving each term a unique type as part of its structure and saying that an application PQ is only defined when P has a function-type $\sigma \to \tau$ and Q the appropriate argument-type σ.[1]

The effect of Church's restriction can be seen on $\lambda x \cdot xx$, which is a well-formed term in type-free λ-calculus but represents the abstract concept of self-application, a concept whose meaningfulness may well be questioned. Self-application was involved in most of the paradoxes that were discovered in mathematics in the early 1900's, and Bertrand Russell devised the first of all type-theories specifically as a language in which these paradoxes could not be expressed. In Church's typed λ-calculus each variable has a unique type, so if x has a function-type $\sigma \to \tau$ it cannot also have type σ, and so the application xx cannot be defined as a typed term. Hence also $\lambda x \cdot xx$ cannot be a typed term.

Curry took a different approach. He pointed out that if we wish to ask questions about the meaningfulness of $\lambda x \cdot xx$, then we need a language in which these questions can be expressed. And Church's type-theory by itself is not adequate for this, because we have just seen that $\lambda x \cdot xx$ is excluded from it. Curry proposed a language which would include all the type-free λ-terms, and a type-theory which would contain rules assigning types to some of these terms but not to others. The term $\lambda x \cdot xx$ would not be given a type by these rules, but would still remain in the system and hence be discussable. (Curry and Feys 1958 §0B, p.5.)

Along with this change Curry proposed another, which is best understood by looking at the identity-combinator $\lambda x \cdot x$ as an example.

In Church's type-theory there is no term $\lambda x \cdot x$. Instead, for each type σ there is

[1] For a definition of typed λ-term and a few examples see HS 86 §13A; for another version, with motivation and more details, see Barendregt 1992 §3.2.

a variable x^σ with type σ and a term $\lambda x^\sigma \cdot x^\sigma$ with type $\sigma \to \sigma$. Informally, this term denotes the identity function on whatever set S may be denoted by σ. Call this function I_S; the only objects it accepts as inputs are members of S, and $I_S(x) = x$ for all $x \in S$. Thus Church's theory has an infinite number of identity functions, one for each set S. This agrees with the view of functions taken by most mathematicians: each function is seen as a set of ordered pairs with a domain and range built into its definition, and the identity functions I_S and I_T on two distinct sets S and T are viewed as different functions.

But this view is not entirely satisfying; an alternative and perhaps more natural view is to see all the separate identity-functions I_S, I_T, etc. as special cases of one intuitive concept, the operation of doing nothing. If we admit that such a concept exists, even though only in an imprecise sense, then a type-theory that tries to make it precise by splitting it into an infinite number of different special cases at the beginning will seem at the very best inefficient.

Curry's aim was a type-theory in which the identity-concept would be expressed by just one term $\lambda x \cdot x$, to which an infinite number of types would be assigned by suitable formal rules. Types would contain variables, and if a term M received a type τ it would also receive all substitution-instances of τ. This kind of theory will be called here a ***type-assignment*** theory or a ***Curry-style*** type-theory. (It is the ancestor of polymorphic type-theories.) In contrast, a theory in which each term has a unique built-in type will be called a ***typed-term*** theory or a ***Church-style*** theory.[1]

TA_λ will be a type-assignment theory.

2A4 Definition A ***type-assignment*** is any expression

$$M : \tau$$

where M is a λ-term and τ is a type; we call M its ***subject*** and τ its ***predicate***.

("$M : \tau$" should be read informally as "*assign to M the type τ*" or "*M has type τ*" or "*M denotes a member of whatever set τ denotes*".)

2A5 Definition A ***type-context*** Γ is any finite, perhaps empty, set of type-assignments

$$\Gamma = \{x_1 : \rho_1, \ \ldots, \ x_m : \rho_m\}$$

whose subjects are term-variables and which is ***monovalent*** or ***consistent*** in the sense that no variable is the subject of more than one assignment. For any such Γ define

$$Subjects(\Gamma) = \{x_1, \ldots, x_m\}.$$

[1] Curry's and Church's lines of thought were not really as distinct as the above seems to imply. In particular Church did not ignore the possibility that a single identity-concept might be formalizable instead of a multitude of particular identity-functions. Indeed his first systems of λ-calculus in the 1930's were part of an attempt to formalize exactly this single-identity view of functions in a type-free theory, and one of the best available expositions of this view is in the introduction to his book Church 1941. Only after his attempt to do this in an extremely general setting proved inconsistent did Church turn to type-theory and a more restricted approach to functions. Also Curry's type-theories began their development in some of his earliest work and were not simply a response to Church's; see Curry 1934.

2A5.1 *Notation* The result of removing from Γ the assignment whose subject is x (if Γ has one) is called

$$\Gamma - x.$$

(If $x \notin Subjects(\Gamma)$ we define $\Gamma - x = \Gamma$.) The result of removing from Γ all assignments $x_i : \rho_i$ with $x_i \notin FV(M)$ (where M is a given term) is called

$$\Gamma \restriction M$$

or "Γ *restricted to* M". And Γ is called an "***M-context***" (for a given M) iff

$$Subjects(\Gamma) = FV(M).$$

2A5.2 *Note* A type-context Γ is a set, not a sequence. Hence it does not change when its members are permuted or repeated. To implement TA_λ as a practical system we would have to represent Γ by an expression in some language and include rewrite-rules to permute Γ's members and make and remove repetitions. Such rules would obscure the main themes of this book so they have been avoided here by simply assuming that contexts are sets.[1]

2A6 Definition We say Γ_1 ***is consistent with*** Γ_2 iff $\Gamma_1 \cup \Gamma_2$ is consistent; and $\Gamma_1, \ldots, \Gamma_n$ are ***mutually consistent*** iff their union is consistent.

2A7 Definition (TA_λ-formulae) For any Γ, M and τ the triple $\langle \Gamma, M, \tau \rangle$ is called a **TA_λ*-formula*** and is written as

$$\Gamma \quad \mapsto \quad M : \tau$$

(or just $\mapsto M : \tau$ when Γ is empty). We shall call M the ***subject*** of this formula and τ its ***predicate*** (despite the fact that in general it contains other subjects and predicates too, namely those of the assignments in Γ).

2A7.1 *Notation* The following abbreviations will often be used:

$$x_1 : \sigma_1, \ldots, x_n : \sigma_n \vdash M : \tau \qquad for \qquad \{x_1 : \sigma_1, \ldots, x_n : \sigma_n\} \vdash M : \tau,$$

$$\Gamma, y_1 : \sigma_1, \ldots, y_n : \sigma_n \vdash M : \tau \qquad for \qquad \Gamma \cup \{y_1 : \sigma_1, \ldots, y_n : \sigma_n\} \vdash M : \tau.$$

2A8 Definition (The system TA_λ) TA_λ has an infinite set of axioms and two deduction-rules (called ($\to$E) or *$\to$-elimination* and ($\to$I) or *$\to$-introduction*), as follows.

Axioms of TA_λ: for every term-variable x and every type τ, TA_λ has an axiom

$$x : \tau \quad \mapsto \quad x : \tau.$$

[1] Type-contexts are also called *environments* in the literature. They play a different role from the sets called *bases* in HS 86 Chs.14–15: there a basis was a set of axioms for a theory, whereas here a context will be used as a set of assumptions for a particular deduction in a theory.

Deduction-rules of $\boldsymbol{TA_\lambda}$:

$$(\to\mathrm{E}) \qquad \frac{\Gamma_1 \mapsto P:(\sigma\to\tau) \quad \Gamma_2 \mapsto Q:\sigma}{\Gamma_1 \cup \Gamma_2 \mapsto (PQ):\tau,} \qquad [\textit{if } \Gamma_1 \cup \Gamma_2 \textit{ is consistent}]$$

$$(\to\mathrm{I}) \qquad \frac{\Gamma \mapsto P:\tau}{\Gamma - x \mapsto (\lambda x.P):(\sigma\to\tau).} \qquad [\textit{if } \Gamma \textit{ is consistent with } x:\sigma]$$

A **TA**$_\lambda$***-deduction*** Δ is a tree of TA$_\lambda$-formulae, those at the tops of branches being axioms and those below being deduced from those immediately above them by a rule. (A detailed definition of such deductions is given in 9C1.) The bottom formula in Δ is called its ***conclusion***; if it is

$$\Gamma \mapsto M:\tau$$

we call Δ a ***deduction of*** $\Gamma \mapsto M:\tau$ or a ***deduction of*** $M:\tau$ ***from*** Γ, and say that $\Gamma \mapsto M:\tau$ is ***TA***$_\lambda$***-deductible.*** In the special case $\Gamma = \emptyset$, Δ may be called a ***proof*** of the assignment $M:\tau$.

2A8.1 *Note* (Rule $(\to\mathrm{I})$) The condition in $(\to\mathrm{I})$ that Γ be consistent with $x:\sigma$ means that either Γ contains $x:\sigma$ or Γ contains no assignment at all whose subject is x. In the first case the rule is said to ***discharge*** or ***cancel*** x from Γ. In the second case it is said to ***discharge*** x ***vacuously.***

In these two cases the rule takes two slightly different forms which may be displayed as follows (using "Γ_1" below to correspond to "$\Gamma - x$" above).

$$(\to\mathrm{I})_{\mathrm{main}} \qquad \frac{\Gamma_1, x:\sigma \mapsto P:\tau}{\Gamma_1 \mapsto (\lambda x.P):(\sigma\to\tau),} \qquad [\textit{if } x \notin \textit{Subjects}(\Gamma_1)]$$

$$(\to\mathrm{I})_{\mathrm{vac}} \qquad \frac{\Gamma_1 \mapsto P:\tau}{\Gamma_1 \mapsto (\lambda x.P):(\sigma\to\tau).} \qquad [\textit{if } x \notin \textit{Subjects}(\Gamma_1)]$$

2A8.2 *Example* Let $\mathbf{B} \equiv \lambda xyz\cdot x(yz)$ as in the list in 1A10.1; the following is a deduction of

$$\mapsto \mathbf{B}:(a\to b)\to(c\to a)\to c\to b.$$

(In it, "Γ" will denote the set $\{x:a\to b,\ y:c\to a,\ z:c\}$.)

$$\cfrac{\cfrac{\cfrac{\cfrac{x:a\to b \mapsto x:a\to b \qquad \cfrac{y:c\to a \mapsto y:c\to a \qquad z:c \mapsto z:c}{y:c\to a,\ z:c \mapsto yz:a}\,(\to\mathrm{E})}{\Gamma \mapsto (x(yz)):b}\,(\to\mathrm{E})}{\Gamma - z \mapsto (\lambda z\cdot x(yz)):c\to b}\,(\to\mathrm{I})_{\mathrm{main}}}{\Gamma - z - y \mapsto (\lambda yz\cdot x(yz)):(c\to a)\to c\to b}\,(\to\mathrm{I})_{\mathrm{main}}}{\mapsto (\lambda xyz\cdot x(yz)):(a\to b)\to(c\to a)\to c\to b}\,(\to\mathrm{I})_{\mathrm{main}}$$

2A8.3 *Example* Let $\mathbf{I} \equiv \lambda x{\cdot}x$; the following is a deduction of

$$\mapsto\ \mathbf{I}:a\to a.$$

$$\frac{x:a \ \mapsto\ x:a}{\mapsto\ (\lambda x{\cdot}x):a\to a}\,(\to\mathrm{I})_{\mathrm{main}}$$

2A8.4 *Example* Let $\mathbf{K} \equiv \lambda xy{\cdot}x$; the following is a deduction of

$$\mapsto\ \mathbf{K}:a\to b\to a.$$

$$\frac{\dfrac{x:a \ \mapsto\ x:a}{x:a\ \mapsto\ (\lambda y{\cdot}x):b\to a}\,(\to\mathrm{I})_{\mathrm{vac}}}{\mapsto\ (\lambda xy{\cdot}x):a\to b\to a}\,(\to\mathrm{I})_{\mathrm{main}}$$

2A8.5 *Example* The following is a deduction of

$$\mapsto\ \mathbf{II}:a\to a.$$

$$\frac{\dfrac{x:a\to a\ \mapsto\ x:a\to a}{\mapsto\ (\lambda x{\cdot}x):(a\to a)\to a\to a}\,(\to\mathrm{I}) \qquad \dfrac{x:a\ \mapsto\ x:a}{\mapsto\ (\lambda x{\cdot}x):(a\to a)\to a}\,(\to\mathrm{I})}{\mapsto\ (\lambda x{\cdot}x)(\lambda x{\cdot}x):a\to a}\,(\to\mathrm{E})$$

2A8.6 *Remark* (Self-application) The above example gave a type to a term involving self-application, namely **II**. This was done by giving a different type to each of the two occurrences of **I**, and to do this we had to give two different types to the one variable x; but there was no inconsistency problem when ($\to$E) was applied because the two applications of ($\to$I) above ($\to$E) removed x from the contexts on the left of "$\mapsto$". Similarly it is possible to give types to several other self-applications in TA_λ, for example **KK** and **BB**.

This may seem surprising, in view of the claim in 2A3 that the original aim of a type-theory was to avoid self-application. But in fact the "dangerous" self-application to be avoided is not any one simple particular case like **II**, but the overall general concept of self-application as represented by the term $\lambda x.xx$. And $\lambda x.xx$ does not receive a type in TA_λ.

To see this, suppose there were a TA_λ-deduction of

$$\mapsto\ (\lambda x{\cdot}xx):\tau$$

for some τ. Then its last step would have to be an application of ($\to$I) to a deduction of

$$x:\rho\ \ \mapsto\ \ xx:\sigma$$

for some ρ and σ such that $\tau \equiv \rho\to\sigma$; and the last step in this deduction would have to be an application of ($\to$E) to two deductions of

$$x:\sigma_1\to\sigma\ \ \mapsto\ \ x:\sigma_1\to\sigma, \qquad x:\sigma_1\ \ \mapsto\ \ x:\sigma_1$$

for some σ_1. But $\sigma_1\to\sigma \not\equiv \sigma_1$ so the consistency condition in ($\to$E) would be violated by these deductions.

Thus the consistency condition in $(\to E)$ prevents $\lambda x \cdot xx$ from having a type. This is in fact its main purpose.[1]

2A8.7 *Exercise** Deduce the following in TA_λ, where $\mathbf{B}' \equiv \lambda xyz \cdot y(xz)$, $\mathbf{C} \equiv \lambda xyz \cdot xzy$, $\mathbf{S} \equiv \lambda xyz \cdot xz(yz)$ and $\mathbf{W} \equiv \lambda xy \cdot xyy$ as in 1A10.1.

(i) $\mapsto \mathbf{B}' : (a \to b) \to (b \to c) \to a \to c$,
(ii) $\mapsto \mathbf{C} : (a \to b \to c) \to b \to a \to c$,
(iii) $\mapsto \mathbf{S} : (a \to b \to c) \to (a \to b) \to a \to c$,
(iv) $\mapsto \mathbf{W} : (a \to a \to b) \to a \to b$.

2A8.8 *Exercise** Deduce the following in TA_λ, where

$$P \equiv (\lambda vxyz \cdot v(y(vxz)))\mathbf{I}, \qquad Q \equiv \lambda xyz \cdot \mathbf{I}(y(\mathbf{I}xz));$$

(i) $\mapsto P : (a \to b) \to (b \to a \to b) \to a \to a \to b$;
(ii) $\mapsto Q : (a \to b) \to (b \to c) \to a \to c$.

2A8.9 *Note* (Comparison with HS 86) The format of TA_λ is what is known as the "***Natural Deduction***" style and was originated by Gerhard Gentzen in his thesis Gentzen 1935. The system called "TA_λ" in HS 86 §15B is another variant of the same style; its main differences from the above system TA_λ are as follows.

(i) In HS 86 the discharging of assumptions by rule $(\to I)$ was shown by enclosing the assumption in brackets at the top of the deduction-tree. But here the set of undischarged assumptions at each stage of the deduction is displayed on the left of the " $\mapsto$ " symbol and when rule $(\to I)$ is used this set is simply reduced. This notation is perhaps more explicit than that in HS 86 and is in common use in recent literature. In both notations deductions have the same tree-structure.

(ii) The version in HS 86 included an α-rule that is not in the present version. This was to ensure that the set of provable formulae would be closed under α-conversion even when the basis of axioms was not. But there are no axioms here in the sense of HS 86 so α-closure will turn out to be provable without adding an α-rule; see 2B6.

2A9 Definition Let Γ be a type-context. Iff there is a TA_λ-deduction of a formula $\Gamma' \mapsto M:\tau$ for some $\Gamma' \subseteq \Gamma$ we shall say

$$\Gamma \vdash_\lambda M:\tau.$$

In the special case $\Gamma = \emptyset$ we shall say ***M has type τ in*** $\mathbf{TA}_\lambda$, or ***τ is a type of M in*** $\mathbf{TA}_\lambda$, or

$$\vdash_\lambda M:\tau.$$

The phrase "in TA_λ" may be omitted when no confusion is likely.

2A9.1 *Lemma* (Weakening) $\Gamma \vdash_\lambda M:\tau,\ \Gamma^+ \supseteq \Gamma \implies \Gamma^+ \vdash_\lambda M:\tau$.

[1] There is at least one interesting type-theory in which this consistency condition is relaxed, the theory of intersection-types that originated in Coppo and Dezani 1978 and Sallé 1978. In this theory xx receives a type and types play a significantly more complex role than in TA_λ, see for example the comment in Hindley 1992 §1.1.

Proof Trivial from 2A9. □

2A9.2 *Warning* Do not confuse "$\mapsto$" with "$\vdash$". The former is part of the language of TA_λ and serves merely to separate two parts of a formula. But "$\vdash_\lambda$" is part of the meta-language in which TA_λ is described, and asserts the existence of a TA_λ-deduction; it is the traditional deducibility symbol.[1] In particular do not confuse the two statements

(a) *the formula* $\Gamma \mapsto M:\tau$ *is deducible,*
(b) $\Gamma \vdash_\lambda M:\tau$.

Statement (b) has the weakening property, as we have just seen in 2A9.1. But (a) does not; the rules of TA_λ have been formulated so that if (a) holds then the subjects of Γ coincide exactly with the free variables of M, and we cannot modify a deduction of $\Gamma \mapsto M:\tau$ to make a deduction of $\Gamma^+ \mapsto M:\tau$ if $\Gamma^+ \supseteq \Gamma$.[2]

The next two lemmas express the above comments more formally.

2A10 Lemma *If* $\Gamma \mapsto M:\tau$ *is deducible in* TA_λ *then Subjects* $(\Gamma) = FV(M)$.

Proof By an easy induction on lengths of deductions. □

2A11 Lemma (i) $\Gamma \vdash_\lambda M:\tau$ *iff Subjects*$(\Gamma) \supseteq FV(M)$ *and there exists a* TA_λ-*deduction of the formula* $\Gamma \restriction M \mapsto M:\tau$.

(ii) $(\exists\Gamma)(\Gamma \vdash_\lambda M:\tau) \iff (\exists\Gamma)\{\Gamma$ *is an M-context and* $\Gamma \vdash_\lambda M:\tau\}$.

(iii) *For closed terms M,*

$$(\exists\Gamma)(\Gamma \vdash_\lambda M:\tau) \iff \vdash_\lambda M:\tau.$$

Proof By 2A9 and 2A10. (The definition of $\Gamma \restriction M$ is in 2A5.1.) □

2A12 Historical Comment Although this book focuses on λ-calculus, type-assignment in fact began in its sister-theory, combinatory logic. The first systems appeared in Curry 1934 and were developed further in Curry and Feys 1958 Chs. 8–10, Seldin 1968 and Curry et al. 1972 Ch. 14, though in his earlier work Curry was aiming at building type-theories with the greatest possible generality and strength and simple type-assignment formed only a small part of each of these. However, when he found his strongest system inconsistent in 1954 he turned to the study of weaker ones and gradually realized that their $\to$-fragment formed a very neat core system that was worth studying on its own and stood a good chance of having some practical value.

This system was essentially a combinatory-logic analogue of TA_λ: Curry called it "*modified basic functionality*" though later in HS86 it was called "TA_C". Its basic properties first appeared in Curry and Feys 1958 §§8C and 9A–F, though even then those authors' main interest was in a slightly stronger system obtained by adding to

[1] Many works use "$\vdash$" where this book uses "$\mapsto$", and introduce no special notation for deducibility.
[2] Many other versions of Natural Deduction in the literature do not have this restriction but I believe its use slightly simplifies the proofs of some properties that depend on analysing the structure of a deduction.

TA_C an equality-invariance rule (see Chapter 4 below). The first papers to feature TA_C exclusively were Curry 1969 and Hindley 1969.

As for TA_λ itself, its first appearance was in Curry and Feys 1958 §9F1 under the name "$F_1(\lambda)^T$", though none of its properties were stated at that date other than a theorem relating it to TA_C. Its properties as an independent system were not described until ten years later in the theses Morris 1968 and Seldin 1968. Seldin's results on TA_λ appeared in Curry et al. 1972 §14D, but Morris' thesis was never published. The next study devoted to TA_λ was another unpublished thesis, Ben-Yelles 1979; some of its material will be the subject of Chapter 8 below.

For subsequent work on TA_λ see the references in Chapters 3–9 below.

2B The subject-construction theorem

Deductions in TA_λ have one very important property that is not shared by deductions in many more complex type-theories; the tree-structure of a deduction of $\Gamma \mapsto M:\tau$ follows the tree-structure of M exactly. To make this correspondence precise we really need the detailed definition of construction-tree of a term given in 9A4 and that of a deduction given in 9C1; but the following example gives a very good idea of what it means.

2B1 Example Let $\mathbf{B} \equiv \lambda xyz \cdot x(yz)$. A deduction of a type-assignment for $\mathbf{B}$ was shown in 2A8.2. If all but the subject is erased from each formula in this deduction the result is the tree shown in Fig. 2B1a. This is the same as the construction-tree of $\mathbf{B}$ (with certain details called position-labels omitted, for these see the full definition of construction-tree in 9A4).

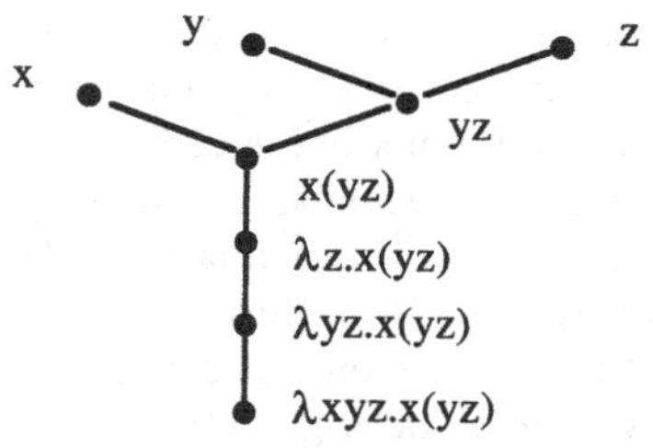

Fig. 2B1a.

The following theorem describes the deductions-to-terms correspondence formally.

2B2 Subject-construction Theorem (Seldin 1968 §3D Thm. 1, Curry et al. 1972 §14D Thm. 1.) *Let Δ be a TA_λ-deduction of a formula $\Gamma \mapsto M:\tau$.*

(i) *If we remove from each formula in Δ everything except its subject, Δ changes to a tree of terms which is exactly the construction-tree for M.*

(ii) *If M is an atom, say $M \equiv x$, then $\Gamma = \{x:\tau\}$ and Δ contains only one formula, namely the axiom*

$$x:\tau \;\mapsto\; x:\tau.$$

(iii) *If $M \equiv PQ$ the last step in Δ must be an application of* (→E) *to two formulae with form*

$$\Gamma\restriction P \;\mapsto\; P:\sigma\to\tau, \qquad \Gamma\restriction Q \;\mapsto\; Q:\sigma,$$

for some σ.

(iv) *If $M \equiv \lambda x\cdot P$ then τ must have form $\rho\to\sigma$; further, if $x \in FV(P)$ the last step in Δ must be an application of $(\to\mathrm{I})_{\mathrm{main}}$ to*

$$\Gamma, x:\rho \;\mapsto\; P:\sigma,$$

and if $x \notin FV(P)$ the last step in Δ must be an application of $(\to\mathrm{I})_{\mathrm{vac}}$ to

$$\Gamma \;\mapsto\; P:\sigma.$$

Proof Induction on $|M|$. Parts (i)–(iii) follow immediately from the full definition of deduction in 9C1. For (iv): if $M \equiv \lambda x\cdot P$ then by 2A8.1 the last step in Δ must have one of the forms

$$(\to\mathrm{I})_{\mathrm{main}}\ \frac{\Gamma, x:\rho \;\mapsto\; P:\sigma}{\Gamma \;\mapsto\; \lambda x\cdot P:\rho\to\sigma}, \qquad (\to\mathrm{I})_{\mathrm{vac}}\ \frac{\Gamma \;\mapsto\; P:\sigma}{\Gamma \;\mapsto\; \lambda x\cdot P:\rho\to\sigma}$$

and by 2A10 $(\to\mathrm{I})_{\mathrm{main}}$ is used when $x \in FV(P)$ and $(\to\mathrm{I})_{\mathrm{vac}}$ is used otherwise. Hence result. □

2B2.1 *Warning* (Deductions are not unique) Given M, let Δ be a deduction of $\Gamma \mapsto M:\tau$. By the subject-construction theorem the structure of M determines both the tree-structure of Δ and the terms at all the nodes in Δ. But this does not mean that the whole of Δ is completely determined by its conclusion, because there is some freedom of choice of the types assigned to terms at non-bottom nodes in Δ. For example, let $\Gamma = \emptyset$ and

$$M \;\equiv\; (\lambda xy\cdot y)(\lambda z\cdot z), \qquad \tau \;\equiv\; a\to a\,,$$

and consider the deduction in Fig. 2B2.1a; the type σ in that figure can be arbitrary.

$$\dfrac{\dfrac{\dfrac{y:a \;\mapsto\; y:a}{\mapsto\; (\lambda xy\cdot y):a\to a}\,(\to\mathrm{I})}{\mapsto\; (\lambda xy\cdot y):(\sigma\to\sigma)\to a\to a}\,(\to\mathrm{I}) \qquad \dfrac{z:\sigma \;\mapsto\; z:\sigma}{\mapsto\; (\lambda z\cdot z):\sigma\to\sigma}\,(\to\mathrm{I})}{\mapsto\; (\lambda xy\cdot y)(\lambda z\cdot z):a\to a.}\,(\to\mathrm{E})$$

Fig. 2B2.1a.

However, if M is a normal form or a λI-term this freedom will disappear and Δ will be completely determined by M, as we shall see in the next lemma and the exercise below it.

2B3 Lemma (Uniqueness of deductions for nf's) (Ben-Yelles 1979 Cor. 3.2.) *Let M be a β-nf and Δ a* TA$_\lambda$*-deduction of* $\Gamma \mapsto M{:}\tau$. *Then*

(i) *every type in Δ has an occurrence in τ or in a type in Γ,*
(ii) *Δ is unique, i.e. if Δ' is also a deduction of $\Gamma \mapsto M{:}\tau$ then $\Delta' \equiv \Delta$.*

Proof Use induction on $|M|$. The cases $M \equiv y$ and $M \equiv \lambda x{\cdot}P$ are easy. Since M is a β-nf, by 1B10 the only other possible case is

$$M \;\equiv\; yP_1 \ldots P_n \qquad (n \geq 1).$$

In this case any deduction Δ of $\Gamma \mapsto M{:}\tau$ must contain an axiom

$$y : (\rho_1 \to \ldots \to \rho_n \to \tau) \;\mapsto\; y : (\rho_1 \to \ldots \to \rho_n \to \tau),$$

as well as n deductions $\Delta_1, \ldots, \Delta_n$ giving

$$\Gamma_1 \mapsto P_1{:}\rho_1,\; \ldots, \Gamma_n \mapsto P_n{:}\rho_n$$

followed by n applications of ($\to$E) to deduce

$$\{y : (\rho_1 \to \ldots \to \rho_n \to \tau)\} \cup \Gamma_1 \cup \ldots \cup \Gamma_n \;\mapsto\; (yP_1 \ldots P_n) : \tau.$$

And Γ must be

$$\{y : (\rho_1 \to \ldots \to \rho_n \to \tau)\} \cup \Gamma_1 \cup \ldots \cup \Gamma_n.$$

To prove (i): by part (i) of the induction hypothesis every type in a Δ_i occurs in ρ_i or Γ_i and hence in Γ; also the type of y occurs in Γ. Hence (i) holds.

To prove (ii): the argument above shows that Δ' must use the same rules at the same positions as in Δ. And the type assigned to y in Δ' is determined by Γ and the assumption that type-contexts are consistent; then the types of $P_1, \ldots, P_n$ are determined by the type of y. □

2B3.1 *Note* (Subformula property) Part (i) of 2B3 corresponds to what is usually called in logic the ***subformula property;*** this says that in a Natural Deduction system every formula in an irreducible deduction occurs in either the conclusion or an undischarged assumption. (The correspondence between types and propositional logic will be fully described in Chapter 6.)

In contrast the TA$_\lambda$-deduction in Fig. 2B2.1a contains a type σ that does not occur in an undischarged assumption or the conclusion.

2B3.2 *Exercise** (Uniqueness of deductions for λI-terms) Show that if Δ is a TA$_\lambda$-deduction of $\Gamma \mapsto M{:}\tau$ and M is a λI-term, then Δ is unique; i.e. if Δ' is also a TA$_\lambda$-deduction of $\Gamma \mapsto M{:}\tau$ then $\Delta' \equiv \Delta$. (Hint (Thierry Coquand): use 2B3 and some facts from 2C and 2D below, and the leftmost-reduction theorem (1B9), plus some thought on the form that a leftmost reduction must have; see the Answers for details.)

The following three lemmas will be needed in the next section. The first is a special case of the third but is stated separately because it is needed in the proof of the third.

2B4 First Substitution Lemma for Deductions *Let* $\Gamma \vdash_\lambda M{:}\tau$ *and let* $[y/x]\Gamma$ *be the result of substituting* y *for a term-variable* x *in* Γ. *If either of the following holds:*

(i) $y \notin \mathit{Subjects}(\Gamma)$,

(ii) y *and* x *receive the same type in* Γ,

then

$$[y/x]\Gamma \vdash_\lambda ([y/x]M) : \tau.$$

Proof First, in both cases (i) and (ii) $[y/x]\Gamma$ satisfies the consistency condition for contexts. Next, by 2A11 there is a deduction of

$$\Gamma^- \mapsto M : \tau$$

for some $\Gamma^- \subseteq \Gamma$ with *Subjects* $(\Gamma^-) = FV(M)$. Then $[y/x]\Gamma^-$ is consistent. An induction on $|M|$ then shows that

$$[y/x]\Gamma^- \vdash_\lambda ([y/x]M) : \tau.^1$$

Then the weakening lemma (2A9.1) gives the result. □

2B5 α-Invariance Lemma *If* $\Gamma \vdash_\lambda P{:}\tau$ *and* $P \equiv_\alpha Q$ *then* $\Gamma \vdash_\lambda Q{:}\tau$.

Proof [Depends on Section 9C] It is enough to prove the result for one change of bound variable, say the replacement of a component $\underline{\lambda x{\cdot}M}$ of P by $\lambda y{\cdot}[y/x]M$ with $y \notin FV(M)$. If $\underline{\lambda x{\cdot}M} \equiv \underline{P}$ the result follows using 2B4. If $\underline{\lambda x{\cdot}M}$ is a proper part of $\underline{P}$, use 9C5 (a replacement lemma). □

2B6 Second Substitution Lemma for Deductions *Let* Γ_1 *be consistent with* Γ_2 *and let*

$$\Gamma_1, x{:}\sigma \vdash_\lambda M{:}\tau, \qquad \Gamma_2 \vdash_\lambda N{:}\sigma$$

Then

$$\Gamma_1 \cup \Gamma_2 \vdash_\lambda [N/x]M : \tau.$$

Proof Assume $x \in FV(M)$. (If not, the result holds trivially.) By 2B5 we can assume no variable bound in M is free in xN. In this case $[N/x]M$ is simply the result of replacing each free x in M by N with no accompanying changes of bound variables. And by 2A11 we can assume that

$$\begin{aligned} \mathit{Subjects}(\Gamma_1) \cup \{x\} &= FV(M), \\ \mathit{Subjects}(\Gamma_2) &= FV(N). \end{aligned}$$

The result is then proved by a straightforward induction on $|M|$. □

[1] By the way, y might be bound in M. To deal with the case that $M \equiv \lambda y{\cdot}P$, it is necessary to use the induction hypothesis twice and use the fact that $|[z/y]P| = |P|$.

2C Subject reduction and expansion

Besides avoiding logical paradoxes another main purpose of type-theories is to avoid errors of mis-matching in programming. If a term P has a type τ we can think of P as being in some sense "safe". If P represents a stage in some computation which continues by $\beta\eta$-reducing P, we would like to know that all later stages in the computation are just as safe as P. The following theorem guarantees this.

2C1 Subject-reduction Theorem (Morris 1968 §4D Thm. 1, Seldin 1968 §3D Thm. 2.) *If* $\Gamma \vdash_\lambda P:\tau$ *and* $P \rhd_{\beta\eta} Q$ *then*

$$\Gamma \vdash_\lambda Q:\tau.$$

Proof [Depends on lemmas in 9C] First, by 2A11 there exists a deduction Δ of $\Gamma^- \mapsto P:\tau$ for some $\Gamma^- \subseteq \Gamma$ with *Subjects* $(\Gamma^-) = FV(P)$. By 1C5.1, $FV(P) \supseteq FV(Q)$. Hence by 9C5 it is enough to prove the theorem when P is a β- or η-redex and Q is its contractum.

Case 1: $P \equiv (\lambda x M)N$, $Q \equiv [N/x]M$. If $x \in FV(M)$ then by the subject-construction theorem (2B2) the lower steps of Δ must have form

$$\dfrac{\dfrac{\Gamma_1, x:\sigma \ \mapsto\ M:\tau}{\Gamma_1 \ \mapsto\ (\lambda x\cdot M):(\sigma\to\tau)}(\to\mathrm{I})_{\mathrm{main}} \qquad \Gamma_2 \ \mapsto\ N:\sigma}{\Gamma_1 \cup \Gamma_2 \ \mapsto\ ((\lambda x\cdot M)N):\tau}(\to\mathrm{E})$$

where $\Gamma_1 \cup \Gamma_2 = \Gamma^-$. Then 2B6 applied to the deductions for M and N gives

$$\Gamma_1 \cup \Gamma_2 \vdash [N/x]M:\tau$$

If $x \notin FV(M)$ the proof is similar.

Case 2: $P \equiv \lambda x\cdot Mx$, $Q \equiv M$, $x \notin FV(M)$. Then $\tau \equiv \rho\to\sigma$ for some ρ and σ, and by 2B2 the last steps in Δ must have form

$$\dfrac{\dfrac{\Gamma^- \ \mapsto\ M:\rho\to\sigma \qquad x:\rho \ \mapsto\ x:\rho}{\Gamma^-, x:\rho \ \mapsto\ Mx:\sigma}(\to\mathrm{E})}{\Gamma^- \ \mapsto\ (\lambda x\cdot Mx):\rho\to\sigma.}(\to\mathrm{I})_{\mathrm{main}}$$

Thus Δ contains a deduction of $\Gamma^- \mapsto M:\tau$ as required. □

The subject-reduction theorem has a partial analogue for expansion as follows.

2C2 Subject-expansion Theorem *If* $\Gamma \vdash_\lambda Q:\tau$ *and* $P \rhd_\beta Q$ *by non-duplicating and non-cancelling contractions, then*

$$\Gamma \vdash_\lambda P:\tau.$$

Proof Exercise. This theorem is a special case of Curry et al. 1972 p.315, §14D Thm. 3 (= Seldin 1968 §3D Thm. 3). □

2C2.1 *Corollary If P is a closed BCIλ-term and $P \triangleright_\beta Q$ then*

$$\Gamma \vdash_\lambda P:\tau \iff \Gamma \vdash_\lambda Q:\tau$$

Proof For "$\Leftarrow$" use 1D6 and 2C2; for "$\Rightarrow$" use 2C1. □

The subject-expansion theorem can be extended to some cancelling contractions under suitable restrictions. (For example see Curry et al. 1972 §14D Thm. 3 or Hindley 1989 Thm. 3.3.) But it cannot be extended to arbitrary contractions, as the following examples show.

2C2.2 *Example $P \triangleright_{1\beta} Q$ by a cancelling contraction and Q has a type but P has no type*:

$$P \equiv (\lambda uv\cdot v)(\lambda x\cdot xx), \qquad Q \equiv \lambda v\cdot v.$$

We have $\vdash_\lambda Q:a{\to}a$ by 2A8.3. But no TA$_\lambda$-deduction has a conclusion with form $\mapsto P:\tau$. Because such a deduction would have to contain a deduction of $\mapsto (\lambda x\cdot xx):\sigma$ for some σ and this is impossible by 2A8.6.

2C2.3 *Example* $P \triangleright_{1\beta} Q$ *by a duplicating contraction and Q has a type but P has none*:

$$P \equiv (\lambda x\cdot xx)\mathbf{I}, \qquad Q \equiv \mathbf{II}.$$

We have $\vdash_\lambda Q:a{\to}a$ by 2A8.5. But P has no type because $\lambda x{\cdot}xx$ has none (by 2A8.6).

2C2.4 *Example* $P \triangleright_{1\beta} Q$ *by a cancellation, P and Q both have types, but Q has more types than P*:

$$P \equiv \lambda xyz\cdot(\lambda u\cdot y)(xz), \qquad Q \equiv \lambda xyz\cdot y.$$

It is easy to prove that

$$\vdash_\lambda P:(c{\to}d){\to}b{\to}c{\to}b, \qquad \vdash_\lambda Q:a{\to}b{\to}c{\to}b;$$

and an application of the principal-type algorithm (3E1) will show that the types possessed by P are exactly the substitution-instances of the one shown above, and similarly for Q. Hence P cannot have the type displayed for Q. (Roughly speaking, the underlying reason is that x has a function position in P and must therefore be assumed to have a function-type $c{\to}d$; since x does not occur at all in Q the type of Q has no such limitation.)

2C2.5 *Example* $P \triangleright_{1\beta} Q$ *by a duplication, P and Q both have types, but Q has more types than P*:

$$P \equiv (\lambda vxyz\cdot v(y(vxz)))\mathbf{I}, \qquad Q \equiv \lambda xyz\cdot\mathbf{I}(y(\mathbf{I}xz)).$$

By 2A8.8 we have

$$\vdash_\lambda P:(a{\to}b){\to}(b{\to}a{\to}b){\to}a{\to}a{\to}b,$$
$$\vdash_\lambda Q:(a{\to}b){\to}(b{\to}c){\to}a{\to}c;$$

and an application of the principal-type algorithm (3E1) will show that P cannot have the type displayed for Q. (The underlying reason is that the two v's in P must receive the same type whereas the two **I**'s in Q are not so limited.)

2C2.6 *Example* *P η-contracts to Q, P and Q both have types, but Q has more types than P:*

$$P \equiv \lambda xy \cdot xy, \qquad Q \equiv \lambda y \cdot y.$$

It is easy to see that

$$\vdash_\lambda P:(a \to b) \to a \to b, \qquad \vdash_\lambda Q:a \to a,$$

and that a TA_λ-deduction of $\mapsto P:a \to a$ is impossible (because x is in a function position in P).

2C3 Definition (Types(M)) If M is closed, define ***Types(M)*** to be the set of all τ such that $\vdash_\lambda M:\tau$.

We shall see in Chapter 3 that if *Types(M)* is not empty its members are exactly the substitution-instances of one type, the *principal type* of M; hence *Types(M)* is either empty or infinite.

2C3.1 *Lemma* *Let P be closed. Then*

(i) $P \rhd_\beta Q \implies Types(P) \subseteq Types(Q)$,
(ii) *if $P \rhd_\beta Q$ by a non-cancelling and non-duplicating reduction, then*

$$Types(P) = Types(Q).$$

Proof By 2C1 and 2C2. □

2C3.2 *Note* (Conversion-invariance) Examples 2C2.2–2C2.6 show that we do not always have

$$M =_\beta N \implies Types(M) = Types(N).$$

Even worse, we shall see an example in 7A2.1 where $M =_\beta N$ but

$$Types(M) \cap Types(N) = \emptyset.$$

Thus *Types(M)* is very definitely not invariant under conversion.

From a theoretical point of view this seems unsatisfactory. In fact, continuing the Church-versus-Curry discussion from 2A3, it must be admitted that conversion-sensitivity of *Types(M)* is the main disadvantage of a Curry-style type system. In a Church system the type of M does not change with conversion (because all terms are typed, including β-redexes, and this fact restricts the β-reduction rule and prevents type-changes). But when we move to a Curry-style system to get the extra expressive power provided by its polymorphism, we do not get it for free, and the price we pay is that *Types(M)* can change with conversion.

However, Chapter 4 will describe the effect of adding a new rule to TA_λ to overcome this defect, and it will give theoretical evidence to suggest that perhaps the price is not so high after all.

In practice too the conversion-sensitivity of *Types(M)* has turned out to be a very small problem. Indeed, if one views an assignment $M:\sigma\to\tau$ as saying that the application of M to every term with type σ is "safe" in some sense, then the most important practical property of a type-system is the subject-reduction theorem, which says that if M has type $\sigma\to\tau$ it will not lose this safety-feature during a reduction. If *Types(M)* happens to increase as M is reduced this is not a drawback but simply means that M is becoming safer. In particular, practical programming languages like ML and its relatives operate very successfully without conversion-invariance.

2D The typable terms

The system TA_λ divides the λ-terms in a natural way into two complementary classes: those which can receive types, such as $\lambda xyz\cdot x(yz)$, and those which cannot, such as $\lambda x\cdot xx$. The former may be regarded as "safe" in the sense that if a term has a type we know there is a way of assigning types to all its components that avoids mis-matches of types. The following is a precise definition of this class.

2D1 Definition A term M is called ***(TA_λ-) typable*** or ***stratified*** iff there exist Γ and τ such that

$$\Gamma \vdash_\lambda M:\tau.$$

2D2 Lemma *The class of all* TA_λ*-typable terms is closed under the following operations:*

(i) *taking subterms (i.e. all subterms of a typable term are typable);*
(ii) *$\beta\eta$-reduction;*
(iii) *non-cancelling and non-duplicating β-expansion;*
(iv) *λ-abstraction (i.e. if M is typable so is $\lambda x\cdot M$).*

Proof (i) by 2B2. (ii) by 2C1. (iii) by 2C2. (iv) by rule ($\to$I). □

2D3 Theorem *The class of all* TA_λ*-typable terms is decidable; that is, there is an algorithm which decides whether a given term is typable in* TA_λ.

Proof The principal-type algorithm (3E1) will be a suitable decision-procedure. □

2D4 Remark (Normalization) A property that nearly every type-theory in the literature possesses is the ***weak normalization (WN)*** property, which says that every typable term can be reduced to a normal form. Many type-theories also have the ***strong normalization (SN)*** property, which says that all reductions of a typable term are finite. Both WN and SN can be regarded as safety-features of the type-theory in question: if reductions are viewed as imitating the process of computing values, WN says that a computation can always be continued to a result if we wish and SN says that all computations terminate.

The next theorems state precisely the position for TA_λ.

2D5 Weak Normalization (WN) Theorem (Turing 1942, Curry and Feys 1958, etc.) *Every* TA_λ*-typable term has both a* β*-nf and a* $\beta\eta$*-nf.*

Proof See 5C1 and 5C1.1 for a proof (from Turing 1942), and 5C1.2 for historical notes. □

2D5.1 *Example* By 2D5 the fixed-point combinator **Y** in 1A10.1 is not typable in TA_λ; because by 1B9.1, **Y** has no β-nf.

2D6 Strong Normalization (SN) Theorem (Sanchis 1967, Diller 1968, etc.) *If M is a* TA_λ*-typable term, every* $\beta\eta$*-reduction that starts at M is finite.*

Proof There are many proofs in the literature besides those of Sanchis and Diller; for example HS 86 Appendix 2 contains an accessible one for β in Thm. A2.3 and one for $\beta\eta$ in Thm. A2.4. For references to some others see 5C2.2. □

2D6.1 *Note* Since SN implies WN there is no real need for a separate treatment of WN. But the Turing proof of WN in 5C1 is both simpler and older than any proof of SN. Further, most applications of normalization turn out to be of WN rather than SN. The following are a couple of such applications.

2D7 Theorem *There is a decision-procedure for* β*-equality of* TA_λ*-typable terms; i.e. an algorithm which, given any typable terms P and Q, will decide whether* $P =_\beta Q$. *Similarly for* $\beta\eta$*-equality.*

Proof Reduce P and Q to their β-nf's (which exist by WN, and can be found using leftmost reductions, by 1B9) and see whether they differ. □

2D7.1 *Note* The complexity of the above decision-procedure can be measured in terms of the Grzegorczyk hierarchy $\mathscr{E}^0$, $\mathscr{E}^1$, $\mathscr{E}^2$, ... of sets of primitive recursive functions (Grzegorczyk 1953 p.29): in fact Statman 1979b pp. 73–75 points out that the procedure can be programmed to operate on a Turing machine in $\mathscr{E}^4$ time but no decision-procedure for β-equality of typable terms can be made to operate in $\mathscr{E}^3$ time. (The members of $\mathscr{E}^3$ are known as *elementary functions.*)

2D8 Theorem *Every BCKλ-term (as defined in 1D2) is typable.*

Proof Hindley 1989 Thm. 4.1, depending on WN. □

2D8.1 *Note* The BCKλ-terms are terms without multiple occurrences of variables (except possibly for binding occurrences), so the above theorem connects untypability with multiple occurrences of variables. On the other hand not every term with multiple occurrences is untypable; consider $\mathbf{S} \equiv \lambda xyz{\cdot}xz(yz)$ in 2A8.7(iii) for example.

3

The principal-type algorithm

A typable term has in general an infinite set of types in TA_λ. For example if $\mathsf{I} \equiv \lambda x{\cdot}x$ it is possible to assign to I every type with form $\sigma{\to}\sigma$, by the following deduction:

$$\frac{x{:}\sigma \quad \mapsto \quad x{:}\sigma}{\mapsto \quad (\lambda x{\cdot}x){:}\,\sigma{\to}\sigma}\ ({\to}\mathrm{I})$$

(like 2A8.3). But all the types in this infinite set are substitution-instances of the one type

$$a{\to}a,$$

and it is easy to see that I has no other types than these. (In fact every deduction for I must have the simple form shown above, by the subject-construction theorem.) The type $a{\to}a$ is called a *principal type* for I.

The aim of the present chapter is to show that the existence of a principal type is a property of all typable terms, not just I. In effect the principal type of a term is the most general type it can receive in TA_λ, and the *principal type theorem* will say that every typable term has one. Further, and most important in practice, an algorithm will be described for finding it.

This algorithm will decide whether a given term M is typable and, if the answer is "yes", will output a principal type for M. Such algorithms are usually called *type-checking* or *principal-type* or *PT* algorithms. The existence of a PT algorithm is what gives TA_λ and its extensions such as ML their practical value, since if the typability of a program is regarded as a safety criterion the programmer will want to be able to decide effectively whether a newly created program satisfies this criterion.

The PT algorithm below will be easy to describe and even easier to apply in practice. But to prove the PT theorem a bald statement of the algorithm will not be enough; we shall need also a proof that the algorithm is correct, i.e. that it does what it claims to do. In the account below a correctness proof will be included with the algorithm in the form of comments to each of its steps, explaining the purpose and effect of each step as the reader meets it.

A little knowledge of substitution, unification and most general unifiers will be needed so introductions to these will be included before the statement of the algorithm.

3A Principal types and their history

3A1 Definition (Type-substitutions) A ***(type-) substitution*** $\mathbb{s}$ is any expression

$$[\sigma_1/a_1,\ldots,\sigma_n/a_n],$$

where $a_1,\ldots,a_n$ are distinct type-variables and $\sigma_1,\ldots,\sigma_n$ are any types. For any τ define $\mathbb{s}(\tau)$ to be the type obtained by simultaneously substituting σ_1 for $a_1,\ldots,\sigma_n$ for a_n throughout τ. In more detail, define

(i) $\mathbb{s}(a_i) \equiv \sigma_i$,

(ii) $\mathbb{s}(b) \equiv b$ *if* b *is an atom* $\notin \{a_1,\ldots,a_n\}$,

(iii) $\mathbb{s}(\rho\to\sigma) \equiv \mathbb{s}(\rho)\to\mathbb{s}(\sigma)$.

We call $\mathbb{s}(\tau)$ an ***instance*** of τ.

3A1.1 *Notation* Letters "$\mathbb{r}$", "$\mathbb{s}$", "$\mathbb{t}$", "$\mathbb{u}$", "$\mathbb{v}$" will denote type-substitutions. If $\mathbb{s} \equiv [\sigma_1/a_1,\ldots,\sigma_n/a_n]$ a frequent alternative notation to $\mathbb{s}(\tau)$ will be

$$[\sigma_1/a_1,\ldots,\sigma_n/a_n]\tau.$$

Recall that the set of all variables occurring in a type τ is called $Vars(\tau)$. The sets of all type-variables occurring in a finite sequence $\langle\tau_1,\ldots,\tau_n\rangle$ of types, or in a deduction Δ, are called respectively

$$Vars(\tau_1,\ldots,\tau_n), \qquad Vars(\Delta).$$

3A2 Definition The action of a substitution $\mathbb{s}$ is extended to finite sequences of types, to contexts and to TA$_\lambda$-formulae thus:

$$\mathbb{s}(\langle\tau_1,\ldots,\tau_n\rangle) = \langle\mathbb{s}(\tau_1),\ldots,\mathbb{s}(\tau_n)\rangle,$$

$$\mathbb{s}(\Gamma) = \{x_1{:}\mathbb{s}(\tau_1),\ldots,x_m{:}\mathbb{s}(\tau_m)\} \qquad \textit{if}\ \Gamma = \{x_1{:}\tau_1,\ldots,x_m{:}\tau_m\},$$

$$\mathbb{s}(\Gamma \mapsto M{:}\tau) = \mathbb{s}(\Gamma) \mapsto M{:}\mathbb{s}(\tau).$$

We also extend $\mathbb{s}$ to act on deductions Δ by defining $\mathbb{s}(\Delta)$ to be the result of applying $\mathbb{s}$ to every TA$_\lambda$-formula in Δ. We call $\mathbb{s}(\Delta)$ an ***instance*** of Δ. (Similarly for instances of type-sequences, etc.)

3A2.1 *Notes* (i) The consistency of Γ implies that of $\mathbb{s}(\Gamma)$.

(ii) If Δ is a TA$_\lambda$-deduction then so is $\mathbb{s}(\Delta)$, because the side-conditions in rules ($\to$E) and ($\to$I) in 2A8 remain true after $\mathbb{s}$ has been applied. Hence

$$\Gamma \vdash_\lambda M{:}\tau \implies \mathbb{s}(\Gamma) \vdash_\lambda M{:}\mathbb{s}(\tau),$$

and the set of all types assigned to a term M is closed under substitution.

3A2.2 *Warning* Two distinct concepts of substitution into deductions have now been mentioned, for term-variables in 2B4 and for type-variables above. Note that $Vars(\Delta)$ is a set of type-variables not term-variables, and when $\mathbb{s}$ is applied to Δ the terms in Δ are completely unchanged.

3A3 Definition (Principal types) In TA_λ, a ***principal type*** or ***PT*** of a term M is a type τ such that

(i) $\Gamma \vdash_\lambda M{:}\tau$ *for some* Γ,
(ii) *if* $\Gamma' \vdash_\lambda M{:}\sigma$ *for some* Γ' *and* σ *then* σ *is an instance of* τ.

3A3.1 *Note* By 3A2.1(ii) a type τ is a PT of M iff, for all types σ,

$$(\exists\Gamma')(\Gamma' \vdash_\lambda M{:}\sigma) \iff \sigma \textit{ is an instance of } \tau.$$

Thus a PT of M can be thought of as completely characterizing the set of all types assignable to M.

3A3.2 *Notation* It will be shown in 3B8.2 that a term's principal type is unique (modulo substitutions of distinct variables for distinct variables), so we shall often say "*the* principal type of M" or

$$PT(M).$$

3A4 Definition (Principal pairs) A ***principal pair*** for a term M is a pair $\langle\Gamma,\tau\rangle$ such that the formula $\Gamma \mapsto M{:}\tau$ is TA_λ-deducible and every other TA_λ-deducible formula $\Gamma' \mapsto M{:}\sigma$ is an instance of $\Gamma \mapsto M{:}\tau$.

3A5 Definition (Principal deductions) A ***principal deduction*** for a term M is a deduction Δ of a formula $\Gamma \mapsto M{:}\tau$ such that every other deduction whose conclusion's subject is M is an instance of Δ. To abbreviate "there exists a principal deduction of $\Gamma \mapsto M{:}\tau$" we shall say

$$\Gamma \vdash_p M{:}\tau.$$

3A5.1 *Notes* (i) If Δ is a principal deduction of $\Gamma \mapsto M{:}\tau$ then clearly τ is a principal type of M and $\langle\Gamma,\tau\rangle$ is a principal pair for M. In fact the PT theorem will prove that every typable term has not only a principal type but a principal deduction, and the PT algorithm will be seen to construct principal deductions as well as types. This observation will slightly simplify the algorithm's correctness-proof. Thus a typable term M will be shown to have not only a most general type but a deduction whose every step is most general.

(ii) Although principal types have been studied since 1969, principal deductions were almost entirely neglected until about 1990 when the structure of a principal deduction was characterized by Sachio Hirokawa (Hirokawa 1991a Thms. 1 and 2). This work is beyond the scope of the present book but it is one of the more interesting recent developments in the study of TA_λ and has led to new results on principal types (for example those in Hirokawa 1991b–c, 1993a) and to simplified proofs of some old results.[1]

[1] To be precise, Hirokawa 1991a uses a weaker definition of principal deduction than that in 3A5 above: Hirokawa calls a deduction of $\Gamma \mapsto M{:}\tau$ principal iff the formula $\Gamma \mapsto M{:}\tau$ is a principal pair in the sense of 3A4. But his characterization theorems can easily be modified to fit the definition in 3A5 by extending the conditions in them to apply to all type-variables in a deduction, not just those in its conclusion and undischarged assumptions.

3A6 Principal Type (PT) Theorem *Every typable term has a principal deduction and a principal type in* TA_λ. *Further, there is an algorithm that will decide whether a given* λ*-term* M *is typable in* TA_λ, *and if the answer is "yes" will output a principal deduction and principal type for* M.

Proof See the PT algorithm and correctness-proof in 3E. □

3A6.1 *Exercise** Let $\mathbf{B} \equiv \lambda xyz{\cdot}x(yz)$. The type assigned to $\mathbf{B}$ in Example 2A8.2 was

$$(a \to b) \to (c \to a) \to c \to b.$$

Using the subject-construction theorem (2B2), show that this type is principal for $\mathbf{B}$. That is, show that every type assigned to $\mathbf{B}$ in TA_λ must have form

$$(\rho \to \tau) \to (\sigma \to \rho) \to \sigma \to \tau,$$

where ρ, σ, τ are arbitrary types.

3A7 Historical Comment The PT problem, that of deciding whether a term is typable and finding its principal type if it is, is one that is crucial to many type-systems, and several different PT algorithms have appeared in the literature over the years. One of the best known is probably *Algorithm W* of Damas and Milner 1982. This was devised originally by Robin Milner for the language ML which includes the present system and a version first appeared in print in Milner 1978.

But the history of PT algorithms goes back a long way before 1978. There seem to have been two mainly independent strands of development, one in λ-calculus with combinatory logic and the other in propositional logic. We shall leave the latter until Chapter 7, but it is almost certainly the older of the two; indeed what amounts to the core of a PT algorithm was formulated in propositional logic as long ago as 1957 and was actually run on a computer at that date, and the informal idea behind such algorithms may go back as far as the 1920's (see 7D3).

The first informal use of a PT algorithm in combinatory logic or λ-calculus was probably due to Haskell Curry in the 1950's. Particular examples of type-computations occur in Curry and Feys 1958 (§9B2, pp.284–293) and show very clearly the equation-solving method on which several later formal algorithms were based. But, as mentioned earlier, Curry was mainly interested in stronger systems at that time and only afterwards began to look at simple type-assignment on its own. When he did, he wrote up his earlier methods as a formal equation-solving PT algorithm for TA_C and added a proof of its correctness; these survive in his notes Curry 1966 and were published in Curry 1969.

A PT algorithm and a correctness-proof were also included in an account of TA_C in Hindley 1969, but these differed from Curry's in that the algorithm made explicit use of the unification algorithm of Robinson 1965 to save itself some work.[1]

[1] The preparation of Curry 1969 and Hindley 1969 took place in about 1967 with the authors discussing matters frequently but deliberately keeping their approaches different.

On the λ-calculus side the first PT algorithm was due to James H. Morris and was written out with a correctness proof in his thesis Morris 1968. This was an equation-solving algorithm and like all such, including Curry's, it automatically did all the unification it needed without calling on an external algorithm.[1]

For about ten years after 1968 type-assignment remained a very specialist topic, then the development of ML by Robin Milner and his group led to a surge of interest in assignment systems and PT algorithms. Milner's own algorithm was invented as a preliminary to this development, and was applied to $\rightarrow$-types and pair-types in a λ-calculus with the extra operator *let* that is characteristic of ML. It was written out formally in Milner 1978 and rewritten and extended in Damas and Milner 1982.[2] Milner's algorithm, like Hindley's, depended on Robinson's unification algorithm to save work.[3]

Since Milner 1978 many modified or extended PT algorithms have been published, some depending on external unification algorithms and others being self-sufficient. See Tiuryn 1990 for a survey.

3A7.1 *Note* The PT algorithm in this chapter will use the method of Hindley 1969 and Milner 1978 rather than equation-solving.

As mentioned above this method depends on a unification algorithm given in advance, but unification algorithms are widely available as packages in practice, so this feature makes a PT algorithm easy to fit into an already given system in a practical implementation.

This method will also turn out to be well suited to deal with the case where the term whose PT is being computed is a combination of other terms $P_1, \ldots, P_n$ whose PT's are already known. This situation is common in practice, where a library of terms and their PT's can be built up and used in determining the PT's of new terms, and one of the original motivations for the method was a belief that it would probably use such accumulated information more efficiently than a straight equation-solving algorithm.

However, the account in this chapter will not be concerned with maximizing efficiency, but only with the (usually incompatible) aim of making the PT algorithm's structure and motivation as clear as possible.

3B Type-substitutions

To make the statement of the PT algorithm reasonably concise it will help to introduce some preliminary definitions and lemmas on type-substitutions.

[1] Morris 1968 was independent of Curry's 1966–67 work and must have been prepared at about the same time. Although Morris 1968 was never published there are later accounts of equation-solving λ-calculus algorithms available in the literature; for example there is one with a correctness-proof in Wand 1987.

[2] Milner's algorithm was discovered independently of earlier work. Milner 1978 did not contain a correctness-proof but there was one in the thesis Damas 1984 to which Damas and Milner 1982 referred.

[3] The history of these early algorithms seems to be a tale of repeated re-discovery of very similar ideas. This is not really very surprising, as the ideas are very simple once they are approached in the right way; it is their applications that make them important, not any intrinsic subtlety.

3B1 Notation As defined in 3A1 a substitution is just a finite sequence of instructions $\mathbb{s} \equiv [\sigma_1/a_1, \ldots, \sigma_n/a_n]$ saying "*simultaneously substitute* σ_1 *for* $a_1, \ldots, \sigma_n$ *for* a_n". The following extra notation will be useful.[1]

The case $n = 0$ will be allowed and called the ***empty substitution***, $\mathbb{e}$. So

$$\mathbb{e}(\tau) \equiv \tau.$$

If $n = 1$, $\mathbb{s}$ will be called a ***single substitution.***

Each part-expression σ_i/a_i of $\mathbb{s}$ will be called a ***component*** of $\mathbb{s}$, and called ***trivial*** if $\sigma_i \equiv a_i$.

If all trivial components are deleted from $\mathbb{s}$ the resulting substitution will be called the ***nontrivial kernel*** of $\mathbb{s}$.

The set $\{a_1, \ldots, a_n\}$ will be called ***Dom***$(\mathbb{s})$ or the ***variable-domain*** of $\mathbb{s}$.

And $Vars(\sigma_1, \ldots, \sigma_n)$ will be called ***Range***$(\mathbb{s})$ or the ***variable-range*** of $\mathbb{s}$.

3B2 Definition Substitutions $\mathbb{s}$ and $\mathbb{t}$ are ***extensionally equivalent*** ($\mathbb{s} =_{\text{ext}} \mathbb{t}$) iff $\mathbb{s}(\tau) \equiv \mathbb{t}(\tau)$ for all τ.

3B2.1 *Lemma* (i) $b \notin Dom(\mathbb{s}) \implies \mathbb{s}(b) \equiv b$.
(ii) $\mathbb{s} =_{\text{ext}} \mathbb{t}$ *iff* $\mathbb{s}$ *and* $\mathbb{t}$ *have the same non-trivial kernel.*

3B3 Definition (Restriction, $\mathbb{s} \restriction \mathbb{V}$) If $\mathbb{s} \equiv [\sigma_1/a_1, \ldots, \sigma_n/a_n]$ and $\mathbb{V}$ is a given set of variables, the ***restriction*** $\mathbb{s} \restriction \mathbb{V}$ of $\mathbb{s}$ to $\mathbb{V}$ is the substitution consisting of the components σ_i/a_i of $\mathbb{s}$ such that $a_i \in \mathbb{V}$.

3B3.1 *Lemma* $(\mathbb{s} \restriction Vars(\tau))(\tau) \equiv \mathbb{s}(\tau)$.

3B4 Definition (Union) If $\mathbb{s} \equiv [\sigma_1/a_1, \ldots, \sigma_n/a_n]$ and $\mathbb{t} \equiv [\tau_1/b_1, \ldots, \tau_p/b_p]$ and either $a_1, \ldots, a_n, b_1, \ldots, b_p$ are all distinct or $a_i \equiv b_j \Rightarrow \sigma_i \equiv \tau_j$, define

$$\mathbb{s} \cup \mathbb{t} \equiv [\sigma_1/a_1, \ldots, \sigma_n/a_n, \tau_1/b_1, \ldots, \tau_p/b_p]$$

(with repetitions omitted).

3B4.1 *Lemma* (i) $Dom(\mathbb{s} \cup \mathbb{t}) = Dom(\mathbb{s}) \cup Dom(\mathbb{t})$.
(ii) *If* $\mathbb{s} =_{\text{ext}} \mathbb{s}'$ *and* $\mathbb{t} =_{\text{ext}} \mathbb{t}'$ *and* $\mathbb{s} \cup \mathbb{t}$ *is defined, then so is* $\mathbb{s}' \cup \mathbb{t}'$ *and*

$$\mathbb{s} \cup \mathbb{t} =_{\text{ext}} \mathbb{s}' \cup \mathbb{t}'.$$

The next definition will be the *composition* of two substitutions $\mathbb{s}$ and $\mathbb{t}$, a simultaneous substitution that will have the same effect as applying $\mathbb{t}$ and $\mathbb{s}$ in succession. To motivate it, consider the case

$$\mathbb{s} \equiv [(c{\to}d)/a, (b{\to}a)/b], \qquad \mathbb{t} \equiv [(b{\to}a)/b]$$

and let $\tau \equiv a{\to}b$. The result of applying first t then s is easily seen to be

$$\mathbb{s}(\mathbb{t}(\tau)) \equiv (c{\to}d){\to}(b{\to}a){\to}(c{\to}d);$$

[1] There seems to be no standard substitution notation in the literature.

the problem is to find a simultaneous substitution having the same effect. A naive attempt to use $\mathbb{s} \cup \mathbb{t}$ would fail, because

$$(\mathbb{s} \cup \mathbb{t})(\tau) \quad \equiv \quad \mathbb{s}(\tau) \quad \equiv \quad (c \to d) \to b \to a.$$

But there does exist a suitable substitution, namely

$$[(c \to d)/a,\ (\mathbb{s}(b \to a))/b]$$

This special case is generalized as follows.

3B5 Definition (Composition) If $\mathbb{s}$ and $\mathbb{t}$ are any substitutions, say

$$\mathbb{s} \equiv [\sigma_1/a_1, \ldots, \sigma_n/a_n], \qquad \mathbb{t} \equiv [\tau_1/b_1, \ldots, \tau_p/b_p],$$

define

$$\mathbb{s} \circ \mathbb{t} \equiv [\sigma_{i_1}/a_{i_1}, \ldots, \sigma_{i_h}/a_{i_h}, \mathbb{s}(\tau_1)/b_1, \ldots, \mathbb{s}(\tau_p)/b_p]$$

where $\{a_{i_1}, \ldots, a_{i_h}\} = Dom(\mathbb{s}) - Dom(\mathbb{t})$ and $0 \le h \le n$.

3B5.1 *Lemma* (i) $Dom(\mathbb{s} \circ \mathbb{t}) = Dom(\mathbb{s}) \cup Dom(\mathbb{t})$.
(ii) $(\mathbb{s} \circ \mathbb{t})(\tau) \equiv \mathbb{s}(\mathbb{t}(\tau))$.
(iii) $\mathbb{r} \circ (\mathbb{s} \circ \mathbb{t}) =_{\text{ext}} (\mathbb{r} \circ \mathbb{s}) \circ \mathbb{t}$.
(iv) $\mathbb{s} =_{\text{ext}} \mathbb{s}', \ \mathbb{t} =_{\text{ext}} \mathbb{t}' \implies \mathbb{s} \circ \mathbb{t} =_{\text{ext}} \mathbb{s}' \circ \mathbb{t}'$.
(v) *By* (ii), *an instance of an instance of* τ *is an instance of* τ.

3B5.2 *Exercise** (i) Write out $\mathbb{s} \circ \mathbb{t}$ in the special case that $s \equiv [a/b]$ and $\mathbb{t} \equiv [b/a]$, and verify that $(\mathbb{s} \circ \mathbb{t})(\tau) \equiv s(t(\tau))$ in the case $\tau \equiv a \to b$.
(ii) Show that the action of any $\mathbb{s}$ on a given type τ can be expressed as a composition $\mathbb{s}_1 \circ \ldots \circ \mathbb{s}_k$ of single substitutions, in the sense that

$$(\mathbb{s}_1 \circ \ldots \circ \mathbb{s}_k)(\tau) \quad \equiv \quad \mathbb{s}(\tau).$$

The next lemma will play an important role in the correctness proof of the PT algorithm: it says that if a composition $\mathbb{s} \circ \mathbb{t}$ is "extended" to $\mathbb{r} \cup (\mathbb{s} \circ \mathbb{t})$, the extended substitution can also be expressed as a composition with $\mathbb{t}$ (under certain conditions on $\mathbb{r}$ to prevent clashes).

3B6 Composition-extension Lemma *Let* $\mathbb{r}$, $\mathbb{s}$, $\mathbb{t}$ *be substitutions such that*
(i) $Dom(\mathbb{r}) \cap (Dom(\mathbb{s}) \cup Dom(\mathbb{t})) = \emptyset$,
(ii) $Dom(\mathbb{r}) \cap Range(\mathbb{t}) = \emptyset$.
Then $\mathbb{r} \cup (\mathbb{s} \circ \mathbb{t})$ *and* $(\mathbb{r} \cup \mathbb{s}) \circ \mathbb{t}$ *are both defined and*

$$\mathbb{r} \cup (\mathbb{s} \circ \mathbb{t}) \quad \equiv \quad (\mathbb{r} \cup \mathbb{s}) \circ \mathbb{t}$$

Proof Suppose $\mathbb{r}$, $\mathbb{s}$, $\mathbb{t}$ are, respectively,

$$[\rho_1/a_1, \ldots, \rho_r/a_r], \quad [\sigma_1/b_1, \ldots, \sigma_s/b_s], \quad [\tau_1/c_1, \ldots, \tau_t/c_t]$$

with $r, s, t \ge 0$, and suppose

(1) $\qquad Dom(\mathbb{s}) - Dom(\mathbb{t}) = \{b_{i_1}, \ldots, b_{i_h}\} \qquad (h \ge 0).$

Then $\mathbb{r} \cup (\mathbb{s} \circ \mathbb{t})$ is

$$[\rho_1/a_1, \ldots, \rho_r/a_r,\ \sigma_{i_1}/b_{i_1}, \ldots, \sigma_{i_h}/b_{i_h},\ \mathbb{s}(\tau_1)/c_1, \ldots, \mathbb{s}(\tau_t)/c_t].$$

(This is defined, since $Dom(\mathbb{s} \circ \mathbb{t}) = Dom(\mathbb{s}) \cup Dom(\mathbb{t})$ by 3B5.1(i) and the latter is disjoint from $Dom(\mathbb{r})$ by assumption (i).) On the other hand $(\mathbb{r} \cup \mathbb{s}) \circ \mathbb{t}$ is

$$[\rho_1/a_1, \ldots, \rho_r/a_r,\ \sigma_1/b_1, \ldots, \sigma_s/b_s] \circ [\tau_1/c_1, \ldots, \tau_t/c_t].$$

(This is defined because $\mathbb{r} \cup \mathbb{s}$ is defined, by (i).) Now by (i) and (1),

$$Dom(\mathbb{r} \cup \mathbb{s}) - Dom(\mathbb{t}) = \{a_1, \ldots, a_r, b_{i_1}, \ldots, b_{i_h}\}$$

so by the definition of composition, $(\mathbb{r} \cup \mathbb{s}) \circ \mathbb{t}$ is

$$[\rho_1/a_1, \ldots, \rho_r/a_r,\ \sigma_{i_1}/b_{i_1}, \ldots \sigma_{i_h}/b_{i_h},\ (\mathbb{r} \cup \mathbb{s})(\tau_1)/c_1, \ldots, (\mathbb{r} \cup \mathbb{s})(\tau_t)/c_t].$$

And $(\mathbb{r} \cup \mathbb{s})(\tau_j) \equiv \mathbb{s}(\tau_j)$ for $j = 1, \ldots, t$ by assumption (ii). Hence result. □

To end the section a proof will be given that the PT of a term is unique in a certain sense. The definition of PT carries with it an intuitive feeling that this should be so, and the following definitions will help to make this intuition precise.

3B7 Definition A ***variables-for-variables*** substitution is a substitution $\mathbb{s} \equiv [b_1/a_1, \ldots, b_n/a_n]$ where $b_1, \ldots, b_n$ are variables (not necessarily distinct).

If $b_1, \ldots, b_n$ are distinct, $\mathbb{s}$ is called ***one-to-one***, and if also $\{a_1, \ldots, a_n\} = Vars(\tau)$ for a given type τ, $\mathbb{s}$ is called a ***renaming (of the variables) in*** τ. (Renamings in deductions and finite type-sequences are defined similarly.)

If $\mathbb{s}$ is one-to-one its ***inverse***, $\mathbb{s}^{-1}$, is defined by

$$\mathbb{s}^{-1} \equiv [a_1/b_1, \ldots, a_n/b_n].$$

3B7.1 *Lemma If* $\mathbb{s}$ *is a renaming in* τ *then* $\mathbb{s}^{-1}$ *is a renaming in* $\mathbb{s}(\tau)$ *and*

$$\mathbb{s}^{-1}(\mathbb{s}(\tau)) \equiv \tau.$$

3B7.2 *Warning* A one-to-one substitution may be a renaming in one type but not in another. For example $[b/a]$ is a renaming in $a \to a$ but not in $a \to b$.

3B8 Definition We say σ ***is an alphabetic variant of*** τ, or σ and τ are ***identical modulo renaming***, iff $\sigma \equiv \mathbb{s}(\tau)$ for some renaming $\mathbb{s}$ in τ. (Alphabetic variants of deductions and of finite type-sequences are defined similarly.)

3B8.1 *Lemma* (i) σ *is an alphabetic variant of* τ *iff* σ *and* τ *are instances of each other.*

(ii) *Part* (i) *also holds for deductions and finite type-sequences.*

Proof For "only if" in (i) use 3B7.1. For "if", let $Vars(\tau) = \{a_1, \ldots, a_n\}$ where $a_1, \ldots, a_n$ are distinct, and suppose $\sigma \equiv \mathbb{s}(\tau)$ and $\tau \equiv \mathbb{t}(\sigma)$, for substitutions $\mathbb{s}$ and $\mathbb{t}$ with

$$Dom(\mathbb{s}) = Vars(\tau), \qquad Dom(\mathbb{t}) = Vars(\sigma).$$

Then $\mathbb{t}(\mathbb{s}(a_i)) \equiv a_i$ for $i = 1,\ldots,n$. Hence $\mathbb{s}(a_i)$ cannot be composite, otherwise $\mathbb{t}(\mathbb{s}(a_i))$ would be composite too. Thus $\mathbb{s}$ has form

$$\mathbb{s} \equiv [b_1/a_1,\ldots,b_n/a_n],$$

and $Vars(\sigma) = \{b_1,\ldots,b_n\}$. Also $b_1,\ldots,b_n$ are distinct, because if $b_i \equiv b_j$ then

$$a_i \equiv \mathbb{t}(\mathbb{s}(a_i)) \equiv \mathbb{t}(b_i) \equiv \mathbb{t}(b_j) \equiv \mathbb{t}(\mathbb{s}(a_j)) \equiv a_j.$$

Thus σ is an alphabetic variant of τ. □

3B8.2 *Corollary* (Uniqueness) *Let τ be a principal type of a term M. Then τ is unique modulo renaming, in the sense that another type σ is a principal type of M iff σ is an alphabetic variant of τ. Principal deductions are unique in a similar sense.*

3B8.3 *Lemma* *For each finite set of type-variables $a_1,\ldots,a_m$ and each type τ there is an alphabetic variant of τ that contains none of $a_1,\ldots,a_m$.*

3C Motivating the PT algorithm

The two main steps in the PT algorithm will be the computation of $PT(\lambda x{\cdot}P)$ from $PT(P)$ and the computation of $PT(PQ)$ from $PT(P)$ and $PT(Q)$. The first will be no problem but the second will need a little work which in fact will be the core of the PT algorithm; the aim of the present section is to motivate the method used in this core.

3C1 Discussion Suppose we are trying to decide whether an application PQ is typable in TA_λ, and we already know that

$$PT(P) \equiv \rho{\rightarrow}\sigma, \qquad PT(Q) \equiv \tau.$$

(And for simplicity suppose PQ has no free variables.) Then by 3A3.1 the types assignable to P are generated from $\rho{\rightarrow}\sigma$ by substitution and those assignable to Q are generated from τ. Hence, if we can find substitutions $\mathbb{s}_1$ and $\mathbb{s}_2$ such that

$$\mathbb{s}_1(\rho) \equiv \mathbb{s}_2(\tau),$$

we will be able to deduce a type for PQ by rule ($\rightarrow$E), thus:

$$\frac{\mapsto P{:}\mathbb{s}_1(\rho){\rightarrow}\mathbb{s}_1(\sigma) \qquad \mapsto Q{:}\mathbb{s}_2(\tau)}{\mapsto PQ{:}\mathbb{s}_1(\sigma).}\,(\rightarrow\mathrm{E})$$

Conversely, by the subject-construction theorem (2B2(iii)), every type deduced for PQ must have been obtained from instances of $\rho{\rightarrow}\sigma$ and τ by ($\rightarrow$E) in this way.

Thus the problem of deciding whether PQ is typable reduces to that of finding $\mathbb{s}_1$ and $\mathbb{s}_2$ such that $\mathbb{s}_1(\rho) \equiv \mathbb{s}_2(\tau)$. This suggests the next two definitions.

3C2 Definition (Common instances) (i) Iff $\nu \equiv \mathbb{s}_1(\rho) \equiv \mathbb{s}_2(\tau)$ we call ν a ***common instance (c.i.)*** of the pair $\langle\rho,\tau\rangle$, and we call $\langle\mathbb{s}_1,\mathbb{s}_2\rangle$ a pair of ***converging substitutions*** for $\langle\rho,\tau\rangle$.

(ii) Iff $\langle \nu_1, \ldots, \nu_n \rangle \equiv s_1(\langle \rho_1, \ldots, \rho_n \rangle) \equiv s_2(\langle \tau_1, \ldots, \tau_n \rangle)$ we call $\langle \nu_1, \ldots, \nu_n \rangle$ a ***common instance*** of $\langle \rho_1, \ldots, \rho_n \rangle$ and $\langle \tau_1, \ldots, \tau_n \rangle$. Common instances of pairs of deductions are defined similarly.

3C2.1 *Example* A common instance of the pair $\langle a \to (b \to c), (a \to b) \to a \rangle$ is the type $((\beta \to \gamma) \to \delta) \to (\beta \to \gamma)$ (where β, γ, δ are any given types), and the corresponding converging substitutions are

$$s_1 \;\equiv\; [((\beta \to \gamma) \to \delta)/a,\ \beta/b,\ \gamma/c], \qquad s_2 \;\equiv\; [(\beta \to \gamma)/a,\ \delta/b].$$

3C2.2 *Note* Not every pair of types has a common instance. For example the pair $\langle a \to a, (b \to b) \to b \rangle$ has none, because if $s_1(a \to a) \equiv s_2((b \to b) \to b)$ we would have

$$s_1(a) \;\equiv\; s_2(b \to b), \qquad s_1(a) \;\equiv\; s_2(b),$$

which would imply the impossible identity $s_2(b) \equiv s_2(b) \to s_2(b)$.

3C3 Definition (M.g.c.i.) (i) A ***most general common instance (m.g.c.i.)*** of $\langle \rho, \tau \rangle$ is a common instance ν_0 such that every other common instance is an instance of ν_0. If ν_0 is an m.g.c.i. of $\langle \rho, \tau \rangle$ we shall call any pair $\langle s_1, s_2 \rangle$ such that $s_1(\rho) \equiv s_2(\tau) \equiv \nu_0$ an ***m.g.c.i.-generator*** for $\langle \rho, \tau \rangle$.

(ii) M.g.c.i.'s of pairs of type-sequences and pairs of deductions are defined similarly.

3C3.1 *Exercise** Show that the pair $\langle a \to (b \to c), (a \to b) \to a \rangle$ in 3C2.1 has the following as an m.g.c.i.:

$$\nu_0 \;\equiv\; ((b \to c) \to d) \to b \to c.$$

3C3.2 *Lemma* (i) *M.g.c.i.'s are unique modulo renaming. That is, if ν is an m.g.c.i. of $\langle \rho, \tau \rangle$ the other m.g.c.i.'s of $\langle \rho, \tau \rangle$ are alphabetic variants of ν.*

(ii) *If ρ' and τ' are alphabetic variants of ρ and τ respectively, then $\langle \rho', \tau' \rangle$ has the same common instances and the same m.g.c.i.'s as $\langle \rho, \tau \rangle$.*

(iii) *Similarly for m.g.c.i.'s of deductions and finite type-sequences.*

3C4 Discussion It will be shown later that every pair $\langle \rho, \tau \rangle$ with a common instance has an m.g.c.i. Given this fact, the discussion in 3C1 suggests that if we know $PT(P) \equiv \rho \to \sigma$ and $PT(Q) \equiv \tau$ and we know somehow that $\langle \rho, \tau \rangle$ has a common instance, we can compute $PT(PQ)$ by just constructing the m.g.c.i. of $\langle \rho, \tau \rangle$, say

$$\nu \;\equiv\; s_1(\rho) \;\equiv\; s_2(\tau),$$

and then letting $PT(PQ) \equiv s_1(\sigma)$.

And this is indeed true, provided we avoid one small snag. Suppose σ contains some variables $b_1, \ldots, b_k$ that do not occur in ρ, and by bad luck the m.g.c.i. ν we have constructed also contains some of these variables. Then $s_1(\sigma)$ might contain two occurrences of one variable b_i, one originally in σ and the other introduced into it by s_1. In this case $s_1(\sigma)$ would not be the most general type assignable to PQ, because we could change ν to an alphabetic variant $\nu' \equiv s_1'(\rho)$ with no variables in common with σ, and then the corresponding $s_1'(\sigma)$ would be a type of PQ that was not an instance of $s_1(\sigma)$.

As a concrete example, let $P \equiv \lambda xy \cdot x$, $Q \equiv \lambda x \cdot x$; it will be shown in 3E that

$$PT(P) \equiv a \rightarrow (b \rightarrow a), \qquad PT(Q) \equiv b \rightarrow b.$$

Thus in this case $\rho \equiv a$, $\sigma \equiv b \rightarrow a$, $\tau \equiv b \rightarrow b$. Clearly an m.g.c.i. of $\langle \rho, \tau \rangle$ is $v \equiv b \rightarrow b$, obtained from ρ by the substitution $s_1 \equiv [(b \rightarrow b)/a]$. And

$$s_1(\sigma) \equiv s_1(b \rightarrow a) \equiv b \rightarrow (b \rightarrow b).$$

It is easy to see that $b \rightarrow (b \rightarrow b)$ is assignable to PQ. But it is not the principal type of PQ. Because if we change s_1 to a new substitution s_1' by replacing b by a new variable c that does not already occur in σ, we get

$$\vdash_\lambda P : (c \rightarrow c) \rightarrow (b \rightarrow (c \rightarrow c)), \qquad \vdash_\lambda Q : c \rightarrow c,$$

and hence PQ has a type $b \rightarrow (c \rightarrow c)$ that is not an instance of $b \rightarrow (b \rightarrow b)$.

To avoid this snag the PT algorithm will be careful to choose an m.g.c.i. v of $\langle \rho, \tau \rangle$ such that

(1) $\quad Vars(v) \cap (Vars(\sigma) - Vars(\rho)) = \emptyset.$

Given this precaution, we have now reduced the problem of finding $PT(PQ)$ to that of finding an m.g.c.i. of $\langle \rho, \tau \rangle$. More precisely, we need an algorithm to decide whether $\langle \rho, \tau \rangle$ has a common instance and, if the answer is "yes", to output a most general one. A suitable algorithm will be given in the next section. It will not be direct, but will apply the *unification algorithm*, which has the advantage that its main properties are so widely known that they will only need to be outlined below.

3D Unification

Most readers have probably met unification before. This section merely summarizes the relevant definitions and basic properties for the reader who has not. The account is based on the classical one in Robinson 1965. (An alternative account is in Aho et al. 1986 §6.7, a thorough survey of major results is in Baader and Siekmann 1994, and a survey of the various applications of unification is in Knight 1989.)

3D1 Definition (Unifiers) (i) Iff there is a substitution s such that $s(\rho) \equiv s(\tau)$ we say $\langle \rho, \tau \rangle$ is ***unifiable***; we call any such s a ***unifier*** of $\langle \rho, \tau \rangle$ and call $s(\rho)$ a ***unification*** of $\langle \rho, \tau \rangle$.

(ii) A ***unifier*** of a pair of sequences $\langle \langle \rho_1, \ldots, \rho_n \rangle, \langle \tau_1, \ldots, \tau_n \rangle \rangle$, both with the same length, is an s such that

$$s(\langle \rho_1, \ldots, \rho_n \rangle) \equiv s(\langle \tau_1, \ldots, \tau_n \rangle).$$

3D1.1 *Note* A unification of $\langle \rho, \tau \rangle$ is just a common instance obtained by making the same substitution in ρ as in τ. But not every common instance is a unification; indeed a pair $\langle \rho, \tau \rangle$ may have a common instance but not be unifiable at all. For example, consider

$$\rho \equiv a \rightarrow (b \rightarrow c), \qquad \tau \equiv (a \rightarrow b) \rightarrow a;$$

this pair was shown in 3C2.1 to have a common instance, but no $\mathbb{s}$ can exist such that $\mathbb{s}(\rho) \equiv \mathbb{s}(\tau)$, because the latter would imply the impossible identity

$$\mathbb{s}(a) \equiv \mathbb{s}(a) \to \mathbb{s}(b).$$

3D1.2 *Note* The problem of finding unifiers for pairs of type-sequences can be reduced to that for pairs of types as follows. Given two sequences $\langle \rho_1, \ldots, \rho_n \rangle$ and $\langle \tau_1, \ldots, \tau_n \rangle$, choose a variable b not occurring in any of these types and define

$$\rho^* \equiv \rho_1 \to \ldots \to \rho_n \to b, \qquad \tau^* \equiv \tau_1 \to \ldots \to \tau_n \to b;$$

then the given pair of sequences is unified by a substitution $\mathbb{s}$ iff $\langle \rho^*, \tau^* \rangle$ is unified by $\mathbb{s} \restriction Vars(\rho_1, \ldots, \rho_n, \tau_1, \ldots, \tau_n)$.

3D2 Definition (M.g.u.) (i) A ***most general unifier (m.g.u.)*** of $\langle \rho, \tau \rangle$ is a unifier $\mathbb{u}$ such that for every other unifier $\mathbb{s}$ of $\langle \rho, \tau \rangle$ we have

$$\mathbb{s}(\rho) \equiv \mathbb{s}'(\mathbb{u}(\rho))$$

for some $\mathbb{s}'$. If $v \equiv \mathbb{u}(\rho)$ for some m.g.u. $\mathbb{u}$ of $\langle \rho, \tau \rangle$ we shall call v a ***most general unification (m.g.u.)*** of $\langle \rho, \tau \rangle$.

(ii) M.g.u.'s of pairs of type-sequences or deductions are defined similarly.

3D2.1 *Exercise** Prove that the pair $\langle a \to (b \to b), (c \to c) \to a \rangle$ is unifiable with a most general unifier $\mathbb{u} \equiv [(b \to b)/a,\ b/c]$, and with the corresponding most general unification being

$$(b \to b) \to (b \to b).$$

3D2.2 *Lemma A type μ is a most general unification of $\langle \rho, \tau \rangle$ iff μ is a unification of $\langle \rho, \tau \rangle$ and all other unifications of $\langle \rho, \tau \rangle$ are instances of μ.*

3D2.3 *Lemma If $\mathbb{u}$ is an m.g.u. of $\langle \rho, \tau \rangle$ and $\mathbb{v}$ is a renaming of variables in $\mathbb{u}(\rho)$, then $\mathbb{v} \circ \mathbb{u}$ is an m.g.u. of $\langle \rho, \tau \rangle$.*

3D2.4 *Notation* From now on we shall often speak of "*the*" m.g.u. of $\langle \rho, \tau \rangle$ as if m.g.u.'s were unique. (By 3D2.2, 3B8.1 and 3D2.3 they are unique modulo renaming.)

3D2.5 *Lemma* (Avoiding variables) (i) *Let $\mathbb{V}$ be any finite set of type-variables. If $\langle \rho, \tau \rangle$ has an m.g.u. $\mathbb{u}$, then it has an m.g.u. $\mathbb{u}'$ such that*

$$Dom(\mathbb{u}') = Vars(\rho) \cup Vars(\tau), \qquad Range(\mathbb{u}') \cap \mathbb{V} = \emptyset.$$

(ii) *Similarly for m.g.u.'s of pairs of type-sequences or deductions.*

Proof If $\mathbb{u}$ contains a component σ/a with $a \notin Vars(\rho) \cup Vars(\tau)$ we can remove this component from $\mathbb{u}$ without affecting $\mathbb{u}(\rho)$ or $\mathbb{u}(\tau)$. We can also add trivial components to enlarge $Dom(\mathbb{u})$ if necessary, and the result can easily be seen to be still an m.g.u. We can then change the range of $\mathbb{u}$ by a renaming. □

3D2.6 *Note* (M.g.u.'s and m.g.c.i.'s) The m.g.u. of a pair $\langle\rho,\tau\rangle$ may differ from its m.g.c.i. For instance the m.g.u. of $\langle a\to(b\to b),(c\to c)\to a\rangle$ was shown in 3D2.1 to be $(b\to b)\to(b\to b)$; but in contrast its m.g.c.i. is easily seen to be $(c\to c)\to(b\to b)$. And as noted in 3D1.1, it is also possible for $\langle\rho,\tau\rangle$ to have an m.g.c.i. but no m.g.u. at all.

However, in the special case that ρ and τ have no common variables every common instance is also a unification, because if

$$\nu \equiv \mathbb{s}_1(\rho) \equiv \mathbb{s}_2(\tau)$$

and $Dom(\mathbb{s}_1)\subseteq Vars(\rho)$ and $Dom(\mathbb{s}_2)\subseteq Vars(\tau)$ then $\mathbb{s}_1\cup\mathbb{s}_2$ is defined and

$$\nu \equiv (\mathbb{s}_1\cup\mathbb{s}_2)(\rho) \equiv (\mathbb{s}_1\cup\mathbb{s}_2)(\tau)$$

This fact gives us the following lemma.

3D3 M.G.U.-M.G.C.I. Lemma (i) *If ρ and τ have no common variables, $\langle\rho,\tau\rangle$ has an m.g.u. iff it has an m.g.c.i., and the two are identical.*

(ii) *For all ρ and τ: if we change τ to an alphabetic variant τ^* with no variables in common with ρ, the unifications of $\langle\rho,\tau^*\rangle$ will be exactly the common instances of $\langle\rho,\tau\rangle$ and the m.g.u. of $\langle\rho,\tau^*\rangle$ will be the m.g.c.i. of $\langle\rho,\tau\rangle$.*

(iii) *Similarly for pairs of type-sequences or deductions.*

Thus the problem of finding m.g.c.i.'s has now been reduced to that of finding m.g.u.'s of pairs $\langle\rho,\tau\rangle$ with no variables in common. But searching for m.g.u.'s of pairs, with or without variables in common, can be done by an algorithm as follows.

3D4 Unification Theorem (J. A. Robinson) (i) *There is an algorithm which decides whether a pair of types $\langle\rho,\tau\rangle$ has a unifier, and, if the answer is "yes", constructs its m.g.u.*

(ii) *If a pair $\langle\rho,\tau\rangle$ has a unifier it has an m.g.u.*

(iii) *Parts* (i)–(ii) *hold also for pairs of deductions and for pairs of finite type-sequences.*

Proof (i) For Robinson's algorithm see 3D5 below; for a proof of its correctness see Robinson 1965 §5 pp. 32–33.

(ii)–(iii) Like (i). □

3D5 Unification Algorithm (Robinson 1965 §5.) ***Input***: any pair $\langle\rho,\tau\rangle$ of types.

Intended output: either a correct statement that $\langle\rho,\tau\rangle$ is not unifiable or an m.g.u. $\mathbb{u}$ of $\langle\rho,\tau\rangle$. [The algorithm will build $\mathbb{u}$ in stages $\mathbb{u}_0,\mathbb{u}_1,\ldots$, each $\mathbb{u}_k$ being a composition of $\mathbb{u}_{k-1}$ with a new substitution: at the k-th stage it will test whether $\mathbb{u}_k(\rho)\equiv\mathbb{u}_k(\tau)$, and if the answer is "yes" it will choose $\mathbb{u}\equiv\mathbb{u}_k$ and stop; but if not, it will "extend" $\mathbb{u}_k$ and go to the next stage.]

***Step* 0**. *Choose $k=0$ and $\mathbb{u}_0\equiv e$ (the empty substitution).*

Step* $k+1$**. *Given k and $\mathbb{u}_k$, construct $\rho_k\equiv\mathbb{u}_k(\rho)$ and $\tau_k\equiv\mathbb{u}_k(\tau)$, and apply the* ***comparison procedure *below to $\langle\rho_k,\tau_k\rangle$. That procedure will output either a correct statement that $\rho_k\equiv\tau_k$ or a* ***disagreement pair*** *$\langle a,\alpha\rangle$ (see below) such that $\alpha\not\equiv a$.*

If $\rho_k\equiv\tau_k$, choose $\mathbb{u}\equiv\mathbb{u}_k$.

If $\rho_k \not\equiv \tau_k$ and the output of the comparison procedure is $\langle a, \alpha \rangle$, decide whether $a \in Vars(\alpha)$.[1]

If $a \in Vars(\alpha)$, state that $\langle \rho, \tau \rangle$ is not unifiable and stop.

If $a \notin Vars(\alpha)$, then replace k by $k+1$, choose $\mathfrak{s}_{k+1} \equiv [\alpha/a] \circ \mathfrak{s}_k$, and go to Step $k+2$.

Comparison Procedure. *Given a pair $\langle \mu, \nu \rangle$ of types, write μ and ν as symbol-strings, say*

$$\mu \equiv s_1 \dots s_m, \qquad \nu \equiv t_1 \dots t_n \qquad (m, n \geq 1)$$

where each of $s_1, \dots, s_m$, $t_1, \dots, t_n$ is an occurrence of a parenthesis, arrow or variable.

If $\mu \equiv \nu$, state that $\mu \equiv \nu$ and stop.

If $\mu \not\equiv \nu$, choose the least $p \leq Min\{m, n\}$ such that $s_p \not\equiv t_p$; it is not hard to show that one of s_p, t_p must be a variable and the other must be a left parenthesis or a different variable. Further, s_p can be shown to be the leftmost symbol of a unique subtype μ^* of μ. (If s_p is a variable, $\mu^* \equiv s_p$.) Similarly t_p is the leftmost symbol of a unique subtype ν^* of ν. Choose one of μ^*, ν^* that is a variable and call it "a". (If both are variables, choose the one that is first in the sequence given in Definition 2A1.) Then call the remaining member of $\langle \mu^*, \nu^* \rangle$ "α"; the pair $\langle a, \alpha \rangle$ is called the ***disagreement pair*** *for $\langle \mu, \nu \rangle$.*

3D5.1 *Note* To prove that p exists in the case that $\mu \not\equiv \nu$ in the comparison procedure we must show that it is not possible to have

$$t_1 \dots t_n \equiv s_1 \dots s_m t_{m+1} \dots t_n$$

with $n > m$. This is left as a (rather dull) exercise for the reader.

3D5.2 *Note* (History) As mentioned earlier, the above unification algorithm is due to J. A. Robinson, see Robinson 1965 §5; it was the first to be published complete with a correctness-proof. Robinson dates its initial implementation to 1962, but he credits a less smooth algorithm implicit in Prawitz 1960 with influence on its origin and mentions that the history of unification algorithms goes back at least as far as Herbrand 1930.[2] Another early unification algorithm is implicit in Maslov 1964. For more on the early history see the start of §3 in Baader and Siekmann 1994.

Although Robinson's algorithm is easy to describe it is not particularly efficient to run, and many better algorithms have been published and implemented since the 1960's. Useful surveys are in Knight 1989 and Baader and Siekmann 1994. A good discussion of efficiency is in §3.3 of the latter; here it is enough just to mention that there are algorithms in Paterson and Wegman 1978 §4 and Martelli and Montanari 1982 that run in linear time if their inputs $\langle \rho, \tau \rangle$ and outputs $\mathfrak{s}$ are coded in a suitably compact way, but that without some coding even the mere printing-out of $\mathfrak{s}(\rho)$ may take exponential time in the worst cases. The problem of deciding whether a given pair $\langle \rho, \tau \rangle$ can be unified is known to be PTIME-complete (Dwork et al. 1984).

[1] This decision is called the "occurs check".

[2] Robinson 1966, Robinson 1979 p. 292.

3D5.3 *Corollary* (i) *There exists an algorithm which decides whether a pair* $\langle \rho, \tau \rangle$ *has a common instance, and if the answer is "yes", outputs an m.g.c.i. and a pair* $\langle \mathbb{s}_1, \mathbb{s}_2 \rangle$ *of m.g.c.i.-generators for* $\langle \rho, \tau \rangle$.

(ii) *Every pair of types with a common instance has an m.g.c.i.*

Proof By 3D3(ii) and the unification algorithm. □

3E The PT algorithm

The PT theorem (3A6) stated that there is an algorithm that decides whether a given untyped term M is typable in TA_λ, and outputs a principal deduction and principal type for M if the answer is "yes". A suitable algorithm will now be described. The proof that it satisfies 3A6 will be given as a series of notes between the algorithm's steps; these notes will also help to motivate the steps.

3E1 Principal Type (PT) Algorithm (Hindley 1969 §3.) ***Input***: any λ-term M, closed or not.

Intended output: either a principal deduction Δ_M for M or a correct statement that M is not typable.

***Case* I**. *If M is a variable, say $M \equiv x$, choose Δ_M to be the one-formula deduction $x{:}a \mapsto x{:}a$, where a is any type-variable.* [Clearly Δ_M is principal for M.]

***Case* II**. *If $M \equiv \lambda x \cdot P$ and $x \in FV(P)$, say $FV(P) = \{x, x_1, \ldots, x_t\}$, apply the algorithm to P. If P is not typable, neither is M. If P has a principal deduction Δ_p its conclusion must have form*

$$x{:}\alpha,\ x_1{:}\alpha_1, \ldots, x_t{:}\alpha_t \quad \mapsto \quad P{:}\beta$$

for some types $\alpha, \alpha_1, \ldots, \alpha_t, \beta$. Apply rule $(\rightarrow I)_{\mathrm{main}}$ to make a deduction of

$$x_1{:}\alpha_1, \ldots, x_t{:}\alpha_t \quad \mapsto \quad (\lambda x.P){:}\,\alpha \rightarrow \beta.$$

Call this deduction $\Delta_{\lambda xP}$.

***Justification of Case* II**. We must show that the above $\Delta_{\lambda xP}$ is principal for $\lambda x \cdot P$. Let Δ be any other deduction of a type for $\lambda x \cdot P$. By the subject-construction theorem (2B2) the last step in Δ must be by rule $(\rightarrow \mathrm{I})_{\mathrm{main}}$, with form

$$\frac{x{:}\alpha',\ x_1{:}\pi_1, \ldots, x_t{:}\pi_t \quad \mapsto \quad P{:}\beta'}{x_1{:}\pi_1, \ldots, x_t{:}\pi_t \quad \mapsto \quad (\lambda x \cdot P){:}\,\alpha' \rightarrow \beta'}$$

for some types α', $\pi_1, \ldots, \pi_t$, β'. Now the steps of Δ above the last one form a deduction Δ' that assigns a type to P; but P has a principal deduction Δ_P, so

$\Delta' \equiv \mathbb{s}(\Delta_P)$ for some $\mathbb{s}$; hence in particular

$$\alpha' \equiv \mathbb{s}(\alpha), \qquad \pi_1 \equiv \mathbb{s}(\alpha_1), \ldots, \pi_t \equiv \mathbb{s}(\alpha_t), \qquad \beta' \equiv \mathbb{s}(\beta).$$

Consequently $\Delta \equiv \mathbb{s}(\Delta_{\lambda xP})$.

***Case* III**. *If $M \equiv \lambda x \cdot P$ and $x \notin FV(P)$, say $FV(P) = \{x_1, \ldots, x_t\}$, apply the algorithm to P. If P is not typable then M is not. If P has a principal deduction Δ_P its conclusion must have form*

$$x_1 : \alpha_1, \ldots, x_t : \alpha_t \quad \mapsto \quad P : \beta$$

for some types $\alpha_1, \ldots, \alpha_t, \beta$. Choose a new type-variable d not in Δ_P and apply $(\rightarrow I)_{\text{vac}}$, vacuously discharging $x{:}d$, to get a deduction of

$$x_1 : \alpha_1, \ldots, x_t : \alpha_t \quad \mapsto \quad (\lambda x \cdot P) : d \rightarrow \beta.$$

Call this deduction $\Delta_{\lambda xP}$.

***Justification of Case* III**. We must show that the above $\Delta_{\lambda xP}$ is principal. Let Δ be any other deduction of a type for $\lambda x \cdot P$. By 2B2 its last step must be an application of rule $(\rightarrow \text{I})_{\text{vac}}$, with form

$$\frac{x_1 : \pi_1, \ldots, x_t : \pi_t \quad \mapsto \quad P : \beta'}{x_1 : \pi_1, \ldots, x_t : \pi_t \quad \mapsto \quad (\lambda x.P) : \alpha' \rightarrow \beta'}$$

for some α', $\pi_1, \ldots, \pi_t$, β'. The steps above the last one form a deduction Δ' of a type for P, and Δ_P is principal, so $\Delta' \equiv \mathbb{s}(\Delta_P)$ for some $\mathbb{s}$. Choose $\mathbb{s}' \equiv \mathbb{s} \cup [\alpha'/d]$; then $\Delta \equiv \mathbb{s}'(\Delta_{\lambda x.P})$.

***Case* IV**. *If $M \equiv PQ$, apply the algorithm to P and Q. If P or Q is untypable then so is M. If P and Q are both typable, suppose they have principal deductions Δ_P and Δ_Q. First rename type-variables, if necessary, to ensure that Δ_P and Δ_Q have no common type-variables. Next list the free term-variables in P and those in Q (noting that these lists may overlap); say*

$$\begin{array}{lcll} FV(P) & = & \{u_1, \ldots, u_p, w_1, \ldots, w_r\} & \quad (p, r \geq 0), \\ FV(Q) & = & \{v_1, \ldots, v_q, w_1, \ldots, w_r\} & \quad (q \geq 0), \end{array}$$

where $u_1, \ldots, u_p$, $v_1, \ldots, v_q$, $w_1, \ldots, w_r$ are distinct.

***Subcase* IVa**: *$M \equiv PQ$ and $PT(P)$ is composite, say $PT(P) \equiv \rho \rightarrow \sigma$. Then the conclusions of Δ_P and Δ_Q have form, respectively,*

(1) $\quad u_1 : \theta_1, \ldots, u_p : \theta_p, \; w_1 : \psi_1, \ldots, w_r : \psi_r \quad \mapsto \quad P : \rho \rightarrow \sigma,$

(2) $\quad v_1 : \phi_1, \ldots, v_q : \phi_q, \; w_1 : \chi_1, \ldots, w_r : \chi_r \quad \mapsto \quad Q : \tau.$

Apply the unification algorithm (3D5) to the pair of sequences

(3) $\quad \langle \psi_1, \ldots, \psi_r, \rho \rangle, \qquad \langle \chi_1, \ldots, \chi_r, \tau \rangle.$

***Subcase* IVa1**: *the pair* (3) *has no unifier. Then PQ is not typable.* [See the justification below.]

***Subcase* IVa2**: *the pair (3) has a unifier. Then the unification algorithm gives a most general unifier* $\mathbb{u}$; *apply a renaming if necessary (3D2.5) to ensure that*

(4) $Dom(\mathbb{u}) = Vars(\psi_1, \ldots, \psi_r, \rho, \chi_1, \ldots, \chi_r, \tau)$,

(5) $Range(\mathbb{u}) \cap \mathbb{V} = \emptyset$,

where

(6) $\mathbb{V} = (Vars(\Delta_P) \cup Vars(\Delta_Q)) - Dom(\mathbb{u})$.[1]

Then apply $\mathbb{u}$ *to* Δ_P *and* Δ_Q; *this changes their conclusions to, respectively,*

$$u_1:\theta_1^*, \ldots, u_p:\theta_p^*,\ w_1:\psi_1^*, \ldots, w_r:\psi_r^* \ \mapsto\ P:\rho^*\to\sigma^*,$$
$$v_1:\phi_1^*, \ldots, v_q:\phi_q^*,\ w_1:\chi_1^*, \ldots, w_r:\chi_r^* \ \mapsto\ Q:\tau^*,$$

where $\theta_1^* \equiv \mathbb{u}(\theta_1)$, *etc. And by the definition of* $\mathbb{u}$ *we have*

$$\psi_1^* \equiv \chi_1^*,\ \ldots, \psi_r^* \equiv \chi_r^*,\ \rho^* \equiv \tau^*.$$

Hence $(\to E)$ *can be applied to the conclusions of* $\mathbb{u}(\Delta_P)$ *and* $\mathbb{u}(\Delta_Q)$. *Call the resulting combined deduction* Δ_{PQ}; *its conclusion is*

(7) $u_1:\theta_1^*, \ldots, u_p:\theta_p^*,\ v_1:\phi_1^*, \ldots, v_q:\phi_q^*,\ w_1:\chi_1^*, \ldots, w_r:\chi_r^* \ \mapsto\ PQ:\sigma^*$.

***Justification of Subcase* IVa.** For IVa1 we must prove that if PQ is typable then $\langle\psi_1, \ldots, \psi_r, \rho\rangle$ and $\langle\chi_1, \ldots, \chi_r, \tau\rangle$ have a unifier, and for IVa2 we must prove that the above Δ_{PQ} is principal for PQ.

***Justification of* IVa1.** If PQ is typable, there is a deduction Δ whose conclusion has form

(8) $u_1:\pi_1, \ldots, u_p:\pi_p,\ v_1:\mu_1, \ldots, v_q:\mu_q,\ w_1:\nu_1, \ldots, w_r:\nu_r \ \mapsto\ PQ:\beta$

for some types $\pi_1, \ldots, \pi_p$, etc. By the subject-construction theorem (2B2), Δ must have been built by applying rule $(\to$ E) to two deductions Δ_1 and Δ_2 whose conclusions are

(9) $u_1:\pi_1, \ldots, u_p:\pi_p,\ w_1:\nu_1, \ldots, w_r:\nu_r \ \mapsto\ P:\alpha\to\beta$,

(10) $v_1:\mu_1, \ldots, v_q:\mu_q,\ w_1:\nu_1, \ldots, w_r:\nu_r \ \mapsto\ Q:\alpha$

for some type α. But Δ_P and Δ_Q are principal deductions for P and Q, so

$$\Delta_1 \equiv \mathbb{r}_1(\Delta_P), \qquad \Delta_2 \equiv \mathbb{r}_2(\Delta_Q)$$

for some substitutions $\mathbb{r}_1$ and $\mathbb{r}_2$ such that

$$Dom(\mathbb{r}_1) = Vars(\Delta_P), \qquad Dom(\mathbb{r}_2) = Vars(\Delta_Q).$$

[1] Roughly speaking, (5) and (6) say that when $\mathbb{u}$ is applied to Δ_P and Δ_Q any new variables it introduces will differ from all those already in Δ_P and Δ_Q, and hence no unnecessary identifications of variables will be made. (Cf. the motivation in 3C4.) By the way, if the aim of the algorithm had been to construct merely a principal type and not a principal deduction, (5) could have been weakened by re-defining $\mathbb{V}$ to consist of just the variables (if any) in σ that do not occur in the types in (3). (Cf. (1) in 3C4.)

Let $r \equiv r_1 \cup r_2$. (This is a well-defined substitution since Δ_P and Δ_Q were chosen such that $Vars(\Delta_P) \cap Vars(\Delta_Q) = \emptyset$.) Then

(11) $\qquad \Delta_1 \equiv \mathfrak{r}(\Delta_P), \qquad \Delta_2 \equiv \mathfrak{r}(\Delta_Q),$

(12) $\qquad Dom(\mathfrak{r}) = Vars(\Delta_P) \cup Vars(\Delta_Q).$

Now look at $v_1, \dots, v_r$ and α in (9). By comparing (9) and (1), since $\Delta_1 \equiv \mathfrak{r}(\Delta_P)$ we have

(13) $\qquad \langle v_1, \dots, v_r, \alpha \rangle \equiv \langle \mathfrak{r}(\psi_1), \dots, \mathfrak{r}(\psi_r), \mathfrak{r}(\rho) \rangle.$

And by comparing (10) and (12), since $\Delta_2 \equiv \mathfrak{r}(\Delta_Q)$,

(14) $\qquad \langle v_1, \dots, v_r, \alpha \rangle \equiv \langle \mathfrak{r}(\chi_1), \dots, \mathfrak{r}(\chi_r), \mathfrak{r}(\tau) \rangle.$

Thus $\langle \psi_1, \dots, \psi_r, \rho \rangle$ and $\langle \chi_1, \dots, \chi_r, \tau \rangle$ have a unifier, namely $\mathfrak{r}$.

***Justification of* IVa2.** We must prove that Δ_{PQ} is principal for PQ, i.e. that an arbitrary deduction Δ of (8) is an instance of Δ_{PQ}. For any such Δ, define Δ_1, Δ_2 and $\mathfrak{r}$ as above. By (6) and (12) we can express $\mathfrak{r}$ as $\mathfrak{r} \equiv \mathfrak{r}' \cup \mathfrak{r}''$, where

(15) $\qquad \mathfrak{r}' \equiv \mathfrak{r} \restriction \mathbb{V}, \qquad \mathfrak{r}'' \equiv \mathfrak{r} \restriction Dom(\mathfrak{u}).$

By (4), (13) and (14), $\mathfrak{r}''$ is a unifier of

$$\langle \psi_1, \dots, \psi_r, \rho \rangle, \qquad \langle \chi_1, \dots, \chi_r, \tau \rangle.$$

But $\mathfrak{u}$ is an m.g.u. of this pair of sequences, so by the definition of m.g.u. (3D2) there exists $\mathfrak{s}$ such that $\mathfrak{r}''(a) \equiv \mathfrak{s}(\mathfrak{u}(a))$ for all $a \in Dom(\mathfrak{u})$. We can clearly also assume

(16) $\qquad Dom(\mathfrak{s}) \subseteq Range(\mathfrak{u}).$

It follows that

(17) $\qquad \mathfrak{r}'' =_{\text{ext}} \mathfrak{s} \circ \mathfrak{u}.$

Since $\mathfrak{r} \equiv \mathfrak{r}' \cup \mathfrak{r}''$, we have by 3B4.1(ii),

(18) $\qquad \mathfrak{r} =_{\text{ext}} \mathfrak{r}' \cup (\mathfrak{s} \circ \mathfrak{u}).$

Now $\mathfrak{r}'$, $\mathfrak{s}$, $\mathfrak{u}$ satisfy conditions (i) and (ii) in the composition-extension lemma (3B6). In fact 3B6(i) holds because by (15) and (16) we have

$$\begin{aligned} Dom(\mathfrak{r}') \cap (Dom(\mathfrak{s}) \cup Dom(\mathfrak{u})) &\subseteq \mathbb{V} \cap (Range(\mathfrak{u}) \cup Dom(\mathfrak{u})) \\ &= \emptyset \qquad \text{by (5), (6),} \end{aligned}$$

and 3B6(ii) holds by (5) and (15). Hence by (18) and 3B6,

$$\mathfrak{r} =_{\text{ext}} (\mathfrak{r}' \cup \mathfrak{s}) \circ \mathfrak{u}.$$

Therefore by (11),

$$\Delta_1 \equiv (\mathfrak{r}' \cup \mathfrak{s})(\mathfrak{u}(\Delta_P)), \qquad \Delta_2 \equiv (\mathfrak{r}' \cup \mathfrak{s})(\mathfrak{u}(\Delta_Q)).$$

But Δ is a combination of Δ_1 and Δ_2 by rule ($\to$E) and Δ_{PQ} is a similar combination of $\mathfrak{u}(\Delta_P)$ and $\mathfrak{u}(\Delta_Q)$. Hence

$$\Delta \equiv (\mathfrak{r}' \cup \mathfrak{s})(\Delta_{PQ}).$$

***Subcase* IVb**: *$M \equiv PQ$ and $PT(P)$ is atomic, say $PT(P) \equiv b$. Then the conclusions of Δ_P and Δ_Q have form, respectively,*

$$(19) \qquad u_1:\theta_1, \ldots, u_p:\theta_p,\ w_1:\psi_1, \ldots, w_r:\psi_r \ \mapsto\ P:b,$$
$$(20) \qquad v_1:\phi_1, \ldots, v_q:\phi_q,\ w_1:\chi_1, \ldots, w_r:\chi_r \ \mapsto\ Q:\tau.$$

Choose any variable $c \notin Vars(\Delta_P) \cup Vars(\Delta_Q)$ and apply the unification algorithm to the pair of sequences

$$(21) \qquad \langle \psi_1, \ldots, \psi_r, b \rangle, \qquad \langle \chi_1, \ldots, \chi_r, \tau \to c \rangle.$$

***Subsubcase* IVb1**: *the pair* (21) *has no unifier. Then PQ is not typable.* [See the justification below.]

***Subsubcase* IVb2**: *the pair* (21) *has a unifier. Then the unification algorithm gives an m.g.u. $\mathbb{u}$; apply* 3D2.5 *to ensure that*

$$(22) \qquad Dom(\mathbb{u}) = Vars(\psi_1, \ldots, \psi_r, b, \chi_1, \ldots, \chi_r, \tau \to c),$$
$$(23) \qquad Range(\mathbb{u}) \cap \mathbb{V} = \emptyset,$$

where $\mathbb{V}$ is the same as in (6)*. Then apply $\mathbb{u}$ to Δ_P and Δ_Q. By the definition of $\mathbb{u}$,*

$$\mathbb{u}(b) \ \equiv\ \mathbb{u}(\tau \to c) \ \equiv\ \mathbb{u}(\tau) \to \mathbb{u}(c),$$

and thus the conclusions of $\mathbb{u}(\Delta_P)$ and $\mathbb{u}(\Delta_Q)$ are

$$u_1:\theta_1^*, \ldots, u_p:\theta_p^*,\ w_1:\psi_1^*, \ldots, w_r:\psi_r^* \ \mapsto\ P:\tau^* \to c^*,$$
$$v_1:\phi_1^*, \ldots, v_q:\phi_q^*,\ w_1:\chi_1^*, \ldots, w_r:\chi_r^* \ \mapsto\ Q:\tau^*,$$

where * denotes application of the substitution $\mathbb{u}$, and

$$\psi_1^* \ \equiv\ \chi_1^*, \ \ldots, \psi_r^* \ \equiv\ \chi_r^*.$$

Choose Δ_{PQ} to be the deduction obtained by applying rule $(\to E)$ to $\mathbb{u}(\Delta_P)$ and $\mathbb{u}(\Delta_Q)$; its conclusion is

$$u_1:\theta_1^*, \ldots, u_p:\theta_p^*,\ v_1:\phi_1^*, \ldots, v_q:\phi_q^*,\ w_1:\chi_1^*, \ldots, w_r:\chi_r^* \ \mapsto\ PQ:c^*.$$

***Justification of Subcase* IVb.** For IVb1 we must prove that if PQ is typable then $\langle \psi_1, \ldots, \psi_r, b \rangle$ and $\langle \chi_1, \ldots, \chi_r, \tau \to c \rangle$ have a unifier, and for IVb2 we must prove that Δ_{PQ} is principal for PQ.

***Justification of* IVb1.** If PQ is typable there is a Δ whose conclusion has the form (8). By 2B2, Δ must have been built by applying ($\to$E) to two deductions Δ_1 and Δ_2 with conclusions (9) and (10). But P and Q have principal deductions Δ_P and Δ_Q, so

$$(24) \qquad \Delta_1 \ \equiv\ \mathbb{r}_1(\Delta_P), \qquad \Delta_2 \ \equiv\ \mathbb{r}_2(\Delta_Q)$$

for some substitutions $\mathbb{r}_1$ and $\mathbb{r}_2$ such that $Dom(\mathbb{r}_1) = Vars(\Delta_P)$ and $Dom(\mathbb{r}_2) = Vars(\Delta_Q)$. Note in particular that

$$\alpha\!\to\!\beta \;\equiv\; \mathbb{r}_1(b), \qquad \alpha \;\equiv\; \mathbb{r}_2(\tau).$$

Define

$$\mathbb{r} \;\equiv\; \mathbb{r}_1 \cup \mathbb{r}_2 \cup [\beta/c].$$

This is well-defined because $c \notin Dom(\mathbb{r}_1) \cup Dom(\mathbb{r}_2)$. And $\mathbb{r}(c) \equiv \beta$, and by (24),

$$\begin{aligned} \mathbb{r}(\Delta_P) \;&\equiv\; \Delta_1, \qquad \mathbb{r}(\Delta_Q) \;\equiv\; \Delta_2,\\ \mathbb{r}(b) \;&\equiv\; \alpha\!\to\!\beta \;\equiv\; \mathbb{r}(\tau\!\to\!c). \end{aligned}$$

Also

$$Dom(\mathbb{r}) = Vars(\Delta_P) \cup Vars(\Delta_Q) \cup \{c\}.$$

Now look at $v_1, \dots, v_r$ and $\alpha\!\to\!\beta$ in (9). By the above, we have

(25) $\quad \langle v_1, \dots, v_r, \alpha\!\to\!\beta\rangle \;\equiv\; \langle \mathbb{r}(\psi_1), \dots, \mathbb{r}(\psi_r), \mathbb{r}(b)\rangle,$

(26) $\quad \langle v_1, \dots, v_r, \alpha\!\to\!\beta\rangle \;\equiv\; \langle \mathbb{r}(\chi_1), \dots, \mathbb{r}(\chi_r), \mathbb{r}(\tau\!\to\!c)\rangle.$

Thus $\langle \psi_1, \dots, \psi_r, b\rangle$ and $\langle \chi_1, \dots, \chi_r, \tau\!\to\!c\rangle$ have a unifier, namely $\mathbb{r}$.

***Justification of* IVb2.** To prove Δ_{PQ} principal we must prove that an arbitrary deduction Δ of (8) is an instance of Δ_{PQ}. For any such Δ, define Δ_1, Δ_2 and $\mathbb{r}$ as above. We can express $\mathbb{r}$ as $\mathbb{r}' \cup \mathbb{r}''$, where

$$\mathbb{r}' \;\equiv\; \mathbb{r}\restriction\mathbb{V}, \qquad \mathbb{r}'' = \mathbb{r}\restriction Dom(\mathbb{u}),$$

where $\mathbb{V}$ and $Dom(\mathbb{u})$ were defined in (6) and (22). By (25) and (26), $\mathbb{r}''$ unifies

$$\langle \psi_1, \dots, \psi_r, b\rangle, \qquad \langle \chi_1, \dots, \chi_r, \tau\!\to\!c\rangle.$$

Hence, just as in the justification of IVa2, $\mathbb{r}'' =_{\text{ext}} \mathbb{s} \circ \mathbb{u}$ for some $\mathbb{s}$ such that

(27) $\quad Dom(\mathbb{s}) \subseteq Range(\mathbb{u}).$

Thus $\mathbb{r} =_{\text{ext}} \mathbb{r}' \cup (\mathbb{s} \circ \mathbb{u})$. Using (23) and (27) it is easy to see that $\mathbb{r}'$, $\mathbb{s}$, $\mathbb{u}$ satisfy the conditions in the composition-extension lemma (3B6), so by that lemma,

$$\mathbb{r} =_{\text{ext}} (\mathbb{r}' \cup \mathbb{s}) \circ \mathbb{u}.$$

Hence, similarly to the justification of IVa2, $\Delta \equiv (\mathbb{r}' \cup \mathbb{s})(\Delta_{PQ})$. □

3E1.1 *Notes* (i) The PT algorithm could have been shortened by combining Subcases IVa and IVb as was done in Hindley 1969: in IVa the unification algorithm could have been applied to

$$\langle \psi_1, \dots, \psi_r, \rho\!\to\!\sigma\rangle, \qquad \langle \chi_1, \dots, \chi_r, \tau\!\to\!c\rangle$$

where c is a new variable, and this modification would have made IVa exactly parallel to IVb and the latter could have been omitted. But this chapter's aim is to explain clearly what is involved in computing a PT and not just to give the slickest presentation, and IVa seems easier to understand when not combined with IVb.

(ii) At the start of Case IV the algorithm could have been made more direct by omitting the renaming of the type-variables in Δ_P and Δ_Q and using common instances instead of unifiers in Subcases IVa and IVb. For example in IVa, instead of seeking an m.g.u. $\mathfrak{u}$ of the sequences

$$\langle\psi_1,\ldots,\psi_r,\rho\rangle, \qquad \langle\chi_1,\ldots,\chi_r,\tau\rangle,$$

we could have sought an m.g.c.i. The justification of the algorithm would then have rested on 3D5.3, the analogue of the unification theorem for common instances.

3E2 Exercise Show that the closed terms in Table 3E2a have the principal types shown there. (The answers to (1)–(7) are displayed in 2A8.2–4 and in the answer to Exercise 2A8.7; these deductions can easily be shown to be principal. The others can be checked by applying the PT algorithm.)

By the way, the terms (10) and (11) in Table 3E2a are not in β-normal form; we shall see in 8B4 and 8B7 that there are no closed β-nfs with the same PT's as these terms.

An extended table of terms and their principal types is given at the end of the book for ease of reference.

Table 3E2a.

	Term	**Principal type**
(1)	$\mathbf{B} \equiv \lambda xyz\cdot x(yz)$	$(a\to b)\to(c\to a)\to c\to b$
(2)	$\mathbf{B}' \equiv \lambda xyz\cdot y(xz)$	$(a\to b)\to(b\to c)\to a\to c$
(3)	$\mathbf{C} \equiv \lambda xyz\cdot xzy$	$(a\to b\to c)\to b\to a\to c$
(4)	$\mathbf{I} \equiv \lambda x\cdot x$	$a\to a$
(5)	$\mathbf{K} \equiv \lambda xy\cdot x$	$a\to b\to a$
(6)	$\mathbf{S} \equiv \lambda xyz\cdot xz(yz)$	$(a\to b\to c)\to(a\to b)\to a\to c$
(7)	$\mathbf{W} \equiv \lambda xy\cdot xyy$	$(a\to a\to b)\to a\to b$
(8)	$\bar{0} \equiv \lambda xy\cdot y$	$a\to b\to b$
(9)	$\bar{1} \equiv \lambda xy\cdot xy$	$(a\to b)\to a\to b$
(10)	$(\lambda xyz\cdot \mathbf{K}(xy)(xz))\mathbf{I}$	$a\to a\to a$
(11)	$\lambda xy\cdot(\lambda z\cdot x)(yx)$	$a\to(a\to b)\to a$
(12)	$\lambda xyz\cdot xy(xz)$	[untypable]
(13)	$\lambda x\cdot xx$	[untypable]

3E3 Theorem *The relation $\vdash_\lambda M:\tau$ is decidable, i.e. there is an algorithm which accepts any M and τ and decides whether or not $\vdash_\lambda M:\tau$.*

Proof Apply the PT algorithm to M. If M is not closed or not typable we cannot have $\vdash_\lambda M:\tau$. If M is closed and typable, decide whether τ is an instance of $PT(M)$. □

3E4 Further Reading For an alternative introduction to PT's and type-checking see Aho et al. 1986 Ch. 6. The early literature on PT algorithms was mentioned in 3A7 above. The more recent literature on their uses and properties is fairly extensive and perhaps the best place to start would be the survey Tiuryn 1990 and the papers in its bibliography, as well as Giannini et al. 1993.

Accounts of PT algorithms that include correctness-proofs are relatively rare, however; besides the proofs in Curry 1969 and Hindley 1969 §3 (and the unpublished ones in Morris 1968 and Damas 1984) there is one in Wand 1987.

3E4.1 *Note* (Efficiency) Results on efficiency and complexity of PT algorithms, mainly focusing on ML, are contained in Kanellakis and Mitchell 1989, Mairson 1990, Kfoury et al. 1990 and Kanellakis et al. 1991. In summary, there is a PT algorithm which can decide in linear time whether a λ-term containing no constants is typable, and if it is, will print out its PT in linear time coded in a suitably compressed form (as a directed acyclic graph or DAG). Also the typability problem for pure λ-terms is PTIME-complete just like the unification problem (3D5.2). (Proofs of this are in Tyszkiewicz 1988 and Mitchell 1996 Ch. 11.)

But when ML's *let* operator is added to the term-language the corresponding typability problem becomes PSPACE-hard (Kanellakis and Mitchell 1989) and DEXPTIME-complete (Mairson 1990, Kfoury et al. 1990).

4

Type assignment with equality

Let M be a closed term and *Types(M)* be the set of all types assignable to M in TA_λ. As we saw in Chapter 2 this set might not stay invariant during a β-conversion of M. In fact Examples 2C2.2–6 and Note 2C3.2 showed that this set may increase during a reduction of M and sometimes M can even be converted to a term with no types at all in common with M.

As noted in 2C3.2 this lack of equality-invariance has not hindered TA_λ from a practical point of view, nor its descendant ML, as the main need in both systems has been simply for the subject-reduction theorem. However, on the theoretical side, equality-invariance of *Types(M)* seems a desirable property from the viewpoint of any of the standard λ-calculus semantics (except possibly an operational semantics): if we believe terms represent functions of some sort and equal terms represent the same function, then equal terms should have the same types.

So this chapter will describe a system obtained by adding an equality-invariance rule to TA_λ. More precisely, two systems will be described in parallel, one for $=_\beta$ and the other for $=_{\beta\eta}$; both will have similar properties.

4A The equality rule

4A1 Definition (The systems $TA_{\lambda+\beta}$, $TA_{\lambda+\beta\eta}$) We define $TA_{\lambda+\beta}$ by adding to rules $(\rightarrow E)$ and $(\rightarrow I)$ in Definition 2A8 the new rule

$$(\mathrm{Eq}_\beta)\ \frac{\Gamma \ \mapsto\ M{:}\tau \qquad M =_\beta N}{\Gamma \ \mapsto\ N{:}\tau.}$$

Iff a formula $\Gamma' \ \mapsto\ M{:}\tau$ is provable in $TA_{\lambda+\beta}$ for some $\Gamma' \subseteq \Gamma$ we say

$$\Gamma \vdash_\beta M{:}\tau.$$

And iff there exist Γ and τ such that $\Gamma \vdash_\beta M{:}\tau$ we call M ***$TA_{\lambda+\beta}$-typable***.

We define $TA_{\lambda+\beta\eta}$, $\vdash_{\beta\eta}$ and ***$TA_{\lambda+\beta\eta}$-typability*** similarly but with "$=_{\beta\eta}$" instead of "$=_\beta$", calling the corresponding new rule "$(\mathrm{Eq}_{\beta\eta})$".[1]

4A1.1 *Notation* When confusion is unlikely (Eq_β) and $(\mathrm{Eq}_{\beta\eta})$ may both be called just "(Eq)".

[1] Strictly speaking, to make the (Eq)-rules meaningful we must also add the axioms and rules for $=_\beta$ and $=_{\beta\eta}$ to the definitions of $TA_{\lambda+\beta}$ and $TA_{\lambda+\beta\eta}$ in some way; the details of this are left to the reader.

The name "$TA_{\lambda+\beta[\eta]}$" will be used to denote $TA_{\lambda+\beta}$ and $TA_{\lambda+\beta\eta}$ simultaneously when stating results that hold for both systems. Deducibility notation in such statements will be

$$\vdash_{\beta[\eta]} .$$

To emphasize the contrast with $\vdash_\beta$ and $\vdash_{\beta\eta}$ we shall call $\vdash_\lambda$, in the present chapter only,

$$\vdash_{\text{no eq}} .$$

4A1.2 *Example* Some terms become typable in $TA_{\lambda+\beta[\eta]}$ that were not typable in TA_λ. For example, consider the term

$$P \equiv (\lambda uv\cdot v)(\lambda x\cdot xx)$$

which was shown in 2C2.2 to have no type although it reduces to **I** which has type $a\to a$. In $TA_{\lambda+\beta[\eta]}$ we can assign a type to P by the following deduction.

$$\dfrac{\dfrac{v:a \quad \mapsto \quad v:a}{\mapsto \quad (\lambda v\cdot v):a\to a}\,(\to\mathrm{I}) \qquad \lambda v\cdot v =_\beta (\lambda uv\cdot v)(\lambda x\cdot xx)}{\mapsto \quad (\lambda uv\cdot v)(\lambda x\cdot xx): a\to a.}\,(\mathrm{Eq}_\beta)$$

4A1.3 *Remark* By adding (Eq) to TA_λ we have trivially solved the problem of making the set of a term's types invariant with respect to conversion. But for this easy gain we pay at least two prices.

(i) Rule (Eq) is undecidable. That is, there is no algorithm that will apply to arbitrary Γ, τ, M, N and decide whether the formula $\Gamma \mapsto N:\tau$ is deducible from $\Gamma \mapsto M:\tau$ by (Eq). (Because the relations $=_\beta$ and $=_{\beta\eta}$ are undecidable.) This defect can be remedied by replacing (Eq) by a series of rules, each one corresponding to an axiom in a suitable definition of $=_\beta$ or $=_{\beta\eta}$, but this solution is far from neat.

(ii) The subject-construction theorem (2B2) breaks down: when there are (Eq)-steps present the structure of a deduction is no longer dictated by that of its subject. Also when the proof of a formula $\Gamma \mapsto M:\tau$ contains (Eq) we cannot infer that $Subjects(\Gamma) = FV(M)$ as we did in Lemma 2A10.

At first sight (i) and (ii) are serious drawbacks. However, the following theorems will show that (ii), at least, is not as bad as it might seem; we shall see that in fact rule (Eq) plays an unexpectedly small role in deductions and that $TA_{\lambda+\beta[\eta]}$ is tied to TA_λ very closely indeed.

4A2 Equality-postponement Theorem *In* $TA_{\lambda+\beta[\eta]}$ *every deduction of* $\Gamma \mapsto M:\tau$ *can be changed into one in which the only use of (Eq) is at the end. That is, if* $\Gamma \vdash_{\beta[\eta]} M:\tau$ *then there exists a term* $M' =_{\beta[\eta]} M$ *such that*

$$\Gamma \vdash_{\text{no eq}} M':\tau.$$

Proof Let Δ be a $TA_{\lambda+\beta[\eta]}$-deduction of $\Gamma \mapsto M:\tau$. If (Eq) occurs in Δ above an occurrence of ($\rightarrow$E), the relevant part of Δ will look like this:

$$\dfrac{\dfrac{\Gamma_1 \mapsto P:\rho\rightarrow\sigma \qquad P =_{\beta[\eta]} P'}{\Gamma_1 \mapsto P':\rho\rightarrow\sigma}\,(\text{Eq}) \qquad \dfrac{\Gamma_2 \mapsto Q:\rho \quad Q =_{\beta[\eta]} Q'}{\Gamma_2 \mapsto Q':\rho}\,(\text{Eq})}{\Gamma_1 \cup \Gamma_2 \mapsto (P'Q'):\sigma.}\,(\rightarrow\text{E})$$

Replace this part by the following, noting that the assumptions and the conclusion stay the same.

$$\dfrac{\dfrac{\Gamma_1 \mapsto P:\rho\rightarrow\sigma \qquad \Gamma_2 \mapsto Q:\rho}{\Gamma_1 \cup \Gamma_2 \mapsto (PQ):\sigma}\,(\rightarrow\text{E}) \qquad PQ =_{\beta[\eta]} P'Q'}{\Gamma_1 \cup \Gamma_2 \mapsto (P'Q'):\sigma.}\,(\text{Eq})$$

If (Eq) occurs in Δ above an occurrence of $(\rightarrow\text{I})_{\text{main}}$, the relevant part of Δ will look like this:

$$\dfrac{\dfrac{\Gamma, x:\rho \mapsto P:\sigma \qquad P =_{\beta[\eta]} P'}{\Gamma, x:\rho \mapsto P':\sigma}\,(\text{Eq})}{\Gamma \mapsto (\lambda x\cdot P'):\rho\rightarrow\sigma.}\,(\rightarrow\text{I})_{\text{main}}$$

Replace this part by the following:

$$\dfrac{\dfrac{\Gamma, x:\rho \mapsto P:\sigma}{\Gamma \mapsto (\lambda x\cdot P):\rho\rightarrow\sigma}\,(\rightarrow\text{I})_{\text{main}} \qquad \lambda x\cdot P =_{\beta[\eta]} \lambda x\cdot P'}{\Gamma - x \mapsto (\lambda x\cdot p'):\rho\rightarrow\sigma.}\,(\text{Eq})$$

If (Eq) occurs above $(\rightarrow\text{I})_{\text{vac}}$ make a similar replacement. (By the way, $(\rightarrow\text{I})_{\text{vac}}$ is distinguished from $(\rightarrow\text{I})_{\text{main}}$ in Definition 2A8 by whether x occurs in the context on its top line, not by whether $x \in FV(P)$, so converting P' to P will not change an application of $(\rightarrow\text{I})_{\text{vac}}$ to one of $(\rightarrow\text{I})_{\text{main}}$ or vice versa.[1])

Finally, if (Eq) occurs in Δ above another (Eq), combine them into one in the obvious way. The above replacement-procedure will terminate in a deduction with (Eq) at the end (if (Eq) occurs in it at all). □

4A2.1 *Note* The above proof depends on little more than the very simple fact that if $P =_{\beta[\eta]} P'$ and $Q =_{\beta[\eta]} Q'$ then

$$PQ =_{\beta[\eta]} P'Q', \qquad \lambda x\cdot P =_{\beta[\eta]} \lambda x\cdot P'.$$

But as a consequence it allows us to extend several important results from TA_λ to $TA_{\lambda+\beta[\eta]}$, as follows.

[1] In TA_λ, x occurred in the context on the top line of ($\rightarrow$I) iff $x \in FV(P)$, but as remarked in 4A1.3(ii), this does not necessarily hold when (Eq) is present.

4A3 Weak Normalization Theorem for $\mathrm{TA}_{\lambda+\beta[\eta]}$ *Every* $\mathrm{TA}_{\lambda+\beta[\eta]}$*-typable term* M *has a* $\beta[\eta]$*-nf* M_**, and furthermore*

$$\Gamma \vdash_{\beta[\eta]} M{:}\tau \iff \Gamma \vdash_{\text{no eq}} M_*{:}\tau.$$

Proof Let $\Gamma \vdash_{\beta[\eta]} M{:}\tau$. Then by 4A2 there exists $M' =_{\beta[\eta]} M$ such that

(1) $\qquad \Gamma \vdash_{\text{no eq}} M'{:}\tau.$

By the weak normalization theorem for TA_λ (2D5), M' has a nf M_*; and by the Church-Rosser theorem M' reduces to M_* and M_* is also the nf of M. They by (1) and the subject-reduction theorem (2C1),

(2) $\qquad \Gamma \vdash_{\text{no eq}} M_*{:}\tau.$

Conversely, if (2) holds then $\Gamma \vdash_{\beta[\eta]} M{:}\tau$ by (Eq). □

4A3.1 *Warning* The weak normalization theorem cannot be strengthened to strong normalization. For example let

$$M \equiv (\lambda uv{\cdot}v)((\lambda x{\cdot}xx)(\lambda x{\cdot}xx)).$$

Then $M =_\beta \mathsf{I}$ so M is typable in both $\mathrm{TA}_{\lambda+\beta}$ and $\mathrm{TA}_{\lambda+\beta\eta}$. But M has an infinite reduction, so strong normalization fails for both systems.

4A3.2 *Corollary* *The relation* $\Gamma \vdash_{\beta[\eta]} M{:}\tau$ *is equivalent to each of the following:*

(i) $\Gamma \vdash_{\text{no eq}} M_*{:}\tau$,
(ii) $\Gamma\restriction M_* \vdash_{\text{no eq}} M_*{:}\tau$,
(iii) $\Gamma \vdash_{\beta[\eta]} M_*{:}\tau$,
(iv) $\Gamma\restriction M_* \vdash_{\beta[\eta]} M_*{:}\tau$,
(v) $\Gamma\restriction M_* \vdash_{\beta[\eta]} M{:}\tau$,
(vi) $\Gamma\restriction M \vdash_{\beta[\eta]} M{:}\tau$.

Proof Each of (i)–(vi) implies $\Gamma \vdash_{\beta[\eta]} M{:}\tau$ by (Eq) and the weakening property of "$\vdash$" (which holds for $\vdash_{\beta[\eta]}$ just as for $\vdash_\lambda$, see 2A9.1).

For the converse, the relation $\Gamma \vdash_{\beta[\eta]} M{:}\tau$ implies (i) by 4A3. And (i) implies (ii) by 2A11. Next, (ii) implies (iv) trivially, and (iv) implies (iii), (v) and (vi) by (Eq) and weakening. □

4A3.3 *Note* When $\Gamma \vdash_{\beta[\eta]} M{:}\tau$ we cannot infer that $Subjects(\Gamma) \supseteq FV(M)$, but by the above corollary and 2A11 we can infer that

$$Subjects(\Gamma) \supseteq FV(M_*).$$

The next theorem will express the content of Corollary 4A3.2 very neatly for the case that M is closed.

4A4 Definition If M is closed, the set of all τ such that $\vdash_{\beta[\eta]} M{:}\tau$ holds will be called

$$Types_{\beta[\eta]}(M).$$

To emphasize the contrast, the set $Types(M)$ defined in 2C3 will be called here $Types_{\text{no eq}}(M)$.

4A5 Theorem *If M is closed and has β- and $\beta\eta$-nf's $M_{*\beta}$ and $M_{*\beta\eta}$ respectively, then*

(i) $Types_{\beta}(M) = Types_{\beta}(M_{*\beta}) = Types_{\text{no eq}}(M_{*\beta})$,
(ii) $Types_{\beta\eta}(M) = Types_{\beta\eta}(M_{*\beta\eta}) = Types_{\text{no eq}}(M_{*\beta\eta})$.

Proof By 4A3.2. □

4A6 Definition (Principal types in TA$_{\lambda+\beta[\eta]}$) In TA$_{\lambda+\beta[\eta]}$ a type τ is a ***principal type*** of a term M iff

(i) $\Gamma \mapsto M{:}\tau$ is deducible for some Γ,
(ii) if $\Gamma' \mapsto M{:}\tau'$ is deducible then τ' is an instance of τ.

4A7 PT Theorem for TA$_{\lambda+\beta[\eta]}$ *In TA$_{\lambda+\beta[\eta]}$ every typable term M has a principal type, and it is the same as the principal type in TA$_\lambda$ of the $\beta[\eta]$-nf of M.*

Proof By 4A3.2 and the PT theorem for TA$_\lambda$ (3A6). □

4A8 Remark Results 4A2–7 show that the effect of adding rule (Eq) has been much less than we might have feared: (Eq) simply transfers types from normal forms to the terms that reduce to them, and consequently TA$_{\lambda+\beta[\eta]}$ is little more than the theory of assigning types to $\beta[\eta]$-normal forms in TA$_\lambda$.

However, this is not quite the whole story. Rule (Eq) was motivated at the start of this section by semantic considerations and the semantics of TA$_{\lambda+\beta[\eta]}$ will be investigated in the next section.

But first two more syntactic results will be stated. The first is an analogue for TA$_{\lambda+\beta}$ of the subject-reduction theorem for TA$_\lambda$: if it merely asserted closure under $\triangleright_\beta$ it would be trivial but it says slightly more.

4A9 Theorem (η-closure of TA$_{\lambda+\beta}$) *If $\Gamma \vdash_\beta P{:}\tau$ and $P \triangleright_{\beta\eta} Q$, then*

$$\Gamma \vdash_\beta Q{:}\tau.$$

Proof If $\Gamma \vdash_\beta P{:}\tau$ then by 4A3, P has a β-nf $P_{*\beta}$ such that

(1) $\qquad \Gamma \vdash_{\text{no eq}} P_{*\beta}{:}\tau.$

Now $P \triangleright_{\beta\eta} Q$ and $P \triangleright_\beta P_{*\beta}$, so by 1C7.1 there exists T such that

$$Q \triangleright_\beta T, \qquad P_{*\beta} \triangleright_{\beta\eta} T.$$

(In fact $P_{*\beta} \triangleright_\eta T$ by 1C9.2.) By (1) and subject-reduction (2C1),

$$\Gamma \vdash_{\text{no eq}} T{:}\tau.$$

Hence by (Eq$_\beta$),

$$\Gamma \vdash_\beta Q{:}\tau.$$ □

4A10 Theorem (Undecidability of $\mathrm{TA}_{\lambda+\beta[\eta]}$) *There is no algorithm that accepts arbitrary Γ, M, τ as inputs and decides whether $\Gamma \vdash_{\beta[\eta]} M{:}\tau$.*

Proof Let $\Gamma = \emptyset$ and $\tau \equiv a{\to}a$. For any M, if $\vdash_{\beta[\eta]} M{:}a{\to}a$ then M is closed and by 4A3, M has a nf M_* which is closed and has the property

$$\vdash_{\text{no eq}} M_*{:}a{\to}a$$

But by the subject-construction theorem (2B2) it is easy to see that a closed $\beta[\eta]$-nf with type $a{\to}a$ in TA_λ must have form $\lambda x{\cdot}x$ for some x. Hence

$$\vdash_{\beta[\eta]} M{:}a{\to}a \iff M =_{\beta[\eta]} \mathbf{I}$$

Thus a test for $\vdash_{\beta[\eta]}$ would give a test for convertibility to $\mathbf{I}$, contrary to standard undecidability results (e.g. Barendregt 1984 Thm. 6.6.2 or HS 86 Cor. 5.6.1). □

4B Semantics and completeness

In this section $\mathrm{TA}_{\lambda+\beta}$ will be interpreted in an arbitrary λ-model and its rules proved sound and complete, and the same will be done for $\mathrm{TA}_{\lambda+\beta\eta}$ in extensional λ-models. The concept of λ-model has been motivated, defined and thoroughly discussed in Barendregt 1984 Ch. 5 (especially Def. 5.2.7), and in HS 86 Ch. 11. There are several definitions of λ-model in these sources, all equivalent, and the one presented below has been chosen mainly because it emphasizes the concepts needed in the completeness proof. It is from HS 86 Def. 11.3.

4B1 Definition (Semantic environments) Given a non-empty set $\mathbb{D}$, a ***semantic environment*** in $\mathbb{D}$ is any function E that assigns to each term-variable v a member $E(v)$ of $\mathbb{D}$. If E is a semantic environment, x a variable and $d \in \mathbb{D}$, the semantic environment

$$[d/x]E$$

is defined to be the same as E except that it assigns d to x. (By the way, if $E(x) = d$ then $[d/x]E = E$.)

4B2 Definition (λ-models) A ***λ-model*** is a triple $\mathscr{D} = \langle \mathbb{D}, \cdot, [\![\ ]\!] \rangle$ where $\mathbb{D}$ is a set with at least two members, $\cdot$ is a 2-place function such that

$$d_1, d_2 \in \mathbb{D} \implies d_1{\cdot}d_2 \in \mathbb{D},$$

and $[\![\ ]\!]$ is a function that assigns to each E and each term M a member of $\mathbb{D}$ called $[\![M]\!]_E$, such that

(i) $[\![x]\!]_E = E(x)$ *for all term-variables x,*
(ii) $[\![PQ]\!]_E = [\![P]\!]_E{\cdot}[\![Q]\!]_E$,
(iii) $[\![\lambda x{\cdot}P]\!]_E{\cdot}d = [\![P]\!]_{[d/x]E}$ *for all $d \in \mathbb{D}$,*
(iv) $[\![M]\!]_{E_1} = [\![M]\!]_{E_2}$ *if $E_1(v) = E_2(v)$ for all $v \in FV(M)$,*
(v) $[\![M]\!]_E = [\![N]\!]_E$ *if $M \equiv_\alpha N$,*
(vi) $[\![\lambda x{\cdot}P]\!]_E = [\![\lambda x{\cdot}Q]\!]_E$ *if $[\![P]\!]_{[d/x]E} = [\![Q]\!]_{[d/x]E}$ for all $d \in \mathbb{D}$.*

4B2.1 *Notation* The function $\cdot$ is called ***application*** and $[\![\;]\!]$ is called the ***interpretation*** mapping.

Note that in the above definition as elsewhere in this book, "=" without a subscript "β" or "$\beta\eta$" means *"is identical to"*.

4B3 Definition A λ-model $\mathcal{D} = \langle \mathbb{D}, \cdot, [\![\;]\!] \rangle$ is called ***extensional*** iff, for all d_1 and $d_2 \in \mathbb{D}$,

$$(\forall e \in \mathbb{D})(d_1 \cdot e = d_2 \cdot e) \quad \Longrightarrow \quad d_1 = d_2.$$

4B4 Lemma (i) *Every λ-model $\mathcal{D}$ satisfies the theory of of β-equality in the sense that*

$$M =_\beta N \quad \Longrightarrow \quad (\forall E)\, [\![M]\!]_E = [\![N]\!]_E.$$

(ii) *A λ-model $\mathcal{D}$ is extensional iff it satisfies $\beta\eta$ in the sense that*

$$M =_{\beta\eta} N \quad \Longrightarrow \quad (\forall E)\, [\![M]\!]_E = [\![N]\!]_E.$$

Proof HS 86 Thms. 11.12 and 11.15. □

4B4.1 *Note* A λ-model $\mathcal{D}$ is a model of *untyped* λ-calculus, i.e. every term receives an interpretation in $\mathbb{D}$ whether it is typable or not. This agrees with the Curry approach to type-theory described in 2A3. In contrast, in a model of Church's type-theory only typed terms are interpreted, and instead of one domain $\mathbb{D}$ the model has a distinct domain for each type. The definition of model for Church's system can be found in Henkin 1950.

Types are interpreted in an arbitrary λ-model as follows.

4B5 Definition (Interpreting types) Let $\mathcal{D} = \langle \mathbb{D}, \cdot, [\![\;]\!] \rangle$ be any λ-model. An ***interpretation of the type-variables*** is any function V that assigns a subset of $\mathbb{D}$ to each type-variable. Each such V generates an ***interpretation of all the types***, $[\![\;]\!]_V$, defined as follows:

(i) $[\![a]\!]_V = V(a)$ *for all type-variables a,*
(ii) $[\![\sigma \to \tau]\!]_V = \{d \in \mathbb{D} : (\forall d' \in [\![\sigma]\!]_V)(d \cdot d' \in [\![\tau]\!]_V)\}$.

4B6 Definition (Satisfaction) Let $\mathcal{D} = \langle \mathbb{D}, \cdot, [\![\;]\!] \rangle$ be a λ-model. A type-assignment $M{:}\tau$ is said to be ***satisfied in $\mathcal{D}$ by E and V*** iff

$$[\![M]\!]_E \in [\![\tau]\!]_V.$$

A set Γ of type-assignments is said to be ***satisfied*** iff all its members are satisfied. A formula $\Gamma \mapsto M{:}\tau$ is said to be ***valid in $\mathcal{D}$*** iff every pair E, V satisfying Γ in $\mathcal{D}$ also satisfies $M{:}\tau$ in $\mathcal{D}$.

Iff $\Gamma \mapsto M{:}\tau$ is valid in all λ-models (respectively, all extensional λ-models), we say

$$\Gamma \models_\beta M{:}\tau, \qquad \Gamma \models_{\beta\eta} M{:}\tau.$$

4B6.1 *Note* The above definition of satisfaction is called the ***simple semantics*** for type-assignment. There are several other semantics-definitions in the literature, for example see Hindley 1983 §§4–5 and Mitchell 1988 §3.

Many different particular λ-models are described in the literature (for some examples see Barendregt 1984 Ch. 18 and HS 86 Ch. 12), but we shall not need to know about them here. In fact the only model used in the completeness-proof below will be the simplest of all kinds of model, a *term-model.*

4B7 Definition (The term-models $\mathbb{TM}_\beta$, $\mathbb{TM}_{\beta\eta}$) The domain $\mathbb{D}$ of $\mathbb{TM}_\beta$ is the set of all β-equality-classes of λ-terms: in more detail, for each M we define

$$[M]^\beta = \{P : P =_\beta M\},$$

and then define

$$\mathbb{D} = \{[M]^\beta : M \text{ is a } \lambda\text{-term}\}.$$

Application in $\mathbb{TM}_\beta$ is defined thus:

$$[M]^\beta \cdot [N]^\beta = [MN]^\beta.$$

Terms are interpreted in $\mathbb{TM}_\beta$ thus: if $FV(M) = \{x_1, \ldots, x_n\}$ and $E(x_i) = [Q_i]^\beta$ for $i = 1, \ldots, n$ (for some terms $Q_1, \ldots, Q_n$), define

$$[\![M]\!]_E = [[Q_1/x_1, \ldots, Q_n/x_n]M]^\beta.$$

The definition of $\mathbb{TM}_{\beta\eta}$ is similar, starting with $[M]^{\beta\eta} = \{P : P =_{\beta\eta} M\}$.

4B7.1 *Definition* A semantic environment in $\mathbb{TM}_{\beta[\eta]}$ called E_0 is defined by setting

$$E_0(x) = [x]^{\beta[\eta]}.$$

4B7.2 *Lemma* (i) *$\mathbb{TM}_\beta$ and $\mathbb{TM}_{\beta\eta}$ are λ-models and $\mathbb{TM}_{\beta\eta}$ is extensional.*
(ii) *In $\mathbb{TM}_{\beta[\eta]}$ we have $[\![M]\!]_{E_0} = [M]^{\beta[\eta]}$ for all M.*

Proof Routine. (For (i) see, e.g., Barendregt 1984 Prop. 5.2.12.) □

4B8 Soundness Theorem *Let Γ be any type-context, M any λ-term and τ any type. Then*

$$\Gamma \vdash_{\beta[\eta]} M:\tau \quad \Longrightarrow \quad \Gamma \models_{\beta[\eta]} M:\tau.$$

Proof Straightforward. (See, e.g., Ben-Yelles 1979 Thm. 4.17.) □

4B9 Completeness Theorem *Let Γ be any type-context, M any λ-term and τ any type. Then*

$$\Gamma \models_{\beta[\eta]} M:\tau \quad \Longrightarrow \quad \Gamma \vdash_{\beta[\eta]} M:\tau.$$

Proof [Hindley 1983a §3.] We shall prove the β-case; the proof of the $\beta\eta$-case is almost identical. By the definition of "type-context", Γ is a finite set of type-assignments

$$\Gamma = \{x_1 : \rho_1, \ldots, x_m : \rho_m\},$$

where $x_1, \ldots, x_m$ are distinct. Extend Γ to an infinite set Γ^+ in which every type in the language of TA_λ is assigned to an infinite number of term-variables (and no variable receives more than one type).

This can be done as follows. First list all the types as an infinite sequence, say $\tau_1, \tau_2, \ldots$. Then note that in 1A1 we assumed the λ-language to contain an infinite number of term-variables, so there are an infinite number of variables distinct from $x_1, \ldots, x_m$ and from the free variables of M; choose from these an infinite number of disjoint infinite sequences, say

$$\{v_{1,1}, v_{1,2}, \ldots\}, \quad \{v_{2,1}, v_{2,2}, \ldots\}, \quad \{v_{3,1}, v_{3,2}, \ldots\}, \ldots.$$

Then define

$$\Gamma^+ = \Gamma \cup \{v_{i,j} : \tau_i : i \geq 1, j \geq 1\}.$$

In what follows, the notation "$\Gamma^+ \vdash_\beta P : \sigma$" (for any given P and σ) will mean that there is a finite subset Γ^* of Γ^+ such that $\Gamma^* \vdash_\beta P : \sigma$.

In $\mathbb{TM}_\beta$ define an interpretation v_0 of the type-variables by setting, for each type-variable a,

$$v_0(a) = \{[P]^\beta : \Gamma^+ \vdash_\beta P : a\}.$$

Extend v_0 to an interpretation $[\![\ ]\!]_{v_0}$ of all types as in 4B5. We shall now prove that, for all σ and all P:

$$(1) \qquad [P]^\beta \in [\![\sigma]\!]_{v_0} \iff \Gamma^+ \vdash_\beta P : \sigma;$$

i.e. that the interpretation of σ is exactly the set of all terms which receive type σ when the assignments in Γ^+ are assumed. □

Proof of (1) Use induction on σ. If σ is an atom we have (1) by the definition of v_0.

For the induction step let $\sigma \equiv \xi \to \eta$. By the definition of $\mathbb{TM}_\beta$ and of the interpretation of $\xi \to \eta$ we have

$$[P]^\beta \in [\![\xi \to \eta]\!]_{v_0} \iff (\forall Q)\,([Q]^\beta \in [\![\xi]\!]_{v_0} \implies [PQ]^\beta \in [\![\eta]\!]_{v_0})$$

and by the induction hypothesis the right-hand side is equivalent to

$$(\forall Q)\,(\Gamma^+ \vdash_\beta Q : \xi \implies \Gamma^+ \vdash_\beta PQ : \eta)$$

So to complete the induction step it is enough to prove

$$(2) \qquad \begin{cases} (\forall Q)\,(\Gamma^+ \vdash_\beta Q : \xi \implies \Gamma^+ \vdash_\beta PQ : \eta) \\ \iff \Gamma^+ \vdash_\beta P : (\xi \to \eta). \end{cases}$$

Proof of (2) For "⇐", use rule (→E). To prove "⇒", suppose the upper clause in (2) holds and, as a special case, take Q to be a variable z not occurring in P and such that Γ^+ contains the assignment $z:\xi$. (By the construction of Γ^+, z exists.) Then by the upper clause in (2),

$$\Gamma^+ \vdash_\beta Pz:\eta.$$

Hence by rule (→I),

$$\Gamma^+ - z \vdash_\beta (\lambda z\cdot Pz):\xi\to\eta.$$

This means that there is a finite subset Γ^* of $\Gamma^+ - z$ such that

$$\Gamma^* \vdash_\beta (\lambda z\cdot Pz):\xi\to\eta;$$

hence by 4B9

$$\Gamma^* \vdash_\beta P:\xi\to\eta,$$

which gives the "⇒" part of (2). Hence (2) holds and the proof of (1) is complete.

Deduction of the theorem from (1) If $\Gamma \models_\beta M:\tau$ then in particular, for $\mathbb{TM}_\beta$ and E_0 and V_0 we have

$$[M]^\beta \in [\![\tau]\!]_{V_0}$$

Hence by (1),

$$\Gamma^+ \vdash_\beta M:\tau.$$

That is $\Gamma^* \vdash_\beta M:\tau$ for some finite $\Gamma^* \subseteq \Gamma^+$. Hence by 4A3.2(vi),

(3) $$\Gamma^* \upharpoonright M \vdash_\beta M:\tau.$$

But $\Gamma^* \upharpoonright M = \Gamma \upharpoonright M$ because $\Gamma^* \subseteq \Gamma^+$ and the extra term-variables in Γ^+ were chosen to be distinct from those in M. Hence by the weakening-property of $\vdash$,

$$\Gamma \vdash_\beta M:\tau.$$ □

4B10 Remark (Too many completeness-proofs?) In the above completeness-proof the full strength of the assumption that $\Gamma \mapsto M:\tau$ was valid in *every* model was not used; all we needed was that it was valid in *one* model, the term-model. There is another completeness proof in Barendregt et al. 1983, which uses a more complex kind of term model called a ***filter model***. And there is a third proof in Coppo 1984 using the ***graph model*** $P\omega$. It looks almost as if the choice of model is quite irrelevant to the success of the completeness-proof.

Furthermore, $TA_{\lambda+\beta}$ and $TA_{\lambda+\beta\eta}$ can be proved sound and complete for at least three other variant definitions of the semantics, see Hindley 1983a §5, Hindley 1983b, and Mitchell 1988 §§3–4.

This richness of completeness-proofs says in effect that the differences which undoubtedly exist between these various kinds of models and definitions of semantics cannot be expressed in the rather limited language of $TA_{\lambda+\beta}$ and $TA_{\lambda+\beta\eta}$.

4B11 Remark By the way, although earlier remarks in this chapter may have given the impression that without equality-invariance a type-theory has no reasonable semantics, this is not strictly true. Plotkin 1994 has described a semantics for TA_{λ} (and some extensions) based on modelling the concept of reduction rather than equality. Plotkin's approach seems closer to the "spirit" of TA_{λ}; in fact TA_{λ} has at its heart the notion of reduction rather than conversion, and has always been seen primarily as a tool for eliminating type-conflicts in practical computations or reductions, rather than as a formal theory of equality.

5

A version using typed terms

In Chapter 2 some care was taken to distinguish the Curry and Church approaches to type-theory from each other. Curry's approach involved assigning types to pre-existing untyped terms with each term receiving either an infinite set of types or none at all, whereas in Church's the terms were defined with built-in types with each term having a single type (see 2A3). In Curry's approach the types contained variables, in Church's they contained only constants.

This book focuses on the Curry approach. However, even in this approach it turns out to be very useful to introduce a typed-term language as an alternative notation for TA_λ-deductions. Although the tree-notation introduced in Chapter 2 shows very clearly what assumptions are needed in deducing what conclusions, it takes up a lot of space and is hard to visualise when the deduction is in any way complicated. And when manipulations and reductions of deductions are under discussion it is almost unmanageable. A much more compact alternative notation is needed, and this is what the typed terms in the present chapter will give.

We shall also define reduction of typed terms; typed terms will be shown in the next chapter to encode deductions in propositional logic as well as in TA_λ, and their reduction will be essentially the same as the reduction of deductions that is a standard tool in proof theory.

By the way, a cynical reader might think we are simply abandoning Curry's approach here and replacing it by Church's, but this is not so; the main positive feature of Curry's approach is the expressive power gained from its use of type-variables and the presence of an underlying language of untyped terms, and we shall not abandon these. All we shall do is replace space-hungry deduction-tree diagrams by neat and compact typed terms. And these terms will differ in several important ways from those in a true Church-style system (see 5A1.5 for example); they will simply be codes for TA_λ-deductions, nothing more.

5A Typed terms

In this section we shall define a system of typed terms isomorphic to TA_λ-deductions: for each Γ a set $\mathbb{TT}(\Gamma)$ of typed terms will be defined that will encode deductions of formulae of form

$$\Gamma^- \mapsto M:\tau \qquad (\Gamma^- \subseteq \Gamma).$$

It might be useful to read the detailed definition of a TA_λ-deduction in 9C in parallel with this section.

5A1 Definition (Typed terms, $\mathbb{TT}(\Gamma)$) Given a type-context Γ the set $\mathbb{TT}(\Gamma)$ of ***typed terms relative to*** Γ is a set of expressions defined thus:

(i) if Γ contains $x{:}\sigma$ then the expression x^σ is in $\mathbb{TT}(\Gamma)$ and is called a ***typed variable***;

(ii) if $\Gamma_1 \cup \Gamma_2$ is consistent and $M^{\sigma\to\tau} \in \mathbb{TT}(\Gamma_1)$ and $N^\sigma \in \mathbb{TT}(\Gamma_2)$, then

$$(M^{\sigma\to\tau}N^\sigma)^\tau \in \mathbb{TT}(\Gamma_1 \cup \Gamma_2);$$

(iii) if Γ is consistent with $\{x{:}\sigma\}$ and $M^\tau \in \mathbb{TT}(\Gamma)$, then

$$(\lambda x^\sigma \cdot M^\tau)^{\sigma\to\tau} \in \mathbb{TT}(\Gamma - x).$$

If M^τ is a typed term (relative to some Γ), τ is called ***the type of*** M^τ.

5A1.1 *Notation* Typed terms will be abbreviated using the same conventions as for untyped terms. Also some type-superscripts may be omitted. For example, depending on which of its types are to be emphasised in a particular discussion, a typed term $(x^{\rho\to\sigma}y^\rho)^\sigma$ may be called any of

$$(xy)^\sigma, \qquad x^{\rho\to\sigma}y^\rho, \qquad x^{\rho\to\sigma}y.$$

5A1.2 *Exercise* (Compare 2A8.2–4.) Show that $\mathbb{TT}(\emptyset)$ contains the typed terms

$$(\lambda x^{a\to b}y^{c\to a}z^c \cdot (x^{a\to b}(y^{c\to a}z^c)^a)^b)^{(a\to b)\to(c\to a)\to c\to b},$$
$$(\lambda x^a \cdot x^a)^{a\to a},$$
$$(\lambda x^a y^b \cdot x^a)^{a\to b\to a}.$$

5A1.3 *Note* (i) In the following term x appears decorated with two different types:

$$Q^b \equiv (x^{(a\to a)\to b}(\lambda x^a \cdot x^a)^{a\to a})^b.$$

Despite this, Q^b is a genuine typed term, and in fact it is easy to verify that $Q^b \in \mathbb{TT}(\Gamma)$, where $\Gamma = \{x{:}(a\to a)\to b\}$. Further, Q^b translates into a genuine TA_λ -deduction in an obvious way.

(ii) In contrast, the following expression is not a typed term (and does not translate into a TA_λ-deduction):

$$(x^{a\to b}x^a)^b.$$

5A1.4 *Warning* The subterms of a term in $\mathbb{TT}(\Gamma)$ need not be in $\mathbb{TT}(\Gamma)$. For example we have

$$(\lambda x^a \cdot x^a)^{a\to a} \in \mathbb{TT}(\emptyset)$$

but the subterm x^a is not in $\mathbb{TT}(\emptyset)$. (It is in $\mathbb{TT}(\{x{:}a\})$.)

5A1.5 *Warning* If $M^{\sigma\to\tau}$ and N^{σ} are typed terms we cannot always say that $(M^{\sigma\to\tau}N^{\sigma})^{\tau}$ is one. (Because if $M^{\sigma\to\tau} \in \mathbb{TT}(\Gamma_1)$ and $N^{\sigma} \in \mathbb{TT}(\Gamma_2)$ we cannot apply 5A1(ii) unless $\Gamma_1 \cup \Gamma_2$ is consistent.)

This is a crucial difference between the present typed terms and those of Church, for example in Church 1940; the latter are typed in an "absolute" sense and have the property that if $M^{\sigma\to\tau}$ and N^{σ} are typed then so is $(M^{\sigma\to\tau}N^{\sigma})^{\tau}$, but the present terms are only typed *relatively* to a given Γ.

5A2 Definition (Type-erasing) The ***type-erasure*** $M^{\not\tau}$ of M^{τ} is the untyped term obtained by erasing all types from M^{τ}.

We shall see in 5A5.1 that $M^{\not\tau}$ is the subject of the conclusion of the TA$_\lambda$-deduction that M^{τ} encodes.

5A3 Lemma *If* $M^{\tau} \in \mathbb{TT}(\Gamma)$, *then* $FV(M^{\not\tau}) \subseteq Subjects(\Gamma)$ *and*

(i) $M^{\tau} \in \mathbb{TT}(\Gamma^{+})$ *for all contexts* $\Gamma^{+} \supseteq \Gamma$,
(ii) $M^{\tau} \in \mathbb{TT}(\Gamma \upharpoonright M^{\not\tau})$,
(iii) *If* $M^{\tau} \in \mathbb{TT}(\Gamma')$ *then* $\Gamma' \upharpoonright M^{\not\tau} = \Gamma \upharpoonright M^{\not\tau}$.

Proof Straightforward induction on $|M^{\not\tau}|$. □

5A4 Definition (Minimum context, *Con*(M^{τ})) If $M^{\tau} \in \mathbb{TT}(\Gamma)$, its *minimum context* is

$$Con(M^{\tau}) = \Gamma \upharpoonright M^{\not\tau}.$$

5A4.1 *Note* $Con(M^{\tau})$ is determined uniquely by M^{τ}. In particular it is independent of Γ, in the sense that if $M^{\tau} \in \mathbb{TT}(\Gamma) \cap \mathbb{TT}(\Gamma')$ then $\Gamma \upharpoonright M^{\not\tau} = \Gamma' \upharpoonright M^{\not\tau}$ (by 5A3(iii)).

We shall see in 5A7 that if M^{τ} encodes a TA$_\lambda$-deduction of $\Gamma \mapsto M^{\not\tau}:\tau$ then $\Gamma = Con(M^{\tau})$. Also it is easy to see that

(i) for all typed terms $M^{\sigma\to\tau}$ and N^{σ}

(a) $(M^{\sigma\to\tau}N^{\sigma})^{\tau}$ is a typed term iff $Con(M^{\sigma\to\tau})$ is consistent with $Con(N^{\sigma})$,
(b) if $Con(M^{\sigma\to\tau})$ is consistent with $Con(N^{\sigma})$ then

$$Con((M^{\sigma\to\tau}N^{\sigma})^{\tau}) = Con(M^{\sigma\to\tau}) \cup Con(N^{\sigma});$$

(ii) for all typed terms M^{τ}

(a) $(\lambda x^{\sigma}.M^{\tau})^{\sigma\to\tau}$ is a typed term iff $Con(M^{\tau})$ is consistent with $x{:}\sigma$ (i.e. iff $Con(M^{\tau})$ either contains $x{:}\sigma$ or does not contain x at all),
(b) if $Con(M^{\tau})$ is consistent with $x{:}\sigma$ then

$$Con((\lambda x^{\sigma}.M^{\tau})^{\sigma\to\tau}) = Con(M^{\tau}) - x.$$

The translation mappings between typed terms and TA$_\lambda$-deductions will now be defined; they are very straightforward but will be given here in full for the sake of precision.

5A5 Definition (Translating deductions to typed terms) Let Δ be a TA_λ-deduction with conclusion $\Gamma \mapsto M{:}\tau$; define a typed term $T^\tau_\Delta \in \mathbb{TT}(\Gamma)$ by following the clauses of the definition of Δ (see 9C1) thus:

(i) if Δ is an axiom $x{:}\tau \mapsto x{:}\tau$, define $T^\tau_\Delta \equiv x^\tau$;
(ii) if Δ is the result of applying ($\to$E) to deductions Δ_1, Δ_2 of

$$\Gamma_1 \mapsto P{:}\,\sigma\to\tau, \qquad \Gamma_2 \mapsto Q{:}\sigma,$$

and $T^{\sigma\to\tau}_{\Delta_1} \in \mathbb{TT}(\Gamma_1)$ and $T^\sigma_{\Delta_2} \in \mathbb{TT}(\Gamma_2)$, define

$$T^\tau_\Delta \equiv (T^{\sigma\to\tau}_{\Delta_1} T^\sigma_{\Delta_2})^\tau;$$

(iii) if Δ is the result of applying rule ($\to$I) to a deduction Δ_1 of

$$\Gamma \mapsto P{:}\sigma,$$

and $\tau \equiv \rho\to\sigma$ and $\Gamma \cup \{x{:}\rho\}$ is consistent and $T^\sigma_{\Delta_1} \in \mathbb{TT}(\Gamma)$, define

$$T^\tau_\Delta \equiv (\lambda x^\rho \cdot T^\sigma_{\Delta_1})^{\rho\to\sigma}.$$

5A5.1 *Lemma* *If Δ is a TA_λ-deduction of $\Gamma \mapsto M{:}\tau$ then*

$$T^\tau_\Delta \in \mathbb{TT}(\Gamma), \qquad T^{\not\tau}_\Delta \equiv M.$$

5A6 Definition (Translating typed terms to deductions) To each typed term M^τ we associate a TA_λ-deduction $\underline{\Delta}(M^\tau)$ as follows:

(i) if $M^\tau \equiv x^\tau$ define $\underline{\Delta}(M^\tau)$ to be the atomic deduction

$$x{:}\tau \mapsto x{:}\tau;$$

(ii) if $M^\tau \equiv (P^{\sigma\to\tau}Q^\sigma)^\tau$, $P^{\sigma\to\tau} \in \mathbb{TT}(\Gamma_1)$, $Q^\sigma \in \mathbb{TT}(\Gamma_2)$, $\Gamma_1 \cup \Gamma_2$ is consistent, and $\underline{\Delta}(P^{\sigma\to\tau})$ and $\underline{\Delta}(Q^\sigma)$ are deductions of

$$\Gamma_1' \mapsto P^{\not\sigma\not\to\not\tau}{:}\sigma\to\tau, \qquad \Gamma_2' \mapsto Q^{\not\sigma}{:}\sigma$$

for some $\Gamma_1' \subseteq \Gamma_1$ and $\Gamma_2' \subseteq \Gamma_2$, define $\underline{\Delta}(M^\tau)$ to be the deduction obtained by applying ($\to$E) to $\underline{\Delta}(P^{\sigma\to\tau})$ and $\underline{\Delta}(Q^\sigma)$;
(iii) if $M^\tau \equiv (\lambda x^\rho \cdot P^\sigma)^{\rho\to\sigma}$, $\tau \equiv \rho\to\sigma$, $P^\sigma \in \mathbb{TT}(\Gamma)$, Γ is consistent with $\{x{:}\rho\}$, and $\underline{\Delta}(P^\sigma)$ is a deduction of

$$\Gamma' \mapsto P^{\not\sigma}{:}\sigma$$

for some $\Gamma' \subseteq \Gamma$, define $\underline{\Delta}(M^\tau)$ to be the deduction obtained by applying ($\to$I) to $\underline{\Delta}(P^\sigma)$, discharging x.

5A7 Theorem *The translation from Δ to T^τ_Δ is a one-to-one correspondence between all TA_λ-deductions and all typed terms, and its inverse is the translation from M^τ to $\underline{\Delta}(M^\tau)$. In particular,*

(i) *if Δ is a deduction of $\Gamma \mapsto M{:}\tau$ then*

$$T^\tau_\Delta \in \mathbb{TT}(\Gamma), \qquad T^{\not\tau}_\Delta \equiv M, \qquad \underline{\Delta}(T^\tau_\Delta) \equiv \Delta,$$

(ii) *if* $M^\tau \in \mathbb{TT}(\Gamma)$ *then* $Con(M^\tau) \subseteq \Gamma$ *and* $\underline{\Delta}(M^\tau)$ *is a deduction of*

$$Con(M^\tau) \quad \mapsto \quad M^{\not\tau}{:}\tau.$$

Proof (i) By 5A5.1 and 5A6. (ii) Easy induction on $|M^{\not\tau}|$. □

5B Reducing typed terms

Most of the term-structure concepts introduced in Section 1A, and those in 9A, can be extended from untyped to typed terms in an obvious way. For example ***position***, ***subterm***, ***occurs*** and ***component*** are all defined for typed terms just as for untyped terms in 9A.

The only difference is that in a typed term every subterm is decorated with a type-superscript; in particular an ***atom*** has form x^τ not just x. For example if $M^\tau \equiv (x^{a \to b} y^a)^b$ we shall say that $x^{a \to b}$ and y^a occur in M^τ but not that x and y occur in M^τ.

Some of the concepts in 1A and 9A do not translate to typed terms quite so unambiguously however, so their typed definitions will be given below and their main properties will be stated.

5B1 Definition The ***length***, $|M^\tau|$, of a typed term M^τ is the same as $|M^{\not\tau}|$, see 1A2.

5B2 Definition (Replacement) Let $\underline{P}^\sigma \equiv \langle P^\sigma, p, M^\tau \rangle$ be a component of a typed term M^τ (see 9A2–3), and let T^σ be any typed term with the same type as P^σ. Define

$$\{T^\sigma/P^\sigma\}_p M^\tau$$

to be the result of replacing P^σ by T^σ at position p in M^τ, just as for untyped terms (see 9A6), but only when (i) or (ii) below holds:[1]

(i) $Con(T^\sigma) \subseteq Con(P^\sigma)$;
(ii) the set $Con(T^\sigma) \cup Con(M^\tau) \cup \{x_1{:}\xi_1, \ldots, x_n{:}\xi_n\}$ is consistent, where $\underline{\lambda x_1^{\xi_1}}, \ldots, \underline{\lambda x_n^{\xi_n}}$ are the abstractors in M^τ whose scopes contain $\underline{P}^\sigma$.

5B2.1 *Lemma* (i) *If* 5B2(i) *holds then* $\{T^\sigma/P^\sigma\}_p M^\tau$ *is a well-defined typed term and*

$$Con(\{T^\sigma/P^\sigma\}_p M^\tau) \subseteq Con(M^\tau).$$

(ii) *If* 5B2(ii) *holds then* $\{T^\sigma/P^\sigma\}_p M^\tau$ *is well-defined and*

$$Con(\{T^\sigma/P^\sigma\}_p M^\tau) \subseteq Con(M^\tau) \cup Con(T^\sigma).$$

Proof Like the proofs of 9C5 and 9C6. □

5B2.2 *Note* If neither (i) nor (ii) holds in 5B2 we do not define $\{T^\sigma/P^\sigma\}_p M^\tau$. In this case the replacement of $\underline{P}^\sigma$ by T^σ in M^τ will still produce an expression of some kind but it might not be a typed term. For example let

$$M^\tau \equiv (x^{a \to b} y^a)^b, \qquad P^\sigma \equiv y^a, \qquad T^\sigma \equiv x^a.$$

[1] Compare the conditions in the replacement lemmas for deductions, 9C5–6.

Then replacing y^a by x^a changes M^τ to $(x^{a\to b}x^a)^b$, which fails to be a typed term because $x{:}a\to b$ is inconsistent with $x{:}a$. (See 5A1.5.)

Also if $\rho \not\equiv \sigma$ we do not define $\{T^\rho/P^\sigma\}_p M^\tau$.

5B3 Definition ***Free*** and ***bound*** variable-occurrences, and the set $FV(M^\tau)$, are defined just as in 1A6. (But all occurrences are now typed.)

5B3.1 *Notes* (i) $x^\sigma \in FV(M^\tau) \iff x{:}\sigma \in Con(M^\tau)$.

(ii) $x \in FV(M^{\not\tau}) \iff (\exists\sigma)(x^\sigma \in FV(M^\tau))$.

(iii) By (i) and the consistency of contexts,

$$x^\sigma, x^\rho \in FV(M^\tau) \implies \sigma \equiv \rho.$$

(iv) But a typed term can contain inconsistently typed variables if one variable is free and the other is bound (or if both are bound). An example is the term Q^b in 5A1.3:

$$Q^b \equiv (x^{(a\to a)\to b}(\lambda x^a.x^a)^{a\to a})^b.$$

5B4 Definition M^τ ***has no bound-variable clashes*** iff $M^{\not\tau}$ has no such clashes (as defined in 1A9).

5B4.1 *Example* Consider the term Q^b above and its type-erasure:

$$Q^b \equiv (x^{(a\to a)\to b}(\lambda x^a.x^a)^{a\to a})^b, \qquad Q^{\not b} \equiv x(\lambda x.x).$$

This erasure has a clash so the above definition says Q^b has a clash. (We might feel like saying that Q^b is without clashes because $x^{a\to a\to b}$ and x^a are distinct typed variables, but this would make the theory of typed terms diverge too far from that of TA_λ-deductions. Definition 5B4 says in effect that a typed term has no clashes iff it represents a deduction whose conclusion has no clashes.)

5B5 Definition (Typed substitution) We define $[N^\sigma/x^\sigma]M^\tau$ by the following clauses. (Compare untyped substitution, 1A7.) These clauses will not cover all cases but all those in which $(\lambda x^\sigma.M^\tau)N^\sigma$ has no bound-variable clashes, which are all the cases needed in this book.

(i) $[N^\sigma/x^\sigma]x^\sigma \equiv N^\sigma$;

(ii) $[N^\sigma/x^\sigma]y^\tau \equiv y^\tau$ if $x \not\equiv y$;

(iii) $[N^\sigma/x^\sigma](P^{\rho\to\tau}Q^\rho)^\tau \equiv ([N^\sigma/x^\sigma]P^{\rho\to\tau}[N^\sigma/x^\sigma]Q^\rho)^\tau$;

(iv) $[N^\sigma/x^\sigma](\lambda x^\xi\cdot P^\eta)^{\xi\to\eta} \equiv (\lambda x^\xi\cdot P^\eta)^{\xi\to\eta}$;

(v) $[N^\sigma/x^\sigma](\lambda y^\xi\cdot P^\eta)^{\xi\to\eta} \equiv (\lambda y^\xi\cdot P^\eta)^{\xi\to\eta}$ if $x \not\equiv y$, $x \notin FV(P^{\not\eta})$;

(vi) $[N^\sigma/x^\sigma](\lambda y^\xi\cdot P^\eta)^{\xi\to\eta} \equiv (\lambda y^\xi\cdot[N^\sigma/x^\sigma]P^\eta)^{\xi\to\eta}$
if $x \not\equiv y$, $x \in FV(P^{\not\eta})$, $y \notin FV(N^{\not\sigma})$;

(vii) $[N^\sigma/x^\sigma](\lambda y^\xi\cdot P^\eta)^{\xi\to\eta} \equiv (\lambda z^\xi\cdot[N^\sigma/x^\sigma][z^\xi/y^\xi]P^\eta)^{\xi\to\eta}$
if $x \not\equiv y$, $x \in FV(P^{\not\eta})$, $y \in FV(N^{\not\sigma})$.

(In (vii) z is the first untyped variable not occurring in $N^{\not\sigma}P^{\not\eta}$.)

5B5.1 *Notes* The restrictions in the above clauses may seem over-strong in that they involve *un*typed variables and terms; but if they were weakened the last part of the useful lemma 5B5.2 below would fail.

Clause (iv) includes the case $\xi \not\equiv \sigma$. But in this case x^σ cannot occur free in P^η, because if it did then $\lambda x^\xi.P^\eta$ would not be a typed term (see Definition 5A1(iii)). Thus substituting for x^σ should change nothing. And this is exactly what (iv) says.

No attempt has been made to define $[N^\rho/x^\sigma]$ when $\rho \not\equiv \sigma$ or $[N^\sigma/x^\sigma]x^\tau$ when $\tau \not\equiv \sigma$.

5B5.2 *Lemma If $((\lambda x^\sigma.M^\tau)N^\sigma)^\tau$ is a typed term with no bound-variable clashes, then*

(i) *$[N^\sigma/x^\sigma]M^\tau$ is defined and is a typed term with type τ,*
(ii) $[N^\sigma/x^\sigma]M^\tau \equiv M^\tau$ *if* $x^\sigma \notin FV(M^\tau)$,
(iii) $Con([N^\sigma/x^\sigma]M^\tau) \subseteq (Con(M^\tau) - x) \cup Con(N^\sigma)$,
(iv) $([N^\sigma/x^\sigma]M^\tau)^{\not\tau} \equiv_\alpha [N^{\not\sigma}/x]M^{\not\tau}$.

Proof Parts (i)–(iv) are proved together by a straightforward but boring induction on $|M^{\not\tau}|$. (The assumption about $((\lambda x^\sigma.M^\tau)N^\sigma)^\tau$ implies in particular that $Con(M^\tau) - x$ is consistent with $Con(N^\sigma)$ and that x does not occur in $N^{\not\sigma}$.) □

5B6 Definition (Typed α-conversion) The relation $\equiv_\alpha$ is defined just as for untyped terms (see 1A8), using replacements with form

$$(\alpha) \qquad \lambda x^\sigma\cdot M^\tau \equiv_\alpha \lambda y^\sigma\cdot[y^\sigma/x^\sigma]M^\tau \qquad (y \notin FV(M^{\not\tau})).$$

5B6.1 *Lemma If $\lambda x^\sigma.M^\tau$ is a typed term and $y \notin FV(M^{\not\tau})$, then $[y^\sigma/x^\sigma]M^\tau$ is defined and both sides of (α) are typed terms with the same type and minimum context. Hence the class of all typed terms is closed under α-conversion, and*

$$P^\tau \equiv_\alpha Q^{\tau'} \implies \tau \equiv \tau' \text{ and } Con(P^\tau) = Con(Q^{\tau'}).$$

5B6.2 *Warning* The condition "$y \notin FV(M^{\not\tau})$" in (α) cannot be weakened to "$y^\sigma \notin FV(M^\tau)$". Because if it were, we could α-convert a typed term to an expression that was not one, thus:

$$\lambda x^{a\to b}\cdot x^{a\to b}y^a \equiv_\alpha \lambda y^{a\to b}\cdot y^{a\to b}y^a.$$

5B7 Definition (Typed redexes and reduction) Typed $\triangleright_\beta$ and $\triangleright_{\beta\eta}$ are defined just like the untyped relations in 1B and 1C. In particular ***typed β- and η-redexes*** have form

$$((\lambda x^\sigma\cdot M^\tau)^{\sigma\to\tau}N^\sigma)^\tau, \qquad (\lambda x^\sigma\cdot(P^{\sigma\to\tau}x^\sigma)^\tau)^{\sigma\to\tau}$$

with $x \notin FV(P^{\not\sigma\not\to\not\tau})$, and their ***contracta*** are, respectively,

$$[N^\sigma/x^\sigma]M^\tau, \qquad P^{\sigma\to\tau}.$$

And, just as in Chapter 1, a ***contraction*** is a replacement of a redex by its contractum.

A ***typed β-nf (η-nf, βη-nf)*** is a typed term containing no β-(η-, βη-) redexes.

5B7.1 *Lemma* (i) *If a β- or η-contraction in a typed term P^τ changes P^τ to an expression X, then X is also a well-defined typed term with type τ.*

(ii) *If $P^\tau \triangleright_{\beta\eta} Q^\tau$, then*

(a) $Con(P^\tau) \supseteq Con(Q^\tau)$,

(b) $P^{\not\tau} \triangleright_{\beta\eta} Q^{\not\tau}$.

Proof Prove (i) and (ii) together: for β use 5B5.2 and 5B2.1(i), and for η the proof is straightforward. □

5B7.2 *Note* (i) When typed terms are interpreted as TA_λ-deductions a β-reduction of a typed term corresponds to a reduction of a deduction. (The idea of reducing deductions originated in Prawitz 1965 and there is a modern account in Troelstra and van Dalen 1988 Vol. 2 Ch. 10 §2; cf. also HS86 Def. 15.30.) In this interpretation the above lemma says that if we reduce a deduction of $\Gamma \mapsto P:\tau$, the result will still be a genuine deduction and will have conclusion $\Gamma^* \mapsto Q:\tau$ for some $\Gamma^* \subseteq \Gamma$ and some Q obtained by β-reducing P.

(ii) Part (ii) of the above lemma is rather like the subject-reduction theorem for TA_λ-deductions (2C1), but is not an exact analogue. A closer analogue is the following lemma which will also be used later.

5B7.3 *Lemma* (i) *Let P^τ be a typed term and $P^{\not\tau} \triangleright_{1\beta} Q$ by contracting a β-redex R at a position r in $P^{\not\tau}$. Then P^τ contains at position r a typed β-redex R^σ such that $R^{\not\sigma} \equiv R$, and contracting this R^σ changes P^τ to a typed term Q^τ such that*

$$Q^{\not\tau} \equiv Q.$$

(ii) *The same holds true for η-redexes.*

Proof Same as the proof of 2C1 but with typed terms instead of TA_λ-deductions. □

5B7.4 *Lemma* (i) *A typed term P^τ has a β-reduction with length n iff $P^{\not\tau}$ has a β-reduction with length n.*

(ii) *A typed term P^τ is a β-nf iff $P^{\not\tau}$ is a β-nf.*

(iii) *Both* (i) *and* (iii) *hold for η.*

Proof Note first that if a typed term P^τ contains a β-redex then so does $P^{\not\tau}$. Then (i)–(iii) follow from this and 5B7.3. □

5B8 Typed Church-Rosser Theorem (i) *If $M^\tau \triangleright_\beta P^\tau$ and $M^\tau \triangleright_\beta Q^\tau$ then there exists a typed term T^τ such that $P^\tau \triangleright_\beta T^\tau$ and $Q^\tau \triangleright_\beta T^\tau$.*

(ii) *The same holds for η- and $\beta\eta$-reductions.*

Proof Like the untyped Church-Rosser theorems in 1B and 1C. □

5B8.1 *Warning* (No typed convertibility relation) No attempt is made here to define a convertibility relation $=_\beta$ or $=_{\beta\eta}$ on typed terms by expansions and contractions of redexes. First, we shall not need one. Second, since the typed terms in this chapter correspond exactly to TA_τ-deductions, any attempt to define such a typed equality would meet the same type-variation problems as were discussed for TA_τ in 2C. In fact, β-expanding a typed term may lead to an expression which is no longer a typed term (cf. 2C2.2–6).

5C Normalization theorems

Along with most other type-theories, TA_λ has what is called the ***weak normalization*** property:

(WN) *every typable term has a normal form.*

And many of them, including TA_λ, also have the ***strong normalization*** property:

(SN) *all reductions of a typable term are finite.*

These properties were stated for TA_λ in Theorems 2D5 and 2D6 without proof. In the present section a proof will be given of the analogue of WN for typed terms, and WN for typable terms will be deduced from it. No proof of SN will be given here as there is already a detailed proof in our main reference (see HS86 Appendix 2).

5C1 Weak Normalization (WN) Theorem (Turing 1942, Curry and Feys 1958 Cor. 9F9.2, etc.) *Every typed term P^π has both a β-nf and a $\beta\eta$-nf.*

Proof The existence of a $\beta\eta$-nf follows from that of a β-nf by the typed analogue of 1C9.4. It remains to prove that P^π has a β-nf, i.e. to give a strategy for reducing P^π and to prove this reduction terminates. This will be done by the method of Turing 1942, the earliest proof known and also the simplest. Some knowledge of 9B will be needed.

Let $P^\pi \in \mathbb{TT}(\Gamma)$. Then each β-redex-occurrence $\underline{R}^\tau$ in P^π has form

$$\underline{R}^\tau \equiv \underline{((\lambda x^\sigma \cdot M^\tau)^{\sigma\to\tau} N^\sigma)^\tau}.$$

We shall call $\underline{(\lambda x \cdot M)^{\sigma\to\tau}}$ the ***function-part*** of $\underline{R}^\tau$ and its type $\sigma\to\tau$ the ***dominant type*** of $\underline{R}^\tau$, and the number of atom-occurrences in $\sigma\to\tau$ the ***degree*** of $\underline{R}^\tau$:

$$Deg(\underline{R}^\tau) = |\sigma\to\tau|.$$

Now let the contraction of $\underline{R}^\tau$ change P^π to Q^π, and consider the residuals in Q^π of β-redex-occurrences in P^π. (Residuals are defined in 9B2.) By 9B2.2(iii) the degree of each residual is the same as that of the residual's parent in P^π.

Further, by the conclusion of 9B5.1, for each newly created β-redex-occurrence in Q^π (i.e. one that is not a residual of one in P^π) its function-part is an occurrence of either N^σ or $[N/x]M^\tau$; thus its type is either σ or τ, and so the degree of each newly created redex-occurrence is strictly less than the degree of $\underline{R}^\tau$.

Now let $d(P^\pi)$ be the maximum of the degrees of all β-redex-occurrences in P^π and let $\mathbb{S}$ be the set of all β-redex-occurrences in P^π with this degree. Reduce P^π by a minimal complete development of $\mathbb{S}$ as defined in 9B4. By 9B4 and 9B4.1 this reduction is finite and its result is a term P_1^π containing no residuals of members of

$\mathbb{S}$. All the redexes in P_1^π are either newly created or residuals of redexes not in $\mathbb{S}$; hence

$$d(P_1^\pi) < d(P^\pi).$$

Continue this procedure by making further minimal complete developments of sets of redexes with maximum degree; since each development strictly decreases $d(P^\pi)$ we must eventually obtain a β-normal form of P^π. □

5C1.1 *Corollary The WN theorem for typable terms (2D5) holds.*

Proof By 5B7.4 and the WN theorem for typed terms. □

5C1.2 *Historical notes* The first known proof of WN for a type-theory equivalent to TA_λ was written around 1941 or '42 in unpublished notes by Alan Turing. (See Gandy 1980a for a transcript of Turing's notes, and Gandy 1977 pp. 178–180 for some comments on Turing's work in type-theory.)

But the first proof to be actually published was carried out by Curry in the late 1950's by a completely different technique (Curry and Feys 1958 §9F, especially Cor. 9F9.2). Its key step was a cut-elimination theorem for a particular formulation of TA_{CL}.[1]

Also there is a WN theorem in Prawitz 1965 for reducing proofs in logic which is essentially equivalent to WN for TA_λ.

From the 1960's onwards the Turing method of proof was re-discovered, probably independently, several times (Morris 1968 §4F Thm. 2, Andrews 1971 Prop. 2.7.3, for example), and WN theorems were proved by various methods for many stronger type-theories than TA_λ.

In particular, the mid-60's saw a spate of proofs of WN for typed λ-calculi enhanced by primitive recursion operators (for example those in Tait 1965, Hanatani 1966, Hinata 1967, Sanchis 1967, Tait 1967, Diller 1968, Dragalin 1968 and Howard 1970); see Troelstra 1973 §§2.2.1–2.3.13 or HS86 Ch. 18 for descriptions of the background setting. At least two of these also included proofs of SN (see below).

5C2 Strong Normalization (SN) Theorem (Sanchis 1967 Thm. 8, Diller 1968 §6, etc.) *Let $P^\pi \in \mathbb{TT}(\Gamma)$ for some Γ; then, for β- and for $\beta\eta$-reductions,*

(i) *all reductions of P^π are finite,*
(ii) *there is an algorithm which accepts P^π as input and outputs a number $k(P^\pi)$ such that all reductions of P^π have length $\leq k(P^\pi)$.*

Proof For (i) there is an accessible proof in HS86 Appendix 2: see Thm. A2.3 for β, and Thm. A2.4 for $\beta\eta$. Alternatively, see Barendregt 1992 Thm. 4.3.6.

For (ii), simply construct a finitely branching tree of reductions starting at P^π by doing all possible contractions at each step. By (i) this tree's branches are all finite

[1] Cut-elimination originated in the study of predicate logic in Gentzen 1935, and the relation between cut-elimination and normalization is explored in Zucker 1974. It depends on the correspondence between formulae and types to be described in the next chapter. Cut-elimination theorems for versions of TA_λ can be found in Seldin 1977 and 1978.

in length, and the famous König's Lemma on trees states that in this case the whole tree must be finite. Hence its branches can all be measured and the maximum of their lengths determined. Call this number $k(P^\pi)$.

But this algorithm is of course inefficient and the proof that $k(P^\pi)$ is well-defined depends on König's Lemma which is usually regarded as non-constructive. To remedy these defects several workers have devised constructive proofs of (ii); see Mints 1979, Gandy 1980b, de Vrijer 1987 and Schwichtenberg 1991. These proofs give more efficient ways of computing suitable bounds $k(P^\pi)$ (though the bounds they give are not always the least possible, see comments in de Vrijer 1987). □

5C2.1 *Corollary The SN theorem for typable terms (2D6) holds.*

Proof By 5B7.4(i) and 5C2. □

5C2.2 *Note* The history of SN began over twenty years later than that of WN. The first known explicit SN proofs were in Sanchis 1967 Thm. 8 and Diller 1968 §6, the former for weak reduction in combinatory logic enhanced by primitive recursion operators and the latter for $\lambda\beta$-reduction similarly enhanced.[1]

Most published proofs have depended on defining what is usually known as a ***computability predicate*** by a suitable induction, and proving first the SN property for all computable terms and then the computability of all terms P^π by induction on $|P^\pi|$. (The proof in HS86 Appendix 2 is typical of this approach, cf. also the WN proof in Tait 1967.) This method has been successfully adapted to so many different type-theories over the years that it is now in effect the standard one. In the early 1970's it was applied by Jean-Yves Girard in a generalised and strengthened form to prove SN for his strong second-order type-theory known as System F (Girard et al. 1989 Ch. 14), and it has since been applied to other second-order type-theories. An analysis with references is in Gallier 1990. Another account is in Barendregt 1992; Barendregt's System $\lambda 2$ is equivalent to Girard's System F.

[1] In each case manuscript versions were made available a couple of years before publication.

6

The correspondence with implication

One of the most interesting facts about TA_λ is that there is a very close correspondence between this system and propositional logic, in which the types assignable to closed terms in TA_λ turn out to be exactly the formulae provable in a certain formal logic of implication. This correspondence is often called the ***Curry-Howard isomorphism*** or the ***formulae-as-types isomorphism***, and will be studied in this chapter.

The logic involved in this correspondence is not the classical logic of truth-tables however, but that of the intuitionist philosophers; it will be defined in the first section below.

The Curry-Howard isomorphism was first hinted at in print in Curry 1934 p.588, and was made explicit in Curry 1942 p.60 footnote 28 and Curry and Feys 1958 §9E. But it was viewed there as no more than a curiosity. The first people to see that it could be extended to other connectives and quantifiers and used as a technical tool to derive results were N. G. de Bruijn, William Howard and H. Läuchli in the 1960's. See Howard 1969, de Bruijn 1980 (an introduction to de Bruijn's AUTOMATH project which began in the 1960's), and Läuchli 1965.

This chapter will also define three rather interesting subsystems of intuitionist logic and show that they correspond to the three restricted classes of λ-terms defined in Section 1D. This correspondence was first noted by Carew Meredith in unpublished work around 1951 and was explored in detail in the thesis Rezus 1981.

6A Intuitionist implicational logic

In this section we shall define the implicational fragment of intuitionist logic. The original formulations of this logic in the 1920's were axiom-based systems and corresponded more closely to combinatory logic than λ-calculus, but it will be defined here in the more modern "Natural Deduction" style due to Gerhard Gentzen.

There is an elementary introduction to Natural Deduction in van Dalen 1980 §1.5, and more detailed accounts are in Gentzen 1935, Prawitz 1965, and Troelstra and van Dalen 1988 Chs. 2 and 10. But the style is so like the definition of TA_λ in 2A8 that the short introduction below will probably be plenty enough for the reader.[1]

[1] This similarity of style is no coincidence; when the earliest formulations of TA_λ were written Gentzen's methods were just beginning to be known more widely; indeed Curry was one of the first to understand their importance.

As mentioned earlier, the formulae provable in the logic defined below will turn out to be exactly the types of closed λ-terms. However, we can also go one step deeper than this and get a correspondence between the proofs of these formulae and the λ-terms themselves. But to make this deeper correspondence work we must be very careful about the definition of "proof" and "deduction" in a Natural Deduction system, and we must clarify some features of such deductions that are not often emphasised in the standard literature on the topic.

Therefore some of the definitions below will involve position-labels and other tedious details that have so far been confined to Chapter 9. These will be needed when determining exactly which deductions correspond to which λ-terms.

6A1 Definition ***Implicational formulae*** (denoted by lower-case Greek letters other than "λ") are built from ***propositional variables*** (denoted by "a", "b", "c", ...) using the implication connective "$\rightarrow$" thus: if σ and τ are formulae, then so is $(\sigma \rightarrow \tau)$. (An infinite sequence of propositional variables is assumed to be given.)

6A1.1 *Note* (i) Of course implicational formulae are exactly the same as types. Parentheses will be omitted using the same association-to-the-right convention as for types, see 2A1.1.

(ii) There are no propositional constants and no other connectives than "$\rightarrow$". (Because this book is only concerned with the Curry-Howard correspondence in its simplest and smoothest form.)

6A1.2 *Background* The intuitionist philosophy of mathematics was developed in the early 1900's by L. E. J. Brouwer and his group in Holland, and a very readable introduction is in Heyting 1955. One feature of this philosophy is that some propositional formulae that are usually accepted as universally valid, and are tautologies in the usual truth-table sense, are regarded by the intuitionists as having only limited validity. One such formula is

(PL) $((a \rightarrow b) \rightarrow a) \rightarrow a,$

which is known as ***Peirce's law***. The logic developed by the intuitionists has attracted continuing interest over the years from many logicians and computer scientists quite independently of their philosophical views. For example many of the polymorphic type-theories in the current literature have intuitionist logic as their basis, not classical logic.

The formulae provable by the rules in the next definition can be shown to coincide exactly with the implicational formulae that the intuitionists accept as universally valid. (See Troelstra and van Dalen 1988, Ch.2 (System IPC) and Ch.10 §5 (separation theorem).)

6A2 Definition ***Intuitionist logic*** (or more precisely, its implicational fragment) has the following two rules:

$$(\to\mathrm{E}):\quad \frac{\sigma\to\tau \quad \sigma}{\tau,} \qquad\qquad (\to\mathrm{I}):\quad \frac{\begin{matrix}[\sigma]\\ \vdots \\ \tau\end{matrix}}{\sigma\to\tau.}$$

Each application of (→I) is said to ***discharge*** (or ***cancel***) some, all, or none of the occurrences of σ above τ, and must be accompanied by a ***discharge label*** that lists all the occurrences of σ it discharges (see below for details). If none are discharged the application of (→I) is called ***vacuous***. Discharged occurrences of σ at the tops of branches must be marked by enclosing them in brackets.[1]

Before formally defining deductions and proofs in this system it will be helpful to look at some examples of how the rules are used. In these examples a position-notation like that in 9A1–4 will be included in the deductions to allow the discharge labels to say precisely which occurrences have been discharged. The position of each formula will be written in parentheses beside it, and discharge labels will be written between braces "{ }".

6A2.1 *Example* A proof of $(a\to a\to c)\to a\to c$.

$$\dfrac{\dfrac{\dfrac{\dfrac{[a\to a\to c]\ (0011) \qquad [a]\ (0012)}{a\to c\ \ (001)}(\to\mathrm{E}) \qquad [a]\ \ (002)}{c\ \ (00)}(\to\mathrm{E})}{a\to c\ \ (0)}(\to\mathrm{I})\ \ \{\text{discharging } a \text{ at } 0012,\ 002\}}{(a\to a\to c)\to a\to a\to c\ \ (\emptyset)}(\to\mathrm{I})\ \ \{\text{discharging } a\to a\to c \text{ at } 0011\}$$

6A2.2 *Example* A proof of $(a\to a\to c)\to a\to a\to c$.

$$\dfrac{\dfrac{\dfrac{\dfrac{\dfrac{[a\to a\to c]\ (00011) \qquad [a]\ (00012)}{a\to c\ \ (0001)}(\to\mathrm{E}) \qquad [a]\ \ (0002)}{c\ \ (000)}(\to\mathrm{E})}{a\to c\ \ (00)}(\to\mathrm{I})\ \ \{\text{discharging } a \text{ at position } 00012\}}{(a\to a\to c)\ \ (0)}(\to\mathrm{I})\ \ \{\text{discharging } a \text{ at } 0002\}}{(a\to a\to c)\to a\to a\to c\ \ (\emptyset)}(\to\mathrm{I})\ \ \{\text{discharging } a\to a\to c \text{ at } 00011\}$$

6A3 Discussion (Partial discharging) The proof in 6A2.2 contains an example of what will be called ***partial discharging***. Suppose rule (→I) in 6A2 is applied to a deduction of τ in which σ has $n\geq 1$ occurrences $\underline{\sigma}_1,\ldots,\underline{\sigma}_n$ as assumptions. Definition

[1] The system defined above is often called ***minimal logic***. But we shall later be interested in subsystems of this system so "minimal" seems inappropriate here.

6A2 allows $(\to\mathrm{I})$ to leave some of $\underline{\sigma}_1,\dots,\underline{\sigma}_n$ undischarged. For example in 6A2.2 the uppermost application of $(\to\mathrm{I})$ has two occurrences of a as assumptions above it but only discharges one.

It is standard practice to allow this in a Natural Deduction system, although few introductory accounts of Natural Deduction emphasise that this is so. Here we shall say that a system which allows it obeys the ***partial discharge convention.*** This convention is discussed in Prawitz 1965 Ch. I §4, Leivant 1979, and Troelstra and van Dalen 1988 Vol. 2, pp.559–560 and p.568 Ex. 10.8.1. (In the extreme, it allows us even to make a vacuous discharge of σ when $n \geq 1$; this would deduce $\sigma\to\tau$ and leave all of $\underline{\sigma}_1,\dots,\underline{\sigma}_n$ undischarged! An example of this extreme is in 6A3.3.)

In any system obeying this convention each occurrence of $(\to\mathrm{I})$ in a deduction must carry a label listing all the occurrences of σ that it discharges. These discharge-labels play so little role in standard accounts of natural deduction that they are almost always omitted, but when we come to make a correspondence between proofs and λ-terms they will be essential because *proofs with different discharge-labels will correspond to different terms.* We shall see this in 6B.

By the way, partial discharging is forbidden in TA_λ. In fact $(\to\mathrm{I})$ in 2A8 has an effect equivalent to discharging every occurrence of $x{:}\sigma$ in Γ that has not been discharged earlier; we shall say TA_λ obeys the ***complete discharge convention.***

6A3.1 *Example* The following is a proof of $(a\to a\to c)\to a\to a\to c$ that is identical to that in 6A2.2 except for having different discharge-labels.

$$\dfrac{\dfrac{\dfrac{\dfrac{\dfrac{[a\to a\to c]\ \ (00011)\qquad [a]\ \ (00012)}{a\to c\ \ (0001)}\,(\to\mathrm{E})\qquad\qquad [a]\ \ (0002)}{c\ \ \ (000)}\,(\to\mathrm{E})}{a\to c\ \ \ (00)}\,(\to\mathrm{I})\quad \{\text{discharging } a \text{ at } 00012,\ 0002\}}{a\to a\to c\ \ \ (0)}\,(\to\mathrm{I})\quad \{\text{discharging } a \text{ vacuously}\}}{(a\to a\to c)\to a\to a\to c\ \ \ (\emptyset)}\,(\to\mathrm{I})\quad \{\text{discharging } a\to a\to c \text{ at } 00011\}$$

6A3.2 *Note* Comparing 6A2.2 with 6A3.1 might suggest that a succession of partial discharges of the same formula can always be replaced by one complete discharge followed by some vacuous ones. And this suggestion is correct. (Though it would fail in restricted logics that forbid vacuous discharging.) Thus if partial discharging were forbidden the class of all provable formulae would not be reduced. However, the class of proofs would then become more restricted than the class of λ-terms.

6A3.3 *Example* The following proof illustrates an earlier remark that the partial discharge convention allows vacuous discharging of σ even when the set of available occurrences of σ is not empty.

$$\cfrac{\cfrac{[a]\quad(00)}{a\to a\quad(0)}\;(\to\mathrm{I})\qquad\{\text{discharging } a \text{ vacuously}\}}{a\to a\to a\quad(\emptyset)}\;(\to\mathrm{I})\qquad\{\text{discharging } a \text{ at position } 00\}$$

Hopefully this and the earlier examples have given the reader some feeling for the concepts involved in a natural deduction. The formal definition of "natural deduction" will now be given for precision's sake, though the reader may omit it without much loss. In it, a natural deduction will be a tree in which each node will carry either two or three labels: (1) a formula, (2) a position, and (3) either a discharge-label (if the node represents the conclusion of ($\to$I)) or a pair of brackets (if the node represents a discharged assumption), or no third label.

6A4 Definition ***Natural deductions in the Intuitionist logic of implication*** (or ***logic deductions*** for short) are trees, defined thus.

(i) An ***atomic*** deduction is a single node with two labels τ, $\emptyset$, where τ is a formula and $\emptyset$ is the empty position.

(ii) If Δ_1 and Δ_2 are natural deductions whose bottom nodes are labelled respectively by $\sigma\to\tau$, $\emptyset$ and σ, $\emptyset$ (and possibly a third label each), define a new deduction by first putting "1" on the left end of each position-label in Δ_1 and "2" on the left end of each position-label in Δ_2, next doing the same to the positions in any discharge-labels in Δ_1 and Δ_2, and finally placing an extra node beneath the two modified deductions, as shown below.

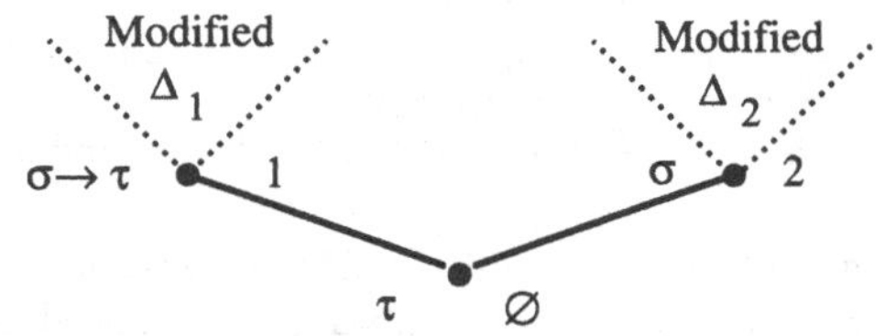

(iii) If Δ_1 is a natural deduction whose bottom node is labelled by τ, $\emptyset$ (and possibly a third label), and σ is any formula, define a new deduction thus. First choose a (possibly empty) set of unbracketed occurrences of σ at the tops of branches in Δ_1 and label them with brackets, then put "0" on the left end of every position in Δ_1, then place an extra node beneath the modified Δ_1 as shown in the diagram below, and finally give this node three labels: (1) $\sigma\to\tau$, (2) $\emptyset$, and (3) a ***discharge-label*** listing the positions of the chosen occurrences of σ. (If the set of chosen occurrences is empty we make the discharge-label say "***vacuous***".)

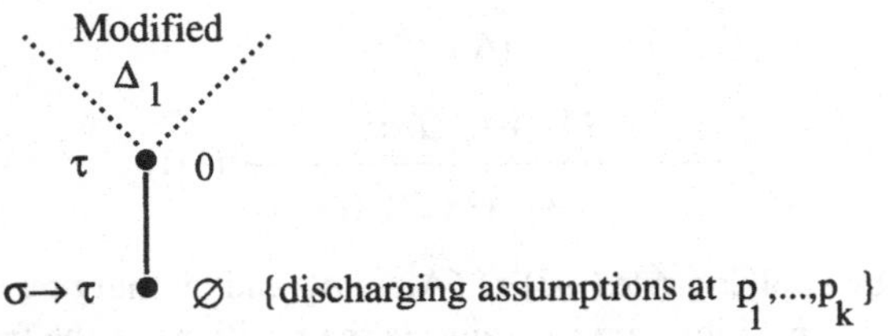

6A4.1 *Notation* In practice natural deductions are never displayed in the space-wasting form shown in these diagrams, but in the horizontal-line form used in the examples earlier.

6A4.2 *Definition* Two occurrences of an assumption at branch-tops in a natural deduction Δ will be called ***discharge-equivalent*** iff they are discharged by the same occurrence of ($\to$I), i.e. iff their names appear on the same non-vacuous discharge-label in Δ.

6A5 Definition (Deducibility and provability) Iff there is a deduction whose conclusion is τ and whose undischarged assumptions are occurrences of members of $\{\sigma_1, \ldots, \sigma_n\}$, we say

$$\sigma_1, \ldots, \sigma_n \vdash_{\text{int}} \tau.$$

(This notation may be used when $\sigma_1, \ldots, \sigma_n$ are not distinct.) Iff $n = 0$ the deduction is called a ***proof*** and τ a ***provable formula*** or ***theorem***, and we say

$$\vdash_{\text{int}} \tau.$$

6B The Curry-Howard isomorphism

The similarity between rules ($\to$E) and ($\to$I) in the previous section and the TA$_\lambda$-rules ($\to$E) and ($\to$I) in Chapter 2 suggests that every TA$_\lambda$-deduction might be changed into a logic deduction by stripping off all the contexts and terms in it. This is in fact true, modulo a few minor points like differences in the discharge conventions. The details are as follows.

6B1 Definition (Curry-Howard mapping from lambda to logic) If Δ is a TA$_\lambda$-deduction of $\Gamma \mapsto M{:}\tau$ (see 2A8), the ***corresponding logic deduction*** Δ_{L} is defined thus.

(i) If $M \equiv x$ and Δ is $x{:}\tau \mapsto x{:}\tau$, choose Δ_{L} to be just τ.
(ii) If $M \equiv PQ$ and $\Gamma = \Gamma_1 \cup \Gamma_2$ and the last step in Δ has form

$$\frac{\begin{matrix}(\Delta_1) & & (\Delta_2)\\ \Gamma' \mapsto P{:}\sigma \to \tau & & \Gamma_2 \mapsto Q{:}\sigma\end{matrix}}{\Gamma_1 \cup \Gamma_2 \mapsto (PQ){:}\tau,}\ (\to\text{E})$$

construct Δ_{L} by applying rule ($\to$E) of 6A2 to $\Delta_{1_{\text{L}}}$ and $\Delta_{2_{\text{L}}}$.

(iii) If $M \equiv \lambda x{\cdot}P$, $\tau \equiv \rho\to\sigma$, $\Gamma = \Gamma' - x$ and the last step in Δ is

$$\dfrac{\begin{matrix}(\Delta')\\ \Gamma' \;\mapsto\; P:\sigma\end{matrix}}{\Gamma' - x \;\mapsto\; (\lambda x{\cdot}P):(\rho\to\sigma),}\,(\to\mathrm{I})$$

construct Δ_{L} by applying rule $(\to\mathrm{I})$ of 6A2 to Δ'_{L} and discharging all occurrences of ρ in Δ'_{L} whose positions are the same as the positions of the free occurrences of x in P.

6B1.1 *Example* If Δ_1 is the following TA_λ-deduction, $(\Delta_1)_{\mathrm{L}}$ is the deduction in 6A2.2.

$$\dfrac{\dfrac{\dfrac{\dfrac{\dfrac{x:a\to a\to c \;\mapsto\; x:a\to a\to c \qquad z:a \;\mapsto\; z:a}{x:a\to a\to c,\; z:a \;\mapsto\; (xz):a\to c}\,(\to\mathrm{E}) \qquad y:a \;\mapsto\; y:a}{x:a\to a\to c,\; y:a,\; z:a \;\mapsto\; (xzy):c}\,(\to\mathrm{E})}{x:a\to a\to c,\; y:a \;\mapsto\; (\lambda z{\cdot}xzy):a\to c}\,(\to\mathrm{I})\ \{\text{discharging } z\}}{x:a\to a\to c \;\mapsto\; (\lambda yz{\cdot}xzy):a\to a\to c}\,(\to\mathrm{I})\ \{\text{discharging } y\}}{\mapsto\; (\lambda xyz{\cdot}xzy):(a\to a\to c)\to a\to a\to c}\,(\to\mathrm{I})\ \{\text{discharging } x\}$$

6B1.2 *Example* If Δ_2 is the TA_λ-deduction below, $(\Delta_2)_L$ is the deduction in 6A3.1.

$$\dfrac{\dfrac{\dfrac{\dfrac{\dfrac{x:a\to a\to c \;\mapsto\; x:a\to a\to c \qquad z:a \;\mapsto\; z:a}{x:a\to a\to c,\; z:a \;\mapsto\; (xz):a\to c}\,(\to\mathrm{E}) \qquad z:a \;\mapsto\; z:a}{x:a\to a\to c,\; z:a \;\mapsto\; (xzz):c}\,(\to\mathrm{E})}{x:a\to a\to c \;\mapsto\; (\lambda z{\cdot}xzz):a\to c}\,(\to\mathrm{I})\ \{\text{discharging } z\}}{x:a\to a\to c \;\mapsto\; (\lambda yz{\cdot}xzz):a\to a\to c}\,(\to\mathrm{I})\ \{\text{vac. dis. } y:a\}}{\mapsto\; (\lambda xyz{\cdot}xzz):(a\to a\to c)\to a\to a\to c}\,(\to\mathrm{I})\ \{\text{discharging } x\}$$

6B1.3 *Note* The λ-terms to which Δ_1 and Δ_2 assign types in the two above examples are distinct, although they have the same tree-structure. Correspondingly $(\Delta_1)_{\mathrm{L}}$ and $(\Delta_2)_{\mathrm{L}}$ are distinct, though they only differ in their discharge-labels.

6B2 Lambda-to-Logic Lemma *Let $x_1,\dots,x_n$ be distinct and Δ a TA_λ-deduction of*

$$x_1:\rho_1,\dots,x_n:\rho_n \;\mapsto\; M:\tau.$$

Then Δ_{L} is a natural deduction in Intuitionist logic and gives

$$\rho_1,\dots,\rho_n \vdash \tau.$$

Proof Induction on $|M|$. □

6B2.1 *Exercise* By applying the Curry-Howard mapping to the TA_λ-proofs in 2A8.2–4 and the answers to 2A8.7, show that the following formulae are provable in Intuitionist logic. (Their names below date from the 1950's and are now standard in the logic literature; of course they are not accidental.)

(B) $(a \to b) \to (c \to a) \to c \to b$,
(B′) $(a \to b) \to (b \to c) \to a \to c$,
(I) $a \to a$,
(K) $a \to b \to a$,
(C) $(a \to b \to c) \to b \to a \to c$,
(W) $(a \to a \to b) \to a \to b$.

6B3 Warning The Curry-Howard mapping is not one-to-one. For example consider the following TA_λ-deductions Δ_3 and Δ_4 which assign types to xyz and xyy.

$$\Delta_3:\quad \dfrac{\dfrac{x{:}a \to a \to c \;\mapsto\; x{:}a \to a \to c \qquad y{:}a \;\mapsto\; y{:}a}{x{:}a \to a \to c,\ y{:}a \;\mapsto\; xy{:}a \to c}\,(\to E) \qquad z{:}a \;\mapsto\; z{:}a}{x{:}a \to a \to c,\ y{:}a,\ z{:}a \;\mapsto\; xyz{:}c}\,(\to E)$$

$$\Delta_4:\quad \dfrac{\dfrac{x{:}a \to a \to c \;\mapsto\; x{:}a \to a \to c \qquad y{:}a \;\mapsto\; y{:}a}{x{:}a \to a \to c,\ y{:}a \;\mapsto\; xy{:}a \to c}\,(\to E) \qquad y{:}a \;\mapsto\; y{:}a}{x{:}a \to a \to c,\ y{:}a \;\mapsto\; xyy{:}c}\,(\to E)$$

It is easy to check that the Curry-Howard mapping assigns the same logic deduction to both, namely

$$\dfrac{\dfrac{a \to a \to c \quad a}{a \to c}\,(\to E) \qquad a}{c}\,(\to E)$$

(More generally, if Δ is a TA_λ-deduction of $\Gamma \mapsto M{:}\tau$ and x and y receive the same type in Γ and we change Δ to a deduction of

$$[v/x, v/y]\Gamma \quad\mapsto\quad [v/x, v/y]M{:}\tau,$$

then Δ_L will not change.)

Since the Curry-Howard mapping is not one-to-one it cannot have an inverse, i.e. there is no logic-to-lambda mapping $(\ )_\lambda$ such that

(1) $(\Delta_\lambda)_L \equiv \Delta$ (for all logic deductions Δ),
(2) $(\Delta_L)_\lambda \equiv \Delta$ (for all TA_λ-deductions Δ).

However there is a "one-sided inverse", a mapping $(\ )_\lambda$ satisfying (1) alone. In fact there are several such inverses, and the next definition will describe one of them; it will be obtained by choosing term-variables to be distinct whenever possible.

6B4 Definition (A logic-to-lambda mapping) To each natural deduction Δ in Intuitionist logic we assign a TA_λ-deduction Δ_λ thus.

(i) If Δ is a single formula τ, choose any term-variable x and let Δ_λ be

$$x{:}\tau \quad \mapsto \quad x{:}\tau.$$

(ii) If the last step in Δ is $(\to E)$ applied to the conclusions of deductions Δ' and Δ'', and Δ'_λ and Δ''_λ have been defined and are deductions of

$$\Gamma' \;\mapsto\; M{:}\sigma\to\tau, \qquad \Gamma'' \;\mapsto\; N{:}\sigma,$$

then replace all term-variables in Δ''_λ by distinct new ones (to make it have no term-variables in common with Δ'_λ, neither free nor bound), and apply the TA_λ-rule $(\to E)$; call the resulting deduction Δ_λ.

(iii) If the last step in Δ is an occurrence of $(\to I)$ with form

$$\dfrac{\left.\begin{matrix}[\rho]\\ \vdots \\ \sigma\end{matrix}\right\}}{\rho\to\sigma} \qquad \begin{matrix}\text{a deduction } \Delta' \\ \{\text{discharging } k\geq 0 \text{ occurrences } \underline{\rho}_1,\ldots,\underline{\rho}_k \text{ of } \rho\},\end{matrix}$$

and Δ'_λ has been defined and its conclusion is

$$\Gamma,\; v_1{:}\rho,\ldots,v_k{:}\rho \quad\mapsto\quad P{:}\sigma$$

where $v_1,\ldots,v_k$ are distinct from each other and from the variables in Γ, and $v_1,\ldots,v_k$ occur free in P at the same positions as $\underline{\rho_1},\ldots,\underline{\rho_k}$ have in Δ' (each v_i occurring only once in P), then proceed as follows.

If $k \geq 1$, replace all of $v_1,\ldots,v_k$ in Δ'_λ by one new variable x that does not occur elsewhere in Δ'_λ; this changes Δ'_λ to a deduction of

$$\Gamma, x{:}\rho \quad\mapsto\quad P^*{:}\sigma \qquad (P^* \;\equiv\; [x/v_1,\ldots,x/v_k]P)$$

where x occurs in P^* at exactly the same positions as $\underline{\rho}_1,\ldots,\underline{\rho}_k$ have in Δ'. Then apply $(\to I)_{\text{main}}$ to this modified Δ'_λ and call the resulting deduction Δ_λ. Its conclusion will be

$$\Gamma \quad\mapsto\quad (\lambda x{\cdot}P^*){:}\,\rho\to\sigma$$

If $k = 0$, the conclusion of Δ'_λ must be simply $\Gamma \mapsto P{:}\sigma$; choose a new variable x not in Δ'_λ and apply $(\to I)_{\text{vac}}$ to deduce

$$\Gamma \quad\mapsto\quad (\lambda x{\cdot}P){:}\,\rho\to\sigma$$

6B4.1 *Note* In the above definition clause (ii) makes as many variables as possible distinct, and then (iii) identifies some of these again. Lemma 6B5 will show that Δ_λ is well-defined for every Δ.

6B4.2 *Examples* (i) If Δ is the following logic deduction, then Δ_λ is the TA_λ-deduction Δ_3 in 6B3 (modulo replacements of distinct term-variables by distinct term-variables).

$$\dfrac{\dfrac{a \to a \to c \quad a}{a \to c}\ (\to\mathrm{E}) \qquad a}{c}\ (\to\mathrm{E})$$

(ii) If Δ is the logic deduction in 6A2.2, Δ_λ is the TA_λ-deduction in 6B1.1 (modulo $\equiv_\alpha$).

(iii) If Δ is the logic deduction in 6A3.1, Δ_λ is the TA_λ-deduction in 6B1.2 (modulo $\equiv_\alpha$).

6B4.3 *Exercise** Construct and compare $(\Delta_5)_\lambda$ and $(\Delta_6)_\lambda$, where Δ_5 is the deduction in 6A3.3 and Δ_6 is the following deduction.

$$\dfrac{\dfrac{[a] \quad (00)}{a \to a \qquad (0)}\ (\to\mathrm{I})}{a \to a \to a \qquad (\emptyset)}\ (\to\mathrm{I}) \qquad \begin{matrix}\{\text{discharging } a \text{ at position } 00\} \\ \{\text{discharging } a \text{ vacouously}\}\end{matrix}$$

6B5 Logic-to-Lambda Lemma *Let $\sigma_1, \ldots, \sigma_n \vdash \tau$ by a logic deduction Δ, and for each $i \leq n$ let*

$$\underline{\sigma}_{i,1}, \ldots, \underline{\sigma}_{i,m_i}$$

be those occurrences of σ_i that are undischarged assumptions at branch-tops in Δ. Then Δ_λ is defined and is a TA_λ-deduction whose conclusion has form

$$x_{1,1}{:}\sigma_1, \ldots, x_{1,m_1}{:}\sigma_1, \ \ldots\ , x_{n,1}{:}\sigma_n, \ldots, x_{n,m_n}{:}\sigma_n \quad \mapsto \quad M{:}\tau$$

where each $x_{i,j}$ occurs exactly once in M (at the same position as $\underline{\sigma}_{i,j}$ has in Δ) and M has no bound-variable clashes. Also

$$(\Delta_\lambda)_\mathrm{L} \equiv \Delta.$$

Proof Straightforward induction on the number of steps in Δ. The change of variables in 6B4(ii) ensures that M has no clashes of bound variables and has only one occurrence of each of its free variables. □

6B5.1 *Note* The Curry-Howard mapping from Δ to Δ_L is usually called the Curry-Howard *isomorphism*: how far can it justify this description? There are three levels to consider:

(i) provable formulae $\leftrightarrow$ types of closed terms,
(ii) logic proofs $\leftrightarrow$ TA_λ-proofs,
(iii) logic deductions $\leftrightarrow$ TA_λ-deductions.

By 6B5, the Δ_L-mapping has a one-sided inverse Δ_λ such that $(\Delta_\lambda)_\mathrm{L} \equiv \Delta$, but for it to be an isomorphism in any real sense we should also have $(\Delta_\mathrm{L})_\lambda \equiv \Delta$. We have seen in 6B3 that this breaks down on level (iii). But on levels (i) and (ii) it holds true, as the next theorem will show.

But before that theorem a lemma will describe exactly how far the identity $(\Delta_L)_\lambda \equiv \Delta$ breaks down.

6B6 Lemma *Let Δ be a TA_λ-deduction of $\Gamma \mapsto P{:}\tau$. Then $(\Delta_L)_\lambda$ differs from Δ only in that some term-variables distinct in $(\Delta_L)_\lambda$ may be identical in Δ. In more detail:*

(i) *$(\Delta_L)_\lambda$ is a TA_λ-deduction of a formula with form*

$$\Gamma' \mapsto M{:}\tau$$

where, just as in 6B5, M has no bound-variable clashes, $FV(M) = \{x_1,\ldots,x_n\}$, and each x_i occurs just once in M; also, for some $v_1,\ldots,v_n$ not necessarily distinct,

$$\begin{aligned} P &\equiv_\alpha [v_1/x_1]\ldots[v_n/x_n]M, \\ \Delta &\equiv_\alpha [v_1/x_1]\ldots[v_n/x_n](\Delta_L)_\lambda; \end{aligned}$$

(ii) *if Δ is a proof of $\mapsto P{:}\tau$ then $(\Delta_L)_\lambda$ is a proof of $\mapsto P'{:}\tau$ for some $P' \equiv_\alpha P$.*

Proof Part (i) is proved by induction on $|M|$ with three cases following the clauses of 6B1. (The notation "$[v_1/x_1]\ldots[v_n/x_n](\Delta_L)_\lambda$" means the deduction obtained by doing the substitutions $[v_1/x_1],\ldots,[v_n/x_n]$ in all subjects in $(\Delta_L)_\lambda$.)

Part (ii) is a special case of (i). □

6B7 Curry-Howard Theorem (i) *The provable formulae of Intuitionist implicational logic are exactly the types of closed λ-terms.*

(ii) *The relation $\sigma_1,\ldots,\sigma_n \vdash \tau$ holds in Intuitionist logic iff there exist M and $x_1,\ldots,x_n$ (distinct) such that*

$$x_1{:}\sigma_1,\ldots,x_n{:}\sigma_n \vdash_\lambda M{:}\tau.$$

(iii) *The Δ-to-Δ_L mapping is a one-to-one correspondence between TA_λ-proofs and proofs in the Natural Deduction version of Intuitionist Implicational logic, and the Δ-to-Δ_λ mapping is its inverse (modulo $\equiv_\alpha$). That is, for all TA_λ-proofs Δ,*

$$(\Delta_L)_\lambda \equiv \Delta$$

(modulo $\equiv_\alpha$ in subjects in $(\Delta_L)_\lambda$), and for all logic proofs Δ,

$$(\Delta_\lambda)_L \equiv \Delta.$$

Proof For (i) and (iii) use 6B2 and 6B6. For (ii) "if", use 6B2.

For (ii) "only if", let $\sigma_1,\ldots,\sigma_n \vdash \tau$ be obtained by a logic deduction Δ, and apply rule ($\to$I) n times to change Δ into a proof, Δ^*, of

$$\sigma_1 \to \ldots \to \sigma_n \to \tau.$$

Then construct $(\Delta^*)_\lambda$. By 6B5 its conclusion will be

$$\mapsto N{:}(\sigma_1 \to \ldots \to \sigma_n \to \tau)$$

for some closed λ-term N with no bound-variable clashes. Hence by the subject-construction theorem, N must have form $\lambda x_1 \dots x_n \cdot M$ for some M and some distinct $x_1, \dots, x_n$, and $(\Delta^*)_\lambda$ must contain the formula

$$x_1 : \sigma_1, \dots, x_n : \sigma_n \;\; \vdash_\lambda \;\; M : \tau.$$

(By the way, M has no bound-variable clashes because N has none.) □

6B7.1 *Note* The one-to-one correspondence in 5A7 between TA_λ-deductions and the typed terms of Chapter 5 can be combined with the above mappings to give a one-to-one correspondence between closed typed terms and logic proofs.

6B7.2 *Corollary To decide whether an implicational formula τ is provable in Intuitionist logic it is enough to decide whether there exists a closed term M such that $\vdash_\lambda M : \tau$, or equivalently, whether there exists a closed typed term with type τ.*

6B7.3 *Note* An algorithm to decide whether there exists a closed typed term M^τ will be described in 8D5.2. Via the above corollary this will give a decision-algorithm for Intuitionist implicational logic. Of course decision-procedures for this logic have been known for a long time,[1] but the one in 8D5.2 will also count the number of closed terms M^τ in β-normal form and will generate them one by one. This can be regarded as counting and generating all the irreducible Natural Deduction proofs of τ if we think of each M^τ as representing a proof via the Curry-Howard mapping.

6B7.4 *Corollary Peirce's Law, the formula $((a \to b) \to a) \to a$ introduced in* 6A1.2, *is not provable in Intuitionist logic.*

Proof By 8B6, Peirce's Law is not the type of a closed normal form; hence by the SN theorem it cannot be the type of any closed term. □

6B8 Note The Curry-Howard theorem has shown that the Intuitionist logic of pure implication corresponds in a very neat and natural way to the pure λ-calculus. Over the years this correspondence has been extended to more expressive logics and even to quite strong mathematical systems, and this has led to some useful techniques in proof theory, for example methods for extracting programs from proofs of existence. (See Crossley and Shepherdson 1993 for a modern account.)

But although each of these extensions is very important from a practical point of view, few of them have the directness and neatness of the original "core" system.

6C Some weaker logics

At the end of Chapter 1 three restricted classes of λ-terms were defined: the λI-terms (roughly speaking, terms without vacuous binding), the BCKλ-terms (terms in which

[1] For example an old one is in Gentzen 1935 pp.405–407 (pp.83–105 of the English translation). A more efficient one is in Dyckhoff 1992 p.800 (the note after the proof of Thm. 1); it has been implemented in the University of St Andrews proof-discovery program MacLogic. Another one is in Hudelmaier 1993 along with a proof that it operates in O($n \log n$)-space. And one involving an explicit translation into λ-calculus is in Zaionc 1988.

each subterm has at most one non-binding occurrence of each variable), and the BCIλ-terms (those that are both BCKλ- and λI-terms).

Suppose we restrict TA_λ by looking only at terms in one of these three classes; does the corresponding logic obtained via the Curry-Howard mapping have any interesting properties? The answer turns out to be "yes" for each class, as we shall see in this section.[1]

6C1 Definition (The relevance logic $R_\rightarrow$) The definition of $R_\rightarrow$ is exactly like that of Intuitionist implicational logic in 6A2 except that vacuous discharging is not allowed. That is, when $\sigma \rightarrow \tau$ is the conclusion of rule ($\rightarrow$I) its discharge-label must show at least one occurrence of σ.

6C1.1 *Note* (Motivation for $R_\rightarrow$) In one important view of implication, a formula $\sigma \rightarrow \tau$ should not be provable unless σ is in some way relevant to τ. In this view the formula

$$a \rightarrow b \rightarrow a$$

is not universally valid, because it says in essence that if a statement a is true then every other statement b implies it, even when b has no connection with the meaning of a. There have been many different attempts to capture the notion of relevant implication by formal systems and $R_\rightarrow$ is one of the earliest and simplest. In it, roughly speaking, we can only prove $\sigma \rightarrow \tau$ when σ has actually been used in the deduction of τ.

More about $R_\rightarrow$ can be found in Anderson and Belnap 1975, especially §§3, 7, 8.3, 8.4, 8.18 and 9–14, and in Anderson et al. 1992, especially §§47.1, 63.2 and 71.2. The system has been invented independently at several different times; see Moh 1950, Church 1951 and the discussion in Dosen 1992b. It is known to be decidable (i.e. there is an algorithm to decide whether a given formula is provable in $R_\rightarrow$); see Anderson and Belnap 1975 §13 and Anderson et al. 1992 §63.[2]

6C1.2 *Examples* Of the proofs in the examples in 6A, those in 6A2.1 and 6A2.2 are correct $R_\rightarrow$-proofs. In particular, by 6A2.2, the formula

$$(a \rightarrow a \rightarrow c) \rightarrow a \rightarrow a \rightarrow c$$

is provable in $R_\rightarrow$. In contrast the proof of the same formula in 6A3.1 contains a vacuous discharge and hence is not an $R_\rightarrow$-proof. Nor is the proof of $a \rightarrow a \rightarrow a$ in 6A3.3.

Of the proofs obtained in Exercise 6B2.1, those of (B), (B′), (I), (C), and (W) are easily seen to be $R_\rightarrow$-proofs, but that of (K) is not.

6C2 Definition (BCK-logic) The system that will be called here ***BCK-logic*** (or more precisely, the implicational fragment of BCK-logic) is defined exactly like Intuitionist

[1] The logics defined in the present section and some others like them have come to be known as ***substructural logics***.

[2] Though in the literature $R_\rightarrow$ is often presented as the implicational fragment of a system R which has other connectives besides "$\rightarrow$" and has been proved undecidable (Urquhart 1984 or Anderson et al. 1992 §65).

logic in 6A2, except that multiple discharging is not allowed. That is, when (→I) is used its discharge-label must either be vacuous or contain only one occurrence of σ.

6C2.1 *Note* Roughly speaking, BCK-logic is a system in which an assumption cannot be used more than once; it is a logic of non-re-usable information. Interest in such logics dates back at least as far as Fitch 1936, and results on BCK logic can be found in a number of sources, for example Meredith and Prior 1963 §§7–8, Jaskowski 1963, Iséki and Tanaka 1978, Bunder 1986, 1991, Komori 1987, 1989, Blok and Pigozzi 1989, Hindley 1989, 1993, Dosen 1992a, Hirokawa 1991c, 1992b, 1993a–b, Komori and Hirokawa 1993, and those mentioned in their bibliographies. The reason for the name "BCK" will be made clear in the next section.

6C2.2 *Examples* Of the proofs constructed in Exercise 6B2.1, it is easy to see that those of (B), (B′), (I), (K) and (C) are correct BCK-proofs.

But the proof of (W) in 6A2.1 is not, because it contains a multiple discharge.

Of the two proofs of $(a{\to}a{\to}c){\to}a{\to}a{\to}c$ in 6A2.2 and 6A3.1, the former is a BCK-proof but the latter is not.

The proof of $a{\to}a{\to}a$ in 6A3.3 is a BCK-proof.

6C3 Definition (BCI-logic) The definition of ***BCI-logic*** (to be precise, its implicational fragment) is like 6A2 except that both vacuous and multiple discharging are forbidden; i.e., when rule (→I) is used its discharge-label must contain exactly one occurrence of σ.

6C3.1 *Note* BCI-logic is a relevance logic of non-re-usable information. Most work on this system has been done in parallel with work on BCK-logic and the majority of the above references for BCK-logic treat both systems. Other references are, for example, Hirokawa 1991b, Avron 1992.

Incidentally, the BCI system above coincides with the implicational fragment of the ***linear logic*** of Girard 1987. Although the latter is a much deeper theory than any logic confined to a single connective and has been studied in many publications, a few of these publications give its implicational fragment some separate attention; an example is Avron 1988.

6C3.2 *Examples* Of the proofs constructed in Exercise 6B2.1, those of (B), (B′), (I), and (C) are correct BCI-proofs.

But the proofs of (K) and (W) are not.

Of the two proofs of $(a{\to}a{\to}c){\to}a{\to}a{\to}c$ in 6A2.2 and 6A3.1, the former is a BCI-proof but the latter is not.

The proof of $a{\to}a{\to}a$ in 6A3.3 is not a BCI-proof.

6C4 Lemma *The sets of provable formulae of the four logics defined in* 6B–C *are related as follows:*

(i) *BCI* $\subseteq$ *BCK* $\subseteq$ *Intuitionist,*
(ii) *BCI* $\subseteq$ $R_{\to}$ $\subseteq$ *Intuitionist.*

6C5 Refined Curry-Howard Theorem (i) *The provable formulae of the three logics defined in* 6C1–3 *are exactly the types of the following λ-terms:*

$R_{\rightarrow}$:	*types of the closed λI-terms;*
BCK-logic :	*types of the closed BCKλ-terms;*
BCI-logic :	*types of the closed BCIλ-terms.*

(ii) *The relation* $\sigma_1, \ldots, \sigma_n \vdash \tau$ *holds in* $R_{\rightarrow}$, *BCK- or BCI-logic iff there exist M and* $x_1, \ldots, x_n$ *(distinct) such that*

$$x_1 : \sigma_1, \ldots, x_n : \sigma_n \ \vdash_\lambda \ M : \tau$$

and M is, respectively, a λI-term, BCKλ-term or BCIλ-term.

Proof By Lemmas 6C5.1 and 6C5.2 below. □

6C5.1 *Lemma Let* Δ *be a* TA_λ*-deduction of* $\Gamma \mapsto M : \tau$ *and let* Δ_{L} *be defined as in* 6B1. *Then*

(i) *if M is a λI-term,* Δ_{L} *is an* $R_{\rightarrow}$*-deduction,*
(ii) *if M is a BCKλ-term,* Δ_{L} *is a BCK-deduction,*
(iii) *if M is a BCIλ-term,* Δ_{L} *is a BCI-deduction.*

Proof Straightforward induction on $|M|$. □

6C5.2 *Lemma Let* Δ *be an* $R_{\rightarrow}$*-, BCK- or BCI-deduction with* Δ_λ *defined as in 6B4, and let the conclusion of* Δ_λ *be* $\Gamma \mapsto M : \tau$. *Then*

(i) *if* Δ *is an* $R_{\rightarrow}$*-deduction, M is a λI-term,*
(ii) *if* Δ *is a BCK-deduction, M is a BCKλ-term,*
(iii) *if* Δ *is a BCI-deduction, M is a BCIλ-term.*

Proof Straightforward induction on the number of steps in Δ. □

6D Axiom-based versions

As a matter of historical fact the four logics discussed in this chapter all made their first appearance not in the Natural Deduction form given above but in an axiom-based version. These axiom-based versions will play a role in the next chapter, so as a preparation they will be defined and discussed in this section.

But before defining the four logics separately some of the properties of axiom-based systems in general will be described, relative to an arbitrary set $\mathbb{A}$ of axioms. Axiomatic systems are often called ***Hilbert-style*** systems to contrast with Natural Deduction.

6D1 Definition ($\mathbb{A}$-logics) Let $\mathbb{A}$ be any set of implicational formulae that are tautologies in the classical truth-table sense. Then $\mathbb{A}$ generates the following Hilbert-style system, which will be called the corresponding ***$\mathbb{A}$-logic***.

Axioms: the members of $\mathbb{A}$.

***Deduction-rules*:**

$$(\to\mathrm{E})\quad \frac{\sigma\to\tau \qquad \sigma}{\tau}$$

$$(\mathrm{Sub})\quad \frac{\tau}{\mathbb{s}(\tau)}$$ *[if* $\mathbb{s}$ *is a substitution and no variable in* Dom($\mathbb{s}$) *occurs in a non-axiom assumption in the deduction above the line]*

Deductions in an $\mathbb{A}$-logic are trees, with axioms and assumptions at the tops of branches and the conclusion at the bottom of the tree. The notation

$$\sigma_1,\ldots,\sigma_n \vdash_{\mathbb{A}} \tau$$

means that there is a deduction whose non-axiom assumptions are some or all of $\sigma_1,\ldots,\sigma_n$ and whose conclusion is τ. ($\sigma_1,\ldots,\sigma_n$ need not all be distinct.)

When $n = 0$ the deduction is called a ***proof*** of τ and we call τ a ***provable formula*** or ***theorem*** of the $\mathbb{A}$-logic in question, and we say

$$\vdash_{\mathbb{A}} \tau.$$

The set of all theorems in an $\mathbb{A}$-logic may be called $\mathbb{A}^{\vdash}$.

6D1.1 *Note* (i) Rule ($\to$E) is often called ***modus ponens*** or the ***detachment rule***. In it, $\sigma\to\tau$ is called its ***major premise*** and τ its ***minor premise***.

(ii) Rule (Sub) is the ***substitution rule***. Its side-condition is standard in propositional logic and says, roughly speaking, that substitutions may be made for variables occurring only in axioms. It excludes such deductions as

$$\frac{a}{b}[b/a].$$

6D1.2 *Example* Let $\mathbb{A}$ contain the formulae (C) and (K) shown in 6B2.1. Then the following deduction gives $\vdash_{\mathbb{A}} a\to a$. (Both its substitution-steps use the substitution $[(a\to b\to a)/b,\ a/c]$.)

$$\dfrac{\dfrac{\dfrac{\overset{(\mathrm{C})}{(a\to b\to c)\to b\to a\to c}}{(a\to(a\to b\to a)\to a)\to(a\to b\to a)\to a\to a}(\mathrm{Sub}) \qquad \dfrac{\overset{(\mathrm{K})}{a\to b\to a}}{a\to(a\to b\to a)\to a}(\mathrm{Sub})}{(a\to b\to a)\to a\to a}(\to\mathrm{E}) \qquad \overset{(\mathrm{K})}{a\to b\to a}}{a\to a}(\to\mathrm{E})$$

6D1.3 *Warning* It is natural to expect the theory of $\mathbb{A}$-logics to be fairly simple, because every such logic is a subsystem of classical propositional logic and the latter is very well known. But this is not so. For example consider the ***provability problem*** for a set $\mathbb{A}$ (the problem of deciding, for each type τ, whether τ is provable in $\mathbb{A}$-logic or not). For at least one $\mathbb{A}$-logic it is not yet known whether its provability problem is decidable although the logic has been studied for over 30 years (see 7D11(ii), system $T_\to$). Further, for every recursively enumerable degree of unsolvability, however high, there is a finite set $\mathbb{A}$ whose provability problem has that degree (Gladstone 1965 §6 Thm 1).

6D2 Definition In any $\mathbb{A}$-logic a ***substitutions-first*** deduction is a deduction in which rule (Sub) is only applied to axioms.

6D2.1 *Lemma In any $\mathbb{A}$-logic, every deduction Δ can be replaced by a substitutions-first deduction Δ^* with the same assumptions, axioms and conclusion.*

Proof Suppose rule (Sub) is applied below an application of rule ($\to$E), as follows:

$$\dfrac{\dfrac{\sigma\to\tau \qquad \sigma}{\tau}(\to\mathrm{E})}{\mathbb{s}(\tau)}(\mathrm{Sub})$$

Then (Sub) can be moved up above ($\to$E), thus:

$$\dfrac{\dfrac{\sigma\to\tau}{\mathbb{s}(\sigma)\to\mathbb{s}(\tau)}(\mathrm{Sub}) \qquad \dfrac{\sigma}{\mathbb{s}(\sigma)}(\mathrm{Sub})}{\mathbb{s}(\tau)}(\to\mathrm{E})$$

Also two successive (Sub)'s can be combined into one. The moving-up procedure ends when all (Sub)'s are at the tops of branches in the deduction-tree. By the restriction on (Sub) in 6D1, the top formula of each of these branches cannot be a non-axiom assumption, so it must be an axiom. □

6D3 Definition ***Hilbert-style Intuitionist logic*** (of implication only) is the $\mathbb{A}$-logic whose $\mathbb{A}$ has just the following four members:

(B) $(a\to b)\to(c\to a)\to c\to b$,
(C) $(a\to b\to c)\to b\to a\to c$,
(K) $a\to b\to a$,
(W) $(a\to a\to b)\to a\to b$.

6D4 Definition ***Hilbert-style $R_\to$*** is the $\mathbb{A}$-logic for $\mathbb{A} = \{(B),(C),(I),(W)\}$, where (I) is

(I) $a\to a$.

6D5 Definition ***Hilbert-style BCK-logic*** (of implication only) is the $\mathbb{A}$-logic for the set $\mathbb{A} = \{(B),(C),(K)\}$.

6D6 Definition ***Hilbert-style BCI-logic*** (of implication only) is the $\mathbb{A}$-logic for the set $\mathbb{A} = \{(B),(C),(I)\}$.

6D6.1 *Note* (i) By Example 6D1.2, (I) is provable in Hilbert-style BCK-logic and Intuitionist logic.

(ii) Of course (B), (C), (I), (K) and (W) are the principal types of the λ-terms **B**, **C**, **I**, **K** and **W**, see Table 3E2a. But each one also expresses a property of implication that has its own interest quite independently of type-theory. Roughly speaking, (I) is the reflexivity property of implication, (C) states that hypotheses can be commuted, (K) that redundant hypotheses can be added, (W) that duplicates can be removed. Finally (B) can be viewed either as a transitivity property of implication or as a "right-handed" replacement property which says that if $a \to b$ holds, then a may be replaced by b in the formula $c \to a$.

(iii) The next theorem will describe the precise connection between $\mathbb{A}$-logics and λ-calculi; it will be a Hilbert-style analogue of the Curry-Howard theorem at the end of the previous section. As mentioned earlier, the type-system that corresponds most naturally to a Hilbert-style logic is combinatory logic not λ-calculus, but we can build a correspondence with λ-calculus if we are careful; the key will be the concept of *applicative combination* defined in 9F1.

6D7 Theorem (Curry-Howard for Hilbert systems) *Let $\{C_1, C_2, \ldots\}$ be a finite or infinite set of typable closed λ-terms and let $\mathbb{A} = \{\gamma_1, \gamma_2, \ldots\}$ where $\gamma_i \equiv PT(C_i)$. Then*

(i) *the theorems of $\mathbb{A}$-logic are exactly the types of the typable applicative combinations of $C_1, C_2, \ldots$,*

(ii) *the relation $\sigma_1, \ldots, \sigma_n \vdash_{\mathbb{A}} \tau$ holds iff there exist an applicative combination M of $C_1, C_2, \ldots$ and some distinct term-variables $x_1, \ldots, x_n$, such that*

$$x_1{:}\sigma_1, \ldots, x_n{:}\sigma_n \;\; \vdash_\lambda \;\; M{:}\tau.$$

Proof Part (i) is the case $n = 0$ of (ii). To prove (ii) we first prove "if". Let M be an applicative combination of $x_1, \ldots, x_n, C_1, C_2, \ldots$, and let Δ be a TA_λ-deduction of

(1) $\quad x_1{:}\sigma_1, \ldots, x_n{:}\sigma_n \;\; \mapsto \;\; M{:}\tau.$

Corresponding to each occurrence of a C_i in M there will be an occurrence of $\mapsto C_i{:}\mathsf{s}(\gamma_i)$ in Δ for some substitution s. Remove from Δ all steps above these occurrences of $C_1, C_2, \ldots$, and replace each formula $\mapsto C_i{:}\mathsf{s}(\gamma_i)$ by the type $\mathsf{s}(\gamma_i)$. Then replace every other formula in Δ, say $\Gamma \mapsto N{:}\rho$, by the type ρ. (Cf. 6B1(i)–(ii).) The result is a Hilbert-style deduction giving

(2) $\quad \sigma_1, \ldots, \sigma_n \vdash_\lambda \tau.$

To prove "only if" in (ii), let $\sigma_1, \ldots, \sigma_n \vdash \tau$ in $\mathbb{A}$-logic. Then by 6D2.1 there is a deduction Δ of τ in which (Sub) is only applied to axioms. Change Δ to a TA_λ-deduction thus. First choose some distinct term-variables $x_1, \ldots, x_n$ and replace each undischarged branch-top occurrence of each σ_i in Δ by

$$x_i{:}\sigma_i \;\; \mapsto \;\; x_i{:}\sigma_i.$$

Next, note that each application of (Sub) in Δ will be applied to an axiom to give, say, $\gamma_j \vdash \mathsf{s}(\gamma_j)$; replace it by a TA_λ-proof of $\mapsto C_j{:}\mathsf{s}(\gamma_j)$. Then replace the logic rule ($\to$E) by the TA_λ-rule ($\to$E) throughout. The result is a TA_λ-deduction of (1) for some term M as required. □

6D7.1 *Corollary The relation* $\sigma_1, \ldots, \sigma_n \vdash \tau$ *holds in the Hilbert version of Intuitionist logic,* $R_{\rightarrow}$*, BCK- or BCI-logic iff*

$$x_1 : \sigma_1, \ldots, x_n : \sigma_n \vdash_\lambda M : \tau$$

holds for some distinct $x_1, \ldots, x_n$ *and some M which is an applicative combination of* $x_1, \ldots, x_n$ *and, respectively,* $\{\mathbf{B}, \mathbf{C}, \mathbf{K}, \mathbf{W}\}$, $\{\mathbf{B}, \mathbf{C}, \mathbf{I}, \mathbf{W}\}$, $\{\mathbf{B}, \mathbf{C}, \mathbf{K}\}$ *or* $\{\mathbf{B}, \mathbf{C}, \mathbf{I}\}$.

6D8 Theorem (Hilbert-Gentzen link) *For the Intuitionist,* $R_{\rightarrow}$*-, BCK- and BCI-logics the relation*

$$\sigma_1, \ldots, \sigma_n \vdash \tau$$

holds in the Natural Deduction version iff it holds in the Hilbert version.

Proof By the Curry-Howard theorems for Natural Deduction (6B7(ii), 6C5(ii)), the combinatory completeness theorems (9F3, 9F5), and Corollary 6D7.1. □

6D8.1 *Note* The Hilbert-Gentzen link is usually proved directly without going through λ-calculus. The key step in a direct proof is a result usually called the *deduction theorem* which is a close analogue of the combinatory completeness theorems in 9F. (The deduction theorem is treated in many standard introductions to classical logic, see for example Hamilton 1988 Proposition 2.8; a study of the theorem in some different logics is in Bunder 1982.)

7

The converse principal-type algorithm

This chapter combines the theme of propositional logic from Chapter 6 with that of principal types from Chapter 3. We saw in the Curry-Howard theorem (6B7) that the types of the closed terms are exactly the theorems of the intuitionist logic of implication: hence the principal types of these terms must form a subset of these theorems, and the very natural question arises of just how large this subset is. Do its members form an aristocracy distinguished in some structural way from the general rabble of theorems, or can every theorem be a principal type?

The main result of the chapter will show that there is in fact no aristocracy: if a type τ is assignable to a closed term M but is not the principal type of M, then it is the principal type of another closed term M^*.

The proof will include an algorithm to construct M^* when τ and M are given. To build M^* an occurrence of M will be combined with some extra terms chosen from a certain carefully defined stock of "building blocks", closed terms with known principal types; and the main aim of this chapter will be to build M^* from as restricted a set of building blocks as possible.

The algorithm in the earliest known proof needed full λ-calculus (Hindley 1969), but two later ones used only λI-terms as building blocks (Mints and Tammet 1991, Hirokawa 1992a §3) and another used an even more restricted class (Meyer and Bunder 1988 §9). The algorithm below will be based on the latter very economical one.

When it was first proved the existence of M^* seemed nothing more than a mere technical curiosity, but several years later it was discovered by David Meredith to be equivalent to the completeness of a neat form of resolution rule for Intuitionist implicational logic. This rule and its completeness problem will be described at the end of the chapter.

7A The converse PT theorems

In fact the situation is not quite as simple as suggested above, as the converse PT theorems for full λ-calculus and λI-calculus are very slightly different. They will be stated separately here.

First, recall that the class of unrestricted λ-terms is sometimes called the ***λK-calculus*** (because it contains $\mathbf{K} \equiv \lambda xy \cdot x$) and its terms ***λK-terms*** to distinguish them from restricted classes of terms.

7A1 Definition A ***λK-PT*** [respectively, ***λI-PT, BCKλ-PT, BCIλ-PT***] is the principal type of a closed λK-term [λI-term, *BCK* λ-term, *BCI* λ-term].

A ***BCKW-PT*** [***BCIW-PT***, etc.] is the principal type of a **BCKW**-combination [**BCIW**-combination, etc.] as defined in 9F1.

7A1.1 *Lemma A type is a λK-PT, λI-PT, BCKλ-PT or BCIλ-PT iff it is, respectively, a* ***BCKW****-,* ***BCIW****-,* ***BCK****- or* ***BCI****-PT.*

Proof By 9F3 and 9F5. □

7A2 Converse PT Theorem for λK (i) *Every type of a closed λK-term is also a λK-PT.*

(ii) *Further, there is an algorithm which accepts any typable closed λK-term M and any type τ of M, and constructs a closed λK-term M^* whose PT is τ.*

(iii) *Furthermore,* $M^* \rhd_\beta M$.

Proof There is proof in Hindley 1969 Thm. 3 of the corresponding result for combinatory logic. This translates straightforwardly into λ-calculus. It contains an algorithm that constructs, for every type σ, a closed λK-term I_σ such that

$$PT(I_\sigma) \equiv \sigma \to \sigma, \qquad I_\sigma \rhd_\beta \mathbf{I}.$$

The last step is to choose $M^* \equiv I_\tau M$. Then an application of the PT algorithm (3E1) shows that $PT(M^*) \equiv \tau$.

(An alternative proof of (i)–(ii) would be to apply Theorem 7A3 below to construct I_σ, but this would not give (iii) but only $M^* \rhd_{\beta\eta} M$.) □

Before going on to the λI-theorem we pause to look at a particularly neat and interesting application of the λK-theorem. The following corollary shows even more clearly than Examples 2C2.2–6 how widely a term's set of types can vary when the term is β- or η-converted.

7A2.1 *Corollary There exist two typable closed λK-terms P and P′ such that* $P =_\beta P'$ *but P and P′ have no types in common at all.*

Proof The following two types have no substitution-instances in common (cf. 3C2.2):

$$\sigma \equiv a \to a, \qquad \tau \equiv (b \to b) \to b.$$

Hence also the following have no instances in common:

$$\sigma \to \sigma, \qquad \tau \to \tau.$$

But by 7A2 there exist I_σ and I_τ such that $I_\sigma =_\beta \mathbf{I} =_\beta I_\tau$ and

$$PT(I_\sigma) \equiv \sigma \to \sigma, \qquad PT(I_\tau) \equiv \tau \to \tau.$$

Define $P \equiv I_\sigma$, $P' \equiv I_\tau$. □

7A3 Converse PT Theorem For λI (i) *Every type of a closed λI-term is also a λI-PT.*

(ii) *Further, there is an algorithm which accepts any typable closed λI-term M and any type τ of M, and builds a closed λI-term M^* whose PT is τ.*

(iii) *Furthermore, $M^* \rhd_{\beta\eta} M$.*

7A3.1 *Proof-note* An algorithm and correctness proof will be given in 7C. Note that (iii) is weaker than the corresponding result for λK in 7A2(iii): in λK we have $\rhd_\beta$ but in λI the proof will only give $\rhd_{\beta\eta}$.

The first known algorithm for λI was devised in 1986 by Robert Meyer (Meyer and Bunder 1988 §9), and another was invented independently by Grigori Mints and Tanel Tammet (Mints and Tammet 1991 §2). Both of these originated in the context of Hilbert-style axiom-based logics and although they can easily be translated into λ-calculus they lose some of their directness when this is done. In 1990 a direct and natural λ-algorithm was described by Sachio Hirokawa (Hirokawa 1992a §3).

The most economical of these algorithms is the Meyer one, in the sense that it does not need all the λI-terms as building blocks but only a certain well-defined proper subset of them. So this algorithm is the one that will be described in 7C.

All three algorithms produce terms M^* satisfying (iii) as well as (ii). Though (iii) was first proved for the Hirokawa algorithm (Hirokawa 1992a §3), a proof will be given below for the Meyer algorithm and a careful reading of Mints and Tammet 1991 shows that (iii) holds for that algorithm too.

7A3.1 *Question* Can 7A3(iii) be strengthened to say "$M^* \rhd_\beta M$"?

7A3.2 *Exercise** If the answer to the above question is "yes" then as a consequence there exist two β-equal typable λI-terms with no types in common (cf. Corollary 7A2.1 for λK). Show that this consequence holds even if the answer to the above question is "no", by constructing two suitable λI-terms directly. (Hint (Martin Bunder): consider the term P in 2A8.8.)

7B Identifications

The construction of M^* from M and τ in the proof of 7A3 will depend on viewing τ as the result of applying certain substitutions to a particularly simple form of type. The present section introduces the notation needed for this.

First recall the substitution notation introduced in 3B. In particular (from 3B7) ***a variables-for-variables*** substitution is one with form

$$\mathbb{s} \equiv [b_1/a_1, \ldots, b_n/a_n]$$

where $b_1, \ldots, b_n$ are any variables; and a ***renaming in*** τ (where τ is a given type) is a variables-for-variables substitution such that $\{a_1, \ldots, a_n\} = Vars(\tau)$ and $b_1, \ldots, b_n$ are distinct.

7B1 Definition For any type τ, an ***identification in*** τ (sometimes called a ***contraction in*** τ) is any substitution $[b/a]$ such that a, b both occur in τ. A type σ is ***obtained from*** τ ***by identifications*** iff

$$\sigma \equiv [b_n/a_n](\ldots([b_1/a_1](\tau))\ldots)$$

where $[b_1/a_1]$ is an identification in τ, $[b_2/a_2]$ is an identification in $[b_1/a_1]\tau$, etc.

7B1.1 *Example* If $\tau \equiv (a\to b\to c)\to(a\to b)\to a\to c$ then $[b/a]$ is an identification in τ, and

$$[b/a]\tau \equiv (b\to b\to c)\to(b\to b)\to b\to c.$$

7B1.2 *Lemma Every variables-for-variables substitution can be performed by a renaming followed by a series of identifications. More precisely, if* $\rho \equiv \mathbb{s}(\tau)$ *and* $\mathbb{s}$ *substitutes variables for variables, then*

$$\rho \equiv [b_n/a_n](\ldots([b_1/a_1](\mathbb{v}(\tau)))\ldots)$$

where $n \geq 0$, $\mathbb{v}$ *is a renaming in* τ, *and each* $[b_i/a_i]$ *is an identification in*

$$[b_{i-1}/a_{i-1}](\ldots(\mathbb{v}(\tau))\ldots).$$

7B2 Definition A type τ is ***skeletal*** iff each variable in τ occurs exactly once. (The property of being skeletal is sometimes called the **1-*property***.)

7B3 Lemma *Every type* τ *can be obtained by identifications from a skeletal type* τ° *(which will be called a* ***skeleton*** *of* τ*).*

Proof If τ is skeletal choose $\tau^\circ \equiv \tau$. If not, then for each variable b with two or more occurrences in τ, replace all but one of these occurrences by distinct new variables□

7C The converse PT proof

This section contains a proof of Theorem 7A3 obtained by translating the proof in Meyer and Bunder 1988 §9 into λ-calculus. The strategy will be to show first that every type of a closed λI-term can be obtained from a λI-PT by a series of identifications, and then that identifications preserve the property of being a λI-PT.

But a preliminary step will be to prove the special case of the theorem in which τ has form $\theta\to\theta$ where θ is skeletal.

7C1 Lemma *Let* θ *be any skeletal type. Then* $\theta\to\theta$ *is the PT of a closed* λ*I-term* I_θ *such that*

$$I_\theta \rhd_{\beta\eta} \mathbf{I}.$$

Proof We shall construct I_θ by induction on $|\theta|$. If θ is an atom, say $\theta \equiv a$, choose

(1) $\quad I_a \equiv \mathbf{I}.$

Next, suppose $\theta \equiv \rho \to \sigma$ and I_ρ and I_σ have already been built such that

(2) $PT(I_\rho) \equiv \rho \to \rho, \qquad PT(I_\sigma) \equiv \sigma \to \sigma,$

(3) $I_\rho \rhd_{\beta\eta} \mathsf{I}, \qquad I_\sigma \rhd_{\beta\eta} \mathsf{I}.$

Choose

(4) $I_{\rho\to\sigma} \equiv \lambda xy \cdot I_\sigma(x(I_\rho y)).$

From (2) and the PT algorithm (3E1) it is easy to deduce that

(5) $PT(I_{\rho\to\sigma}) \equiv (\rho\to\sigma)\to(\rho\to\sigma).$

(Note that the proof of (5) depends on the fact that $Vars(\rho) \cap Vars(\sigma) = \emptyset$, which holds because $\rho\to\sigma$ is skeletal.) Also, by (3),

$$\begin{aligned} I_{\rho\to\sigma} &\rhd_{\beta\eta} \lambda xy \cdot \mathsf{I}(x(\mathsf{I}y)) \\ &\rhd_\beta \lambda xy \cdot xy \\ &\rhd_\eta \mathsf{I}. \end{aligned}$$

□

7C2 Lemma *Every type of a closed λI-term can be obtained from a λI-PT by identifications. In detail: if M is a closed λI-term and* $\vdash_\lambda M:\tau$, *there exists a closed typable λI-term* M^+ *such that*

(i) $\tau \equiv \mathsf{s}_k(\mathsf{s}_{k-1}(\ldots\mathsf{s}_1(PT(M^+))\ldots))$ *for some identifications* $\mathsf{s}_1,\ldots,\mathsf{s}_k$,

(ii) $M^+ \rhd_{\beta\eta} M$,

(iii) *if* τ *is skeletal then* $PT(M^+) \equiv \tau$.

Proof First construct a skeleton τ° of τ as in 7B3. (If τ itself is skeletal, $\tau^\circ \equiv \tau$.) By 7C1 there is a closed λI-term I_{τ° with

(1) $PT(I_{\tau^\circ}) \equiv \tau^\circ \to \tau^\circ, \qquad I_{\tau^\circ} \rhd_{\beta\eta} \mathsf{I}.$

Let $\vdash_\lambda M:\tau$. Then M has a PT, call it σ. And by renaming variables in σ we can ensure that

(2) $Vars(\sigma) \cap Vars(\tau^\circ) = \emptyset.$

Define

(3) $M^+ \equiv I_{\tau^\circ} M.$

Then (ii) holds by (1). To prove (i), apply the PT algorithm to M^+. The first step is to find an m.g.u. of $\langle\tau^\circ, \sigma\rangle$. To see that one exists, note that τ is an instance of τ° by the definition of τ°, and τ is an instance of σ because σ is principal, so $\langle\tau^\circ,\sigma\rangle$ has a common instance, namely τ; and by (2) this instance is a unification of $\langle\tau^\circ,\sigma\rangle$; hence $\langle\tau^\circ,\sigma\rangle$ has an m.g.u. τ^+ and τ is an instance of τ^+, say $\tau \equiv \mathsf{s}(\tau^+)$. Then

(4) $PT(M^+) \equiv \tau^+.$

To complete the proof of (i) the next step is to show that s is a variables-for-variables substitution. For this it is enough to show that

(5) $|\tau| \le |\tau^+|,$

because if $\mathbb{s}$ substituted a composite type for a variable in τ^+ it would increase $|\tau^+|$. But $|\tau| = |\tau^\circ|$ because τ is obtained from τ° by identifications; and τ^+ is an instance of τ° since τ^+ unifies $\langle\tau^\circ, \sigma\rangle$, so $|\tau^+| \geq |\tau^\circ|$; hence (5) holds.

Thus τ is obtained from a λI-PT τ^+ by a variables-for-variables substitution $\mathbb{s}$. By 7B1.2, $\mathbb{s}$ can be split into a renaming (which changes τ^+ to another PT of M^+) followed by some identifications. Hence (i) holds.

To prove (iii) note that if τ is skeletal then $\tau^\circ \equiv \tau$, so $M^+ \equiv I_\tau M$ and the PT of the latter is clearly τ. □

7C2.1 *Note* By the above lemma, the proof of Theorem 7A3 will be complete if we can prove that identifications preserve the property of being a λI-PT. This will be done in the next three lemmas.

In them the following notation will be useful: if $a_1, \ldots, a_n$ are distinct and each has exactly one occurrence in a given type τ, we may say

$$\tau\langle a_1, \ldots, a_n\rangle, \qquad \tau\langle\sigma_1, \ldots, \sigma_n\rangle$$

for τ and $[\sigma_1/a_1, \ldots, \sigma_n/a_n]\tau$ respectively.

7C3 Single-Replacement Lemma *If τ is skeletal and $a \in Vars(\tau)$ and $b \notin Vars(\tau)$, there exists a closed λI-term Q whose PT is*

(i) $\quad (a\to b)^* \to \tau\langle a\rangle \to \tau\langle b\rangle,$

where $(a\to b)^* \equiv a\to b$ if the sole occurrence of a in τ is positive in the sense of Definition 9D3, but $(a\to b)^* \equiv b\to a$ if it is negative. Further,

(ii) $\quad Q\mathbf{I} \rhd_{\beta\eta} \mathbf{I}.$

Proof Q will be constructed by induction on $|\tau|$.

Basis: $\tau \equiv a$. Then $(a\to b)^* \equiv a\to b$. Choose $Q \equiv \lambda xy{\cdot}xy$; then $Q\mathbf{I} \rhd_\beta \mathbf{I}$, and by the PT algorithm (3E1),

$$PT(Q) \equiv (a\to b)\to(a\to b).$$

Induction step: $\tau \equiv \rho\to\sigma$. Then ρ and σ are skeletal, so by 7C1 there exist λI-terms I_ρ and I_σ with

(1) $\quad PT(I_\rho) \equiv \rho\to\rho, \qquad PT(I_\sigma) \equiv \sigma\to\sigma,$

(2) $\quad I_\rho \rhd_{\beta\eta} \mathbf{I}, \qquad I_\sigma \rhd_{\beta\eta} \mathbf{I}.$

Case 1: the sole occurrence of a in τ is positive and is in ρ. Then $(a\to b)^* \equiv a\to b$. But the positive occurrence of a in τ corresponds to a negative occurrence in ρ, so by the induction hypothesis there is a λI-term $Q_{\rho-}$ such that

(3) $\quad PT(Q_{\rho-}) \equiv (b\to a)\to\rho\langle a\rangle\to\rho\langle b\rangle,$

and $Q_{\rho-}\mathbf{I} \rhd_{\beta\eta} \mathbf{I}$. By renaming the variables in (3) we get

$$PT(Q_{\rho-}) \equiv (a\to b)\to\rho\langle b\rangle\to\rho\langle a\rangle$$

Choose

(4) $\quad Q \equiv \lambda xyz{\cdot}I_\sigma(y(Q_{\rho-}xz)).$

Since $(a{\to}b)^* \equiv a{\to}b$, we must prove that

(5) $\quad PT(Q) \;\equiv\; (a{\to}b){\to}(\rho\langle a\rangle{\to}\sigma){\to}(\rho\langle b\rangle{\to}\sigma).$

But this comes easily from applying the PT algorithm to Q. Finally it is simple to check that $Q\mathbf{I} \rhd_{\beta\eta} \mathbf{I}$, using (2).

Case 2: the occurrence of a in τ is positive and is in σ. Then a occurs positively in σ, so by the induction hypothesis there exists $Q_{\sigma+}$ such that

(6) $\quad PT(Q_{\sigma+}) \;\equiv\; (a{\to}b){\to}\sigma\langle a\rangle{\to}\sigma\langle b\rangle,$

and $Q_{\sigma+}\mathbf{I} \rhd_{\beta\eta} \mathbf{I}$. Choose

(7) $\quad Q \;\equiv\; \lambda xyz{\cdot}Q_{\sigma+}x(y(I_\rho z)).$

Then $Q\mathbf{I} \rhd_{\beta\eta} \mathbf{I}$ easily. Now $(a{\to}b)^* \equiv a{\to}b$ since a occurs positively in τ; and by the PT algorithm and perhaps some renaming we get

(8) $\quad PT(Q) \;\equiv\; (a{\to}b){\to}(\rho{\to}\sigma\langle a\rangle){\to}(\rho{\to}\sigma\langle b\rangle).$

Case 3: the occurrence of a in τ is negative and is in ρ. Then a occurs positively in ρ, so by the induction hypothesis there exists $Q_{\rho+}$ such that

(9) $\quad PT(Q_{\rho+}) \;\equiv\; (a{\to}b){\to}\rho\langle a\rangle{\to}\rho\langle b\rangle,$

and $Q_{\rho+}\mathbf{I} \rhd_{\beta\eta} \mathbf{I}$. Choose

(10) $\quad Q \;\equiv\; \lambda xyz{\cdot}I_\sigma(y(Q_{\rho+}xz)).$

Then $Q\mathbf{I} \rhd_{\beta\eta} \mathbf{I}$. Now $(a{\to}b)^* \equiv b{\to}a$ since a occurs negatively in τ; and by the PT algorithm and perhaps some renaming, we get

(11) $\quad PT(Q) \;\equiv\; (b{\to}a){\to}(\rho\langle a\rangle{\to}\sigma){\to}(\rho\langle b\rangle{\to}\sigma).$

Case 4: the occurrence of a in τ is negative and is in σ. Then a occurs negatively in σ, so the induction hypothesis gives $Q_{\sigma-}$ such that

(12) $\quad PT(Q_{\sigma-}) \;\equiv\; (b{\to}a){\to}\sigma\langle a\rangle{\to}\sigma\langle b\rangle$

and $Q_{\sigma-}\mathbf{I} \rhd_{\beta\eta} \mathbf{I}$. Choose

(13) $\quad Q \;\equiv\; \lambda xyz{\cdot}Q_{\sigma-}x(y(I_\rho z)).$

Then $Q\mathbf{I} \rhd_{\beta\eta} \mathbf{I}$. Now $(a{\to}b)^* \equiv b{\to}a$ since a occurs negatively in τ; and by the PT algorithm and perhaps some renaming we get

(14) $\quad PT(Q) \;\equiv\; (b{\to}a){\to}(\rho{\to}\sigma\langle a\rangle){\to}(\rho{\to}\sigma\langle b\rangle).$ □

7C4 Double-Replacement Lemma *If τ is skeletal and a_1, a_2 are distinct variables in τ, and b_1, b_2 are distinct variables not in τ, then there is a closed λI-term R whose PT is*

(i) $\quad (a_1{\to}b_1)^*{\to}(a_2{\to}b_2)^*{\to}\tau\langle a_1, a_2\rangle{\to}\tau\langle b_1, b_2\rangle,$

where, for each $i \le 2$, $(a_i{\to}b_i)^* \equiv a_i{\to}b_i$ if the occurrence of a_i in τ is positive, but $(a_i{\to}b_i)^* \equiv b_i{\to}a_i$ if it is negative. Also

(ii) $\quad R\mathbf{II} \rhd_{\beta\eta} \mathbf{I}.$

Proof By 7C3 there exist λI-terms P and Q such that

$$PT(P) \equiv (a_1 \to b_1)^* \to \tau\langle a_1, a_2\rangle \to \tau\langle b_1, a_2\rangle,$$
$$PT(Q) \equiv (a_2 \to b_2)^* \to \tau\langle b_1, a_2\rangle \to \tau\langle b_1, b_2\rangle,$$

and $P\mathbf{I} \rhd_{\beta\eta} \mathbf{I}$ and $Q\mathbf{I} \rhd_{\beta\eta} \mathbf{I}$. Choose

(1) $R \equiv \lambda xyz \cdot Qy(Pxz).$ □

7C5 Identification Lemma *If τ is a λI-PT then so are all types obtained from τ by identifications. Further, there is an algorithm which, when given a λI-term M and $\tau \equiv PT(M)$ and $\sigma \equiv [b/a]\tau$ with a, $b \in Vars(\tau)$, will construct a λI-term N such that*

$$PT(N) \equiv \sigma, \qquad N \rhd_{\beta\eta} M.$$

Proof Let $\tau \equiv PT(M)$ for some closed λI-term M and let $\sigma \equiv [b/a]\tau$ where a, $b \in Vars(\tau)$. We must prove that σ is a λI-PT. Let

$$Vars(\tau) = \{a, b, c_1, \ldots, c_k\}$$

where a, b, $c_1, \ldots, c_k$ are distinct, and let p, q, $n_1, \ldots, n_k$ respectively be the number of occurrences of each of these variables in τ.

Define τ° to be the result of replacing each occurrence of each variable in τ by a distinct new variable; say

$$\tau^\circ \equiv \tau^\circ\langle a_1, a_2, \ldots, a_p, b_1, b_2, \ldots, b_q, c_{1,1}, \ldots, c_{1,n_1}, \ \ldots, \ c_{k,1}, \ldots, c_{k,n_k}\rangle,$$

where $a_1, \ldots, a_p$ replace the occurrences of a, etc. Then replace a_1 and b_1 in τ° by two new variables f and g distinct from all those above, and call the result τ':

$$\tau' \equiv \tau^\circ\langle f, a_2, \ldots, a_p, g, b_2, \ldots, b_q, c_{1,1}, \ldots, c_{1,n_1}, \ \ldots, \ c_{k,1}, \ldots, c_{k,n_k}\rangle.$$

Apply the double-replacement lemma (7C4) to a_1, b_1, f, g and τ°: this gives a closed λI-term R such that

(1) $PT(R) \equiv (a_1 \to f)^* \to (b_1 \to g)^* \to (\tau^\circ \to \tau')$

where $(a_1 \to f)^*$, $(b_1 \to g)^*$ are defined as in 7C4 depending on whether a_1, b_1 occur positively or negatively in τ°. Define

(2) $N \equiv (\lambda x \cdot Rxx)\mathbf{I}M.$

We shall see that $PT(N) \equiv [b/a]\tau$. First, the PT algorithm gives

$$PT(\lambda x \cdot Rxx) \equiv (a_1 \to f)^* \to [a_1/b_1, f/g](\tau^\circ \to \tau').$$

Hence

$$PT((\lambda x \cdot Rxx)\mathbf{I}) \equiv [a_1/f][a_1/b_1, f/g](\tau^\circ \to \tau')$$

(3) $$\equiv [a_1/b_1]\tau^\circ \to [a_1/f, a_1/g]\tau'.$$

To finish computing $PT(N)$ we need an m.g.c.i. of $\langle [a_1/b_1]\tau^\circ, \tau\rangle$. Now $[a_1/b_1]\tau^\circ$ is

$$\tau^\circ\langle a_1, a_2, \ldots, a_p, a_1, b_2, \ldots, b_q, c_{1,1}, \ldots, c_{1,n_1}, \ \ldots, \ c_{k,1}, \ldots, c_{k,n_k}\rangle$$

and τ is

$$\tau^\circ\langle a, a, \ldots, a, b, b, \ldots, b, c_1, \ldots, c_1, \ \ldots, \ c_k, \ldots, c_k\rangle.$$

Consider any common instance ρ of $\langle [a_1/b_1]\tau^\circ, \tau\rangle$: since $[a_1/b_1]\tau^\circ$ has a_1 in the position that was occupied by b_1 in τ°, the types in ρ at the a_1- and b_1-positions must be the same. Also, since ρ is an instance of τ, the types in ρ at the positions of $a_1,\ldots,a_p$ must be the same, and those at the positions of $b_1,\ldots,b_q$ must be the same. Hence an m.g.c.i. of $\langle [a_1/b_1]\tau^\circ, \tau\rangle$ is

$$\tau^\circ\langle b, b, \ldots, b, b, b, \ldots, b, c_1, \ldots, c_1, \ \ldots, \ c_k, \ldots, c_k\rangle.$$

The substitution that generates this from $[a_1/b_1]\tau^\circ$ is

$$[b/a_1, b/a_2, \ldots, b/a_p, b/b_2, \ldots, b/b_q, c_1/c_{1,1}, \ldots].$$

Hence by the PT algorithm and (3), $PT(N)$ is

$$[b/a_1, b/a_2, \ldots, b/a_p, b/b_2, \ldots, b/b_q, c_1/c_{1,1}, \ldots]([a_1/f, a_1/g]\tau'),$$

which is

$$\tau^\circ\langle b, b, \ldots, b, b, b, \ldots, b, c_1, \ldots, c_1, \ \ldots, \ c_k, \ldots, c_k\rangle,$$

and this is $[b/a]\tau$ as required.

Finally, $N \rhd_{\beta\eta} M$ by (2) and 7C4(ii). □

The following lemma and algorithm complete the proof of Theorem 7A3.

7C6 Lemma *Algorithm 7C7 below accepts any τ and any M such that $\vdash_\lambda M{:}\tau$, and outputs a closed term M^* such that $PT(M^*) \equiv \tau$ and $M^* \rhd_{\beta\eta} M$. Further, if M is a λI-term so is M^*.*

Proof See 7C7 and 7C1–5. □

7C7 Converse PT Algorithm (Meyer and Bunder 1988 §9.) ***Input:*** *any pair $\langle \tau, M\rangle$ such that $\vdash_\lambda M{:}\tau$.* (The relation $\vdash_\lambda M{:}\tau$ is decidable by 3E3.)

Step 1. *Follow the proof of* 7C2 *to construct M^+ and $\tau^+ \equiv PT(M^+)$ and to find a series of identifications $\mathsf{s}_1, \ldots, \mathsf{s}_k$ $(k \geq 0)$ such that*

$$\tau \ \equiv \ \mathsf{s}_k(\ldots(\mathsf{s}_1(\tau^+))\ldots).$$

Step 2. *If $k = 0$ in Step 1, choose $M^* \equiv M^+$. If $k \geq 1$, apply* 7C5 *first to τ^+, then to $\mathsf{s}_1(\tau^+)$, then to $\mathsf{s}_2(\mathsf{s}_1(\tau^+))$, etc., and choose M^* to be the last term N produced.*

7C7.1 *Note* By the proofs of 7C1–5 we can see that the M^* produced by the above algorithm has form

$$M^* \ \equiv \ T_k(T_{k-1}(\ldots(T_1(I_{\tau^\circ}M))\ldots))$$

where $T_1, \ldots, T_k$ and I_{τ° are typable closed λI-terms that $\beta\eta$-reduce to I.

7C7.2 *Exercise** Apply the above algorithm to construct a term M^* whose PT is τ in the following cases:

(i) $\quad \tau \equiv (b{\to}b){\to}b{\to}b, \qquad M \equiv \mathsf{I};$

(ii) $\quad \tau \equiv b{\to}b{\to}b, \qquad M \equiv \mathsf{K}.$

(By the way, in (ii) M is not a λI-term; but the algorithm works despite this, though in such a case it produces an M^* that is also not a λI-term.)

7C7.3 *Note* As mentioned earlier the above converse PT proof is not quite the one in Meyer and Bunder 1988 §9 but a λ-adaptation of it. The unadapted Meyer-Bunder proof is slightly stronger, and shows that the converse PT theorem holds not only for the class of all λI-terms but for a more restricted class too, namely the **BB′IW**-combinations as defined in 9F1.[1] For completeness' sake this result will now be stated as a formal theorem.

7C8 Theorem (Meyer and Bunder 1988 §9.) (i) *Every type of a* **BB′IW**-*combination is also a* **BB′IW**-*PT*.

(ii) *In detail: there is an algorithm which accepts any typable closed term M and any type τ of M, and outputs an applicative combination M^* of M and the closed λ-terms* **B**, **B′**, **I**, **W**, *such that*

$$PT(M^*) \equiv \tau, \qquad M^* \rhd_{\beta\eta} M.$$

Proof Using the PT algorithm and some patience, it is easy to show that the proofs of Lemmas 7C1–5 stay valid if the definitions of $I_{\rho\to\sigma}$, Q, R and N in them are replaced by the following:

in 7C1 (4):	$I_{\rho\to\sigma}$	$\equiv$	$\mathbf{B}(\mathbf{B}'\mathbf{B})(\mathbf{BBB}')I_\rho I_\sigma$,
in 7C3 (4):	Q	$\equiv$	$\mathbf{BB}(\mathbf{B}(\mathbf{B}'\mathbf{B}')(\mathbf{BBB}))I_\sigma Q_{\rho-}$,
in 7C3 (7):	Q	$\equiv$	$\mathbf{BB}(\mathbf{B}(\mathbf{B}'\mathbf{B})(\mathbf{BBB}'))I_\rho Q_{\sigma+}$,
in 7C3 (10):	Q	$\equiv$	$\mathbf{BB}(\mathbf{B}(\mathbf{B}'\mathbf{B}')(\mathbf{BBB}))I_\sigma Q_{\rho+}$,
in 7C3 (13):	Q	$\equiv$	$\mathbf{BB}(\mathbf{B}(\mathbf{B}'\mathbf{B})(\mathbf{BBB}'))I_\rho Q_{\sigma-}$,
in 7C4 (1):	R	$\equiv$	$\mathbf{B}(\mathbf{B}'\mathbf{B}')(\mathbf{BB}')PQ$,
in 7C5 (2):	N	$\equiv$	$\mathbf{W}R\mathbf{I}M$. □

7D Condensed detachment

We now come to the connection with the resolution-style rule for propositional logic mentioned in the introduction to this Chapter. This rule was originally devised in the early 1950's under the name of the ***condensed detachment rule***. It will be described here in the context of the $\mathbb{A}$-logic generated by an arbitrary set $\mathbb{A}$ of axioms, see 6D1.

7D1 Definition ***Rule (D)***, the ***condensed detachment rule***, makes the deduction

$$(D) \quad \frac{\rho\to\sigma \qquad \tau}{D(\rho\to\sigma)\tau},$$

where $D(\rho\to\sigma)\tau$ is an implicational formula defined thus: if ρ and τ have a common

[1] This class is a proper subclass of the closed λI-terms because it does not contain $\mathbf{C} \equiv \lambda xyz{\cdot}xzy$. (When $\mathbf{C}\,xyz$ is β-reduced the occurrence of z moves away from the rightmost position, and it is easy to see that no **BB′IW**-combination has this property.)

instance, construct an m.g.c.i. $v \equiv \mathbb{s}_1(\rho) \equiv \mathbb{s}_2(\tau)$ of $\langle \rho, \tau \rangle$ such that

(i) $Vars(v) \cap (Vars(\sigma) - Vars(\rho)) = \emptyset$,

(ii) $Dom(\mathbb{s}_1) = Vars(\rho)$, $Dom(\mathbb{s}_2) = Vars(\tau)$,

and define

(iii) $D(\rho \to \sigma)\tau \equiv \mathbb{s}_1(\sigma)$.

(If ρ and τ have no common instance $D(\rho \to \sigma)\tau$ is undefined and rule (D) is not applicable.)

7D1.1 *Lemma If* $D(\rho \to \sigma)\tau$ *is defined, it is the most general conclusion that can be obtained by* (→E) *from instances of* $\rho \to \sigma$ *and* τ *using an instance of* $\rho \to \sigma$ *as major premise. More precisely, if* $v \equiv \mathbb{s}_1(\rho) \equiv \mathbb{s}_2(\tau)$ *is an m.g.c.i. of* $\langle \rho, \tau \rangle$ *satisfying* 7D1(i)–(ii) *and* $\mathbb{r}_1$ *and* $\mathbb{r}_2$ *are any substitutions such that* $\mathbb{r}_1(\rho) \equiv \mathbb{r}_2(\tau)$, *then* $\mathbb{r}_1(\sigma)$ *is an instance of* $\mathbb{s}_1(\sigma)$.

Proof The definition of $D(\rho \to \sigma)\tau$ is almost identical to the procedure described in 3C4 for computing $PT(PQ)$ when $PT(P) \equiv \rho \to \sigma$ and $PT(Q) \equiv \tau$; hence the argument in 3C4 proves the present lemma. (By the way, condition 7D1(i) corresponds to (1) in 3C4.) □

7D1.2 *Notes* (i) $D(\rho \to \sigma)\tau$ is unique modulo renaming of variables (by 3C3.2), so in future we may think of it as uniquely defined.

(ii) $D(\rho \to \sigma)\tau$ is also independent of renaming in $\rho \to \sigma$ and τ; that is, if $D(\rho \to \sigma)\tau$ is defined and $\rho' \to \sigma'$ and τ' are alphabetic variants of $\rho \to \sigma$ and τ respectively then $D(\rho' \to \sigma')\tau'$ is defined and is an alphabetic variant of $D(\rho \to \sigma)\tau$. (By 3C3.2).

(iii) In any system whose rules include (→E) and (Sub) we can derive rule (D) as follows.

$$\dfrac{(\text{Sub})\ \dfrac{\rho \to \sigma}{\mathbb{s}_1(\sigma) \to \mathbb{s}_1(\sigma)} \qquad (\text{Sub})\ \dfrac{\tau}{\mathbb{s}_2(\tau)}}{\mathbb{s}_1(\sigma)}\ (\to\text{E}) \qquad (\mathbb{s}_2(\rho) \equiv \mathbb{s}_2(\tau))$$

The following lemma expresses formally the fact that the definition of $D(\rho \to \sigma)\tau$ is the same as the procedure in 3C4 for computing $PT(PQ)$ when $PT(P) \equiv \rho \to \sigma$ and $PT(Q) \equiv \tau$.

7D2 Lemma (D. Meredith.) *If* P *and* Q *are typable closed terms with* $PT(P) \equiv \rho \to \sigma$ *and* $PT(Q) \equiv \tau$, *then*

(i) PQ *is typable iff* $D(\rho \to \sigma)\tau$ *is defined,*

(ii) $PT(PQ) \equiv D(\rho \to \sigma)\tau$ *modulo permutation of variables.*

7D3 Historical Note Although rule (D) is so close to the PT algorithm each of the two concepts was developed in total ignorance of work on the other until around 1978, when David Meredith was the first to realise the parallel. (Hindley and Meredith 1990.)

Rule (D) was invented by Carew Meredith, and David Meredith (his cousin) recalled learning it from him in 1954. Its first appearance in print was in Lemmon et al. 1957 §9. A definition of the rule with historical comments appears in D. Meredith 1977 and further historical comments are in Kalman 1983.

Precursors of the rule date back perhaps as far as the 1920's, however. In Poland, a particular D-computation was published in Lukasiewicz 1939 (p. 276 of the English translation); and there is indirect evidence[1] that Alfred Tarski, then a colleague of Lukasiewicz, might have formulated the D-concept (and therefore perhaps also an algorithm for computing $D(\rho\to\sigma)\tau$) even before 1930.

Carew Meredith's work on propositional logics involved computing $D(\rho\to\sigma)\tau$ in many special cases, for example those in Lemmon et al. 1957, but he does not seem to have written out his method as a formal algorithm, at least not in print. However, in 1957 an algorithm for constructing $D(\rho\to\sigma)\tau$ was formalized by David Meredith and implemented by him as a program for the computer UNIVAC I.[2]

Now by 7D2 the D-construction is the same as the core of the PT algorithm; hence David Meredith's 1957 D-program was probably in essence the first formal PT algorithm. It was also the first one to be run on a machine. (Cf. Comment 3A7 on the history of PT algorithms.)

7D4 Definition (Condensed logics) For any set $\mathbb{A}$ of formulae, ***condensed $\mathbb{A}$-logic*** is obtained by replacing the two rules ($\to$E) and (Sub) in the definition of "$\mathbb{A}$-logic" in 6D1 by the single rule (D). We shall call its deductions ***D-deductions***; they are trees constructed from axioms and assumptions by rule (D). For deducibility, etc. in a condensed logic we shall say ***D-deducible***, ***D-provable***, ***D-proof***, ***D-theorem***, and shall use the notation

$$\sigma_1,\ldots,\sigma_n \vdash_{\mathbb{A}\mathrm{D}} \tau, \qquad \vdash_{\mathbb{A}\mathrm{D}} \tau.$$

The set of all theorems of condensed $\mathbb{A}$-logic may be called $\mathbb{A}^{\mathrm{D}\vdash}$.

7D4.1 *Note* By 7D1.2(iii), $\mathbb{A}^{\mathrm{D}\vdash} \subseteq \mathbb{A}^{\vdash}$.

7D5 Definition Rule (D) is said to be ***complete*** for a given set $\mathbb{A}$ of axioms (or $\mathbb{A}$ is said to be ***D-complete***) iff

$$\mathbb{A}^{\mathrm{D}\vdash} = \mathbb{A}^{\vdash}.$$

7D5.1 *Note* The concepts of condensed logic and D-completeness have not been defined for Natural Deduction systems but only for Hilbert-style (axiom-based) logics.

7D5.2 *Question* It is natural to ask which sets $\mathbb{A}$ are D-complete: in particular, which of the axiom-sets for Intuitionist, $R_\to$-, BCK- and BCI-logics in 6D3–6 are D-complete? This is the question that the converse PT theorem will help to answer, and the key to the answer is the following preliminary theorem.

[1] Mentioned in Kalman 1983 p. 447.

[2] Noted in Kalman 1983 p. 449 and in correspondence from David Meredith to the present author.

7D6 Meredith's Curry-Howard Theorem (D. Meredith.) *Let* $\{C_1, C_2, \ldots\}$ *be a finite or infinite set of typable closed* λ*-terms, let* $PT(C_i) \equiv \gamma_i$*, and let* $\mathbb{A} = \{\gamma_1, \gamma_2, \ldots\}$*. Then the theorems of condensed* $\mathbb{A}$*-logic are exactly the PTs of the typable applicative combinations of* $C_1, C_2, \ldots$.

Proof By 7D2. □

7D7 Theorem *The axiom-set* $\{(\mathrm{B}), (\mathrm{C}), (\mathrm{I}), (\mathrm{W})\}$ *for* $\mathrm{R}_\rightarrow$ *given in* 6D4 *is D-complete.*

Proof Let τ be provable in $\mathrm{R}_\rightarrow$. Then by 6D7.1, τ is the type of an applicative combination M of **B**, **C**, **I** and **W**. Hence by 7C8, $\tau \equiv PT(M^*)$ for some applicative combination M^* of M, **B**, **B**$'$, **I** and **W**. Let M^{**} be the result of replacing **B**$'$ in M^* by the following combination of **C**, **B** and **I**:

$$\mathbf{B(B(CIB)B)(CI)}.$$

It is straightforward to check that this combination has the same PT as **B**$'$ (in fact it also reduces to **B**$'$); so $PT(M^{**}) \equiv PT(M^*) \equiv \tau$. Hence τ is a **BCIW**-PT. But by 7D6 every **BCIW**-PT is a D-theorem of the logic whose axioms are the PT's of **B**, **C**, **I**, **W**, and this logic is $\mathrm{R}_\rightarrow$. □

The next step in answering Question 7D5.2 is to prove the D-completeness of the axiom-set $\{(\mathrm{B}), (\mathrm{C}), (\mathrm{K}), (\mathrm{W})\}$ for Intuitionist logic. This logic is stronger than $\mathrm{R}_\rightarrow$, and if we view the D-completeness of a set of axioms as saying that deductions obtained by rule (Sub) can be imitated using rule (D) in combination with some of the axioms, it is natural to conjecture that if we strengthen a D-complete set it will remain D-complete. The following definition and lemma make this conjecture precise.

7D8 Definition For any sets $\mathbb{A}$ and $\mathbb{B}$ of formulae: $\mathbb{B}$-logic is called an ***extension*** of $\mathbb{A}$-logic iff $\mathbb{B}^{\vdash} \supseteq \mathbb{A}^{\vdash}$; it is called a ***D-extension*** of $\mathbb{A}$-logic iff

$$\mathbb{B}^{\mathrm{D}\vdash} \supseteq \mathbb{A}^{\mathrm{D}\vdash}.$$

7D8.1 *Note* If $\mathbb{B} \supseteq \mathbb{A}$ then $\mathbb{B}$-logic is both an extension and a D-extension of $\mathbb{A}$-logic.

7D9 D-Extension Lemma *If* $\mathbb{A}$ *is D-complete and* $a \rightarrow a$ *is an* $\mathbb{A}$*-theorem, then every set* $\mathbb{B}$ *whose logic is a D-extension of* $\mathbb{A}$*-logic is D-complete.*

Proof Let $\mathbb{B}^{\mathrm{D}\vdash} \supseteq \mathbb{A}^{\mathrm{D}\vdash}$; to prove $\mathbb{B}$ is D-complete we must show that if Δ is a deduction from $\mathbb{B}$ by rules ($\rightarrow$E) and (Sub), each application of ($\rightarrow$E) or (Sub) in Δ can be replaced by one of (D).

***Case*($\rightarrow$E).** ($\rightarrow$E) is already a special case of (D).

Case (Sub). It is enough to show that if s is any substitution then

$$\tau \in \mathbb{B}^{\mathrm{D}\vdash} \implies \mathrm{s}(\tau) \in \mathbb{B}^{\mathrm{D}\vdash}.$$

First note that $a \to a \in \mathbb{A}^{\vdash}$ by assumption, so by (Sub),

$$\mathbb{s}(\tau) \to \mathbb{s}(\tau) \in \mathbb{A}^{\vdash}.$$

But we have assumed $\mathbb{A}^{\vdash} = \mathbb{A}^{D\vdash}$ and $\mathbb{A}^{D\vdash} \subseteq \mathbb{B}^{D\vdash}$, so

$$\mathbb{s}(\tau) \to \mathbb{s}(\tau) \in \mathbb{B}^{D\vdash}.$$

Now it is easy to see from Definition 7D1 that

$$D(\mathbb{s}(\tau) \to \mathbb{s}(\tau), \tau) \equiv \mathbb{s}(\tau).$$

Hence by rule (D) applied to the D-theorems $\mathbb{s}(\tau) \to \mathbb{s}(\tau)$ and τ we get

$$\mathbb{s}(\tau) \in \mathbb{B}^{D\vdash}. \qquad \square$$

7D10 Theorem *The axiom-set* {(B), (C), (K), (W)} *for Intuitionist logic given in* 6D3 *is D-complete.*

Proof By 7D7 and 7D9, since this logic is a D-extension of $R_{\to}$. □

7D11 Note (Other D-complete logics) (i) ***Classical logic.*** The implicational fragment of classical logic is a Hilbert-style system defined by the axioms (B), (C), (K), (W) and

(PL) $((a \to b) \to a) \to a$.

((PL) is called ***Peirce's law***, see 6A1.2 and 6B7.4.) It can be shown that a formula is provable in this system iff it is a tautology in the usual truth-table sense. (Prior 1955 Part I, Ch. III.) By 7D9–10 this system is D-complete.

(ii) ***Ticket entailment.*** A Hilbert-style logic defined by the axioms (B), (B′), (I) and (W) listed in 6B2.1 was introduced in Anderson and Belnap 1975 (see especially Ch. 1 §§6, 8.3.2), where it was called $T_{\to}$ or ***the logic of ticket entailment***. The details of $T_{\to}$ and its motivation are not the concern of this book, but in a sense (B) and (B′) are "right-handed" and "left-handed" replacement properties: if $a \to b$ holds, (B) says that a can be replaced by b in the formula $c \to a$ and (B′) says that b can be replaced by a in $a \to c$. (Meanings for (I) and (W) were suggested in 6D6.1(ii).) This logic can be shown to be weaker than $R_{\to}$ but by 7D6 and 7C8 it is nevertheless D-complete.[1]

(iii) A set of axioms whose logic is strictly weaker than $T_{\to}$ was proved D-complete by N. Megill in unpublished notes in 1993, and an infinite series of ever weakening D-complete axiom-sets has since been constructed (Megill and Bunder 1996).

But not all axiom-sets are D-complete, as the next theorem will show.

7D12 Theorem *The axiom-sets* {(B), (C), (K)} *and* {(B), (C), (I)} *given in* 6D5–6 *are D-incomplete.*

[1] By the way, it is not yet known whether there is a decision-procedure for provability in $T_{\to}$.

Proof By 7D9 it is enough to prove the result for $\{(\mathrm{B}),(\mathrm{C}),(\mathrm{K})\}$. And by 7D6 it is enough to find a type τ that can be assigned to an applicative combination of **B**, **C**, **K** but is not the PT of such a combination. One such type (pointed out by A. Wronski, cf. Bunder 1986) is

$$\tau \equiv ((a \to a) \to a) \to a.$$

It is easy to deduce from the types of **C** and **K** in Table 3E2a that

$$\vdash_\lambda (\mathbf{C}(\mathbf{CKK})(\mathbf{CKK})) : \tau.$$

On the other hand, τ cannot be the PT of an applicative combination M of **B**, **C**, **K**. Because if it were, M would be a BCKλ-term and hence $M\mathbf{I}$ would be one too by the definition of BCKλ-terms in 1D2; then by 2D8 $M\mathbf{I}$ would be typable. The last step in a deduction of a type for $M\mathbf{I}$ must have form

$$\frac{\mapsto \; M:(\rho\to\rho)\to\sigma \qquad \mapsto \; \mathbf{I}:\rho\to\rho}{\mapsto \; M\mathbf{I}:\sigma.}\;(\to\mathrm{E})$$

Hence $(\rho\to\rho)\to\sigma$ would have to be an instance of $PT(M)$ which is τ. But then $\rho\to\rho$ would be an instance of $(a\to a)\to a$, which is impossible. □

7D12.1 *Warning* D-completeness or -incompleteness is a property of sets of axioms, not of the logics they generate. In fact it is possible to have two sets $\mathbb{A}$ and $\mathbb{B}$ of axioms with $\mathbb{A}^{\vdash} = \mathbb{B}^{\vdash}$ but such that $\mathbb{A}$ is D-complete and $\mathbb{B}$ is not. One example is $\mathbb{B} = \{(\mathrm{B}),(\mathrm{C}),(\mathrm{K})\}$ and $\mathbb{A} = \mathbb{B}^{\vdash}$. There are also examples with $\mathbb{A}$ and $\mathbb{B}$ both finite (Martin Bunder, unpublished notes 1994).

This brings our excursion into propositional logic to an end. (Except that if one identifies λ-terms with deductions the whole of this book is a look at the proof-theory of propositional logic from a particular point of view.)

8

Counting a type's inhabitants

Given a type τ, how many closed terms can receive type τ in TA_λ? As stated this question is trivial, since if the answer is not zero it is always infinite; for example the type $a \rightarrow a$ can be assigned to all members of the sequence **I**, **II**, **III**, etc. But if we change the question to ask only for terms in normal form, the answer is often finite and interesting patterns show up which are still not completely understood.

The aim of this chapter is to describe an algorithm from Ben-Yelles 1979 that answers the "how many" question for normal forms. For each τ it will decide in a finite number of steps whether the number of closed β-normal forms that receive type τ is finite or infinite, will compute this number in the finite case, and will list all the relevant terms in both cases.

Ben-Yelles' algorithm can be used in particular to test whether the number of terms with type τ is zero or not, and as mentioned in 6B7.3 this gives a test for provability in Intuitionist implicational logic.

The first section below will describe the sets to be counted. The next will show some examples of the algorithm's strategy in action. Then in 8C–D the algorithm will be stated formally, and the rest of the chapter will be occupied by a proof that the algorithm does what it claims to do.[1]

8A Inhabitants

This section gives precise definitions and notations for the sets to be counted.

8A1 Definition (Inhabitants) An ***untyped inhabitant*** of τ is a closed term M such that $\vdash_\lambda M : \tau$. A ***typed inhabitant*** of τ is a closed typed term M^τ. The sets of all typed and untyped inhabitants of τ will be called $Habs_{\mathbf{t}}(\tau)$ and $Habs_{\mathbf{u}}(\tau)$ respectively, or, when no confusion is likely, just

$$Habs(\tau).$$

A ***(β-)normal inhabitant*** of a type is an inhabitant in β-nf. The sets of all typed and untyped normal inhabitants of τ will be called $Nhabs_{\mathbf{t}}(\tau)$ and $Nhabs_{\mathbf{u}}(\tau)$ respectively, or, when no confusion is likely, just

$$Nhabs(\tau).$$

[1] This fact was first proved mostly in Ben-Yelles 1979 and partly in Hirokawa 1993c.

A ***βη-normal inhabitant*** of a type is an inhabitant in $\beta\eta$-nf. The sets of all typed and untyped $\beta\eta$-normal inhabitants of τ will both be called

$$Nhabs_\eta(\tau).$$

A type with at least one inhabitant is said to be ***inhabited***.

As remarked earlier the aim of this chapter is to count β-normal inhabitants. The following lemma will show that it does not matter whether we count typed or untyped inhabitants.

8A2 Lemma *If $M^\tau \in Nhabs_t(\tau)$ then $M^{\not t} \in Nhabs_u(\tau)$; further, the type-erasing mapping is a one-to-one correspondence between the typed and the untyped β-normal inhabitants of τ (modulo $\equiv_\alpha$). The same holds for $\beta\eta$-normal inhabitants.*

Proof Let $M \in \beta$-nf; then M inhabits τ iff there exists a proof Δ of $\mapsto M{:}\tau$; and by 2B3 this Δ is uniquely determined by M. And such proofs correspond one-to-one with typed closed terms by 5A7. □

8A2.1 *Notation* All terms in this chapter will be typed unless explicitly stated otherwise. But for ease of reading they will often be written with some or all of their types omitted.

8A3 Definition The number (0, 1, 2, ... or ∞) of members of a set $\mathbb{S}$, counted modulo $\equiv_\alpha$ if $\mathbb{S}$ is a set of λ-terms, is called the ***cardinality*** of $\mathbb{S}$ or

$$\#(\mathbb{S}).$$

For $\#(Nhabs(\tau))$ and $\#(Nhabs_\eta(\tau))$ we shall usually say just

$$\#(\tau), \qquad \#_\eta(\tau).$$

8A4 Definition (Counting, enumerating) A distinction will be made in this book between ***counting*** and ***enumerating*** a set $\mathbb{S}$ of β-normal inhabitants of a type τ:

(i) to ***count*** $\mathbb{S}$ will mean to compute $\#(\mathbb{S})$ after a finite number of steps (even when $\#(\mathbb{S}) = \infty$);

(ii) to ***enumerate*** or ***list*** $\mathbb{S}$ will mean to enumerate $\mathbb{S}$ in the usual recursion-theoretic sense, i.e. to output a sequence consisting of all the members of $\mathbb{S}$ (and no non-members!), continuing for ever if $\mathbb{S}$ is infinite.

8A4.1 *Comment* The aim of Ben-Yelles' algorithm is to count inhabitants as well as enumerate them. Mere enumeration would be easy: we could simply list all closed typed β-nf's in some standard order and for each one decide whether it is an inhabitant of a given τ by looking at its type. But counting is not so easy: we must find a way of enumerating $Nhabs(\tau)$ which will tell us after only a finite number of steps whether the enumeration will continue for ever or not.

The strategy will be to do the counting in order of increasing *depth* in a sense to be defined below, and to first count certain inhabitants called *long β-nf's* from which all others can be generated by η-reduction. Before defining "depth" and "long" we shall look briefly at the structure of arbitrary typed β-nf's (cf. untyped β-nf's, 1B10).

8A5 Lemma (Structure of a typed β-nf) *Let Γ be a type-context. Every β-nf $M^\tau \in \mathbb{TT}(\Gamma)$ can be expressed uniquely in the form*

$$\text{(i)} \qquad (\lambda x_1^{\tau_1} \dots x_m^{\tau_m} \cdot (v^{(\rho_1 \to \dots \rho_n \to \tau^*)} M_1^{\rho_1} \dots M_n^{\rho_n})^{\tau^*})^{(\tau_1 \to \dots \tau_m \to \tau^*)}$$

where $m \geq 0$, $n \geq 0$, and

$$\text{(ii)} \qquad \tau \equiv \tau_1 \to \dots \to \tau_m \to \tau^*$$

for some τ^*, possibly composite, and each $M_j^{\rho_j}$ is a β-nf that is typed relative to

$$\text{(iii)} \qquad \Gamma \cup \{x_1 : \tau_1, \dots, x_m : \tau_m\}$$

(and the set displayed in (iii) *is consistent). Further, if M^τ is closed then $m \geq 1$ and there is an $i \leq m$ such that*

$$\text{(iv)} \qquad v \equiv x_i, \qquad \tau_i \equiv \rho_1 \to \dots \to \rho_n \to \tau^*.$$

Proof Straightforward induction on $|M^{\natural}|$. Note that m, n etc. are determined uniquely, just as in 1B10 for untyped β-nf's. □

8A5.1 *Notation* In the term in 8A5(i) the displayed occurrences of

$$\lambda x_1^{\tau_1}, \dots, \lambda x_m^{\tau_m}, \qquad v^{(\rho_1 \to \dots \rho_n \to \tau^*)}, \qquad M_1^{\rho_1}, \dots, M_n^{\rho_n}$$

are called respectively the term's ***initial abstractors***, ***head*** and ***arguments***.

8A6 Definition (Depth(M^τ)) Define the ***depth*** of a typed or untyped β-nf thus:

(i) $Depth(y) = Depth(\lambda x_1 \dots x_m \cdot y) = 0$;
(ii) $Depth(\lambda x_1 \dots x_m \cdot y M_1 \dots M_n) = 1 + \underset{1 \leq j \leq n}{Max}\, Depth(M_j)$ if $n > 0$.

8A6.1 *Examples* $Depth(\lambda uv \cdot uxvx) = Depth(z(\lambda w \cdot y)) = 1$,
$Depth(\lambda x \cdot x(z(\lambda w \cdot y))(\lambda uv \cdot uxvx)) = 2$.

8A6.2 *Lemma* $Depth(M^\tau) = Depth(M^{\natural}) < |M^{\natural}|$.

8A7 Definition (Long β-nf's) A typed β-nf M^τ is called ***long*** or ***maximal*** iff every variable-occurrence $\underline{z}$ in M^τ is followed by the longest sequence of arguments allowed by its type, i.e. iff each component with form $(zP_1 \dots P_n) (n \geq 0)$ that is not in a function position has atomic type.[1] An untyped β-nf M is called ***long*** relative to a type τ iff it is the type-erasure of a typed long β-nf M^τ. (By 8A2 M^τ is unique.)

The sets of all long normal inhabitants of τ (typed or untyped) will both be called

$$Long(\tau).$$

[1] Sometimes "*long η-normal form*" is used in the literature for long β-nf's but this is misleading, as these terms are β-nf's but not necessarily η-nf's.

8A7.1 *Example* Let $\tau \equiv ((a \to b) \to c) \to (a \to b) \to c$. Then the following normal inhabitant of τ is not long:

$$M^\tau \equiv \lambda x^{(a\to b)\to c} y^{a\to b} . x^{(a\to b)\to c} y^{a\to b}$$

(because $y^{a\to b}$ has a type which "demands" an argument but none is provided). On the other hand the following one is long:

$$N^\tau \equiv \lambda x^{(a\to b)\to c} y^{a\to b} . x^{(a\to b)\to c} (\lambda z^a . y^{a\to b} z^a).$$

8A7.2 *Definition* The sets of all long normal inhabitants of τ (typed or untyped) with depth $\leq d$ will both be called

$$Long(\tau, d).$$

The next lemma shows that if we could enumerate long normal inhabitants the others would be obtainable from these by η-reduction.

8A8 Lemma (Completeness of Long(τ)) (Ben-Yelles 1979 Lemma 3.9.) *Every normal inhabitant of τ can be η-expanded to a long normal inhabitant of τ. And this long inhabitant is unique (modulo $\equiv_\alpha$); i.e.*

$$\{M^\tau, N^\tau \in Long(\tau) \text{ and } M^\tau =_\eta N^\tau\} \implies M^\tau \equiv_\alpha N^\tau.$$

Proof Let $P^\tau \in Nhabs(\tau)$. First we must η-expand P^τ to a term $P^{\tau+} \in Long(\tau)$. Then we must show that $P^{\tau+}$ is unique, i.e. that

(1) $\quad M^\tau \in Long(\tau), \quad M^\tau \rhd_\eta P^\tau \implies M^\tau \equiv_\alpha P^{\tau+}.$

Suppose P^τ contains a ***short component***, i.e. a component with form

$$(yQ_1 \ldots Q_n)^\sigma \qquad (n \geq 0)$$

that is not in function position and whose type σ is composite, say

$$\sigma \equiv \sigma_1 \to \ldots \to \sigma_k \to a \qquad (k \geq 1).$$

Choose distinct new variables $z_1, \ldots, z_k$ not occurring in P^τ and replace this component by

$$(\lambda z_1^{\sigma_1} \ldots z_k^{\sigma_k} . ((yQ_1 \ldots Q_n)^\sigma z_1^{\sigma_1} \ldots z_k^{\sigma_k})^a)^\sigma.$$

This replacement is an η-expansion; it is easy to check that its result is still a β-normal form. (cf. Example 8A7.1.)

Make similar replacements until there are no short components left in P^τ. (Each replacement may introduce new short components with types $\sigma_1, \ldots, \sigma_k$, but these types are shorter than σ so the replacement process will terminate.)

Call the result $P^{\tau+}$. The proof that this term satisfies (1) is a routine induction on $|P^\tau|$. □

8A8.1 *Corollary* $Nhabs(\tau) = \emptyset \iff Long(\tau) = \emptyset.$

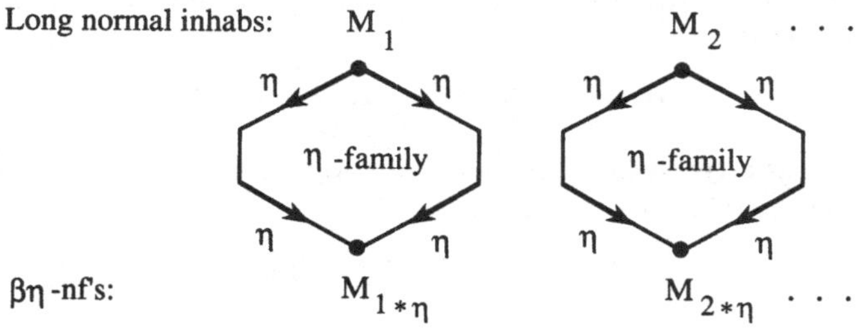

Fig. 8A10a.

8A9 Definition (η-family) The set of all terms obtained by η-reducing M^{τ} will be called the η-family of M^{τ} (just as for untyped terms in 1C3), or

$$\{M^{\tau}\}_{\eta}.$$

8A9.1 *Note* Let $M^{\tau} \in \mathbb{TT}(\Gamma)$ for some Γ. Then $\{M^{\tau}\}_{\eta}$ is finite (by the typed analogue of 1C3.1) and all its members are in $\mathbb{TT}(\Gamma)$ (by 5B7.1). If M^{τ} is a β-nf then so are all the members of $\{M^{\tau}\}_{\eta}$ (by the typed analogue of 1C9.3). Hence

(i) $\quad M^{\tau} \in Nhabs(\tau) \implies \{M^{\tau}\}_{\eta} \subseteq Nhabs(\tau).$

Also, if M^{τ} is a β-nf its η-family contains exactly one $\beta\eta$-nf (by the typed analogue of 1C9.3). Finally, each normal inhabitant of τ is in the η-family of exactly one long normal inhabitant, by 8A8.

The following lemma summarises this situation.

8A10 Lemma (i) *The η-families of the long typed normal inhabitants of τ partition $Nhabs(\tau)$ into non-overlapping finite subsets, each η-family containing just one long member and just one $\beta\eta$-nf.* (*See Fig. 8A10a.*)

(ii) $\#(\tau)$ *is finite or infinite or zero according as* $\#_{\eta}(\tau)$ *is finite or infinite or zero.*

(iii) $\#_{\eta}(\tau) = \#(Long(\tau))$.

8A11 Definition (Principal inhabitants) An untyped inhabitant M of τ is called ***principal*** iff τ is a principal type of M. A typed inhabitant M^{τ} of τ is called ***principal*** iff the deduction of $\mapsto M^{\not\tau} : \tau$ that it encodes (see 5A7) is principal.

The sets of all principal inhabitants of τ (typed or untyped) will both be called

$$Princ(\tau).$$

The sets of all principal β-normal inhabitants of τ (typed or untyped) will both be called

$$Nprinc(\tau).$$

8A11.1 *Lemma* M^{τ} *is a typed principal β-normal inhabitant of τ iff $M^{\not\tau}$ is an untyped principal β-normal inhabitant of τ.*

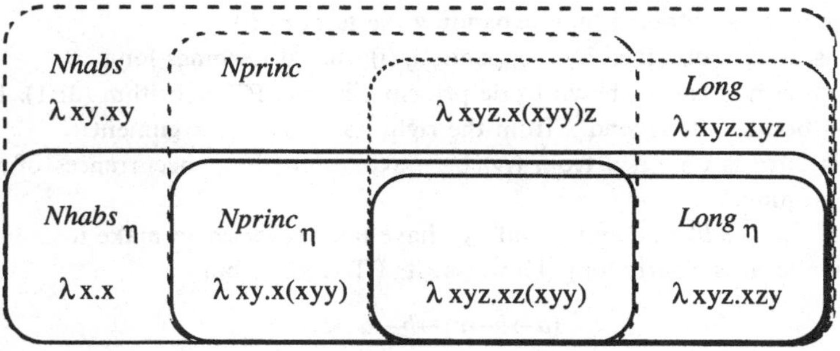

Fig. 8A12a.

8A11.2 *Lemma* *Let $M^{\tau+}$ be the unique member of $Long(\tau)$ to which M^{τ} η-expands (see 8A8). Then*

$$M^{\tau} \in Nprinc(\tau) \quad \Longrightarrow \quad M^{\tau+} \in Nprinc(\tau).$$

Proof The η-expansion in the proof of 8A8 preserves principality because of the way the types given to $z_1, \ldots, z_k$ are determined by the type σ of the component that is replaced. □

8A12 Comment (Sets of nf's) Three sets of β-nf's have been defined so far in this section, namely

$$Nhabs(\tau), \qquad Long(\tau), \qquad Nprinc(\tau),$$

and the sets of all $\beta\eta$-nf's in these sets will be called respectively

$$Nhabs_{\eta}(\tau), \qquad Long_{\eta}(\tau), \qquad Nprinc_{\eta}(\tau).$$

To clarify the relations between these six sets consider the type

$$\tau \;\equiv\; (a{\to}a{\to}a){\to}a{\to}a{\to}a.$$

(See Fig. 8A12a.) For this τ the six sets are all distinct and in fact there is a term in every space in Fig. 8A12a except one. In detail:

(i) $\lambda x^{a\to a\to a}.\, x^{a\to a\to a} \in Nhabs_{\eta} - (Nprinc \cup Long)$;

(ii) $\lambda x^{a\to a\to a} y^{a}.(xy)^{a\to a} \in Nhabs - Nhabs_{\eta} - (Nprinc \cup Long)$;

(iii) $\lambda x^{a\to a\to a} y^{a} z^{a}.(xyz)^{a} \in Long - Nhabs_{\eta} - Nprinc$;

(iv) $\lambda x^{a\to a\to a} y^{a}.(x(xyy))^{a\to a} \in Nprinc_{\eta} - Long_{\eta}$;

(v) $\lambda x^{a\to a\to a} y^{a} z^{a}.(x(xyy)z)^{a} \in Nprinc \cap Long - Nhabs_{\eta}$;

(vi) $\lambda x^{a\to a\to a} y^{a} z^{a}.(xz(xyy))^{a} \in Nprinc_{\eta} \cap Long_{\eta}$;

(vii) $\lambda x^{a\to a\to a} y^{a} z^{a}.(xzy)^{a} \in Long_{\eta} - Nprinc_{\eta}$.

Proof of 8A12 (i) The term shown in (i) is clearly a $\beta\eta$-nf and is not long. It fails to encode a principal deduction for $\lambda x \cdot x$ because the $PT(\lambda x \cdot x)$ is not τ but $a \to a$.

(ii) This term is obtained by η-expanding the term in (i).

(iii) This term is obtained by η-expanding (i) until it becomes long.

(iv) This term is easily shown to be principal by the PT algorithm (3E1). It fails to be long because its second x from the right has only one argument.

(v) This term is obtained from (iv) by η-expansion; both occurrences of x now have two arguments.

(vi) This term is like (v) but z and xyy have been reversed to make it an η-nf.

(vii) This term is clearly long. However, its PT is not τ but

$$(a \to b \to c) \to b \to a \to c.$$

8A12.1 *Exercise** In Fig. 8A12a one of the eight spaces is empty: show that if τ is changed to the following type then every space in that figure will contain a term:

$$\tau \equiv (a \to a \to a \to a) \to a \to a \to a \to a.$$

8A13 Remark (Sets containing non-nf's) This chapter is concerned mainly with counting normal forms so the sets $Habs(\tau)$ and $Princ(\tau)$ will play almost no role. However, it is worth noting their relation to $Nhabs(\tau)$ and $Nprinc(\tau)$ before going on.

(i) If τ has an inhabitant M then M has a β-nf $M*_\beta$ by WN (5C1) and $M*_\beta$ is also an inhabitant of τ by subject-reduction (2C1); hence

$$Habs(\tau) \neq \emptyset \iff Nhabs(\tau) \neq \emptyset.$$

(ii) Next, by the converse PT theorem (7A2) every type with an inhabitant has a principal one, so

$$Habs(\tau) \neq \emptyset \iff Princ(\tau) \neq \emptyset.$$

(iii) In contrast it is not true that $Habs(\tau) \neq \emptyset \Rightarrow Nprinc(\tau) \neq \emptyset$. It is not even true that $Princ(\tau) \neq \emptyset \Rightarrow Nprinc(\tau) \neq \emptyset$. Because τ may have an inhabitant M, even a principal one, such that $PT(M)$ changes when M is reduced to $M*_\beta$. An example is

$$\tau \equiv a \to a \to a;$$

by 8B4 this type's only normal inhabitants are $\lambda xy \cdot x$ and $\lambda xy \cdot y$ and it is easy to check that neither of these is principal; on the other hand Table 3E2a(10) showed that τ has a non-normal principal inhabitant

$$(\lambda xyz \cdot \mathbf{K}(xy)(xz))\mathbf{I}.$$

8B Examples of the search strategy

The core of the counting algorithm will be a *search algorithm* which will seek long normal inhabitants of τ with increasing depths $d = 0, 1, 2, \ldots$. The strategy of this algorithm will depend on nothing more than some surprisingly simple comments about the structure of long typed terms. These comments will be collected in 8B2 below and then applied in some examples which will show the search strategy in action.

8B1 Lemma *Every type τ can be expressed uniquely in the following form, where $m \geq 0$ and e is an atom:*

$$\tau \equiv \tau_1 \rightarrow \ldots \rightarrow \tau_m \rightarrow e.$$

Proof Easy induction on $|\tau|$. □

8B1.1 *Notation* The occurrences of $\tau_1, \ldots, \tau_m$ and e displayed above will be called the ***premises*** and ***conclusion*** (or ***tail***) of τ respectively, and m will be called the ***arity*** of τ. (See Definition 9E5 for more details.)

Two type-occurrences will be called ***isomorphic*** iff they are occurrences of the same type. (cf. Definition (iv).) Iff the tail-components of σ and τ are isomorphic we may say

$$Tail(\sigma) \cong Tail(\tau).$$

8B2 Comments (Long typed β-nf's) Let τ be any type; say τ has form

$$\tau \equiv \tau_1 \rightarrow \ldots \rightarrow \tau_m \rightarrow e \qquad (m \geq 0,\ e \text{ an atom})$$

and let M^τ be any β-nf with type τ. By 8A5, M^τ has form

$$(\lambda x_1^{\tau_1} \ldots x_k^{\tau_k} \cdot (v^{(\rho_1 \rightarrow \ldots \rho_n \rightarrow \tau^*)} M_1^{\rho_1} \ldots M_n^{\rho_n})^{\tau^*})^{(\tau_1 \rightarrow \ldots \tau_k \rightarrow \tau^*)}$$

where $0 \leq k \leq m$ and $\tau^* \equiv \tau_{k+1} \rightarrow \ldots \tau_m \rightarrow e$. If M^τ is long (see 8A7), then

(i) $k = m$,
(ii) $\tau^* \equiv e$,
(iii) the types of $x_1, \ldots, x_m$ coincide with the premises of τ,
(iv) the tail of the type of v is isomorphic to that of τ,
(v) if M^τ is closed then $m \geq 1$ and v is an x_i $(1 \leq i \leq m)$ and

$$\tau_i \equiv \rho_1 \rightarrow \ldots \rightarrow \rho_n \rightarrow e.$$

The following examples show how the above comments are applied.

8B3 Example (A type τ with $\#(\tau) = 1$) (Ben-Yelles 1979 p. 42.) The following type has exactly one normal inhabitant:

$$\tau \equiv (a \rightarrow b \rightarrow c) \rightarrow (a \rightarrow b) \rightarrow a \rightarrow c.$$

And its normal inhabitant (which is also both long and principal) is

$$\mathbf{S}^\tau \equiv \lambda x^{a \rightarrow b \rightarrow c} y^{a \rightarrow b} z^a \cdot xz(yz).$$

Proof We shall start by proving that $Long(\tau) = \{\mathbf{S}^\tau\}$.

Step 1. First look at the structure of τ: in the notation of 8B2 we have $m = 3$ and

$$e \equiv c, \qquad \tau_1 \equiv a \rightarrow b \rightarrow c, \qquad \tau_2 \equiv a \rightarrow b, \qquad \tau_3 \equiv a.$$

Hence any $M^\tau \in Long(\tau)$ must have just three initial abstracted variables, say

$$M^\tau \equiv (\lambda x_1^{\tau_1} x_2^{\tau_2} x_3^{\tau_3} \cdot (v^{(\rho_1 \rightarrow \ldots \rho_n \rightarrow c)} M_1^{\rho_1} \ldots M_n^{\rho_n})^c)^{(\tau_1 \rightarrow \tau_2 \rightarrow \tau_3 \rightarrow c)}.$$

Now by 8B2(iv), v must be one of x_1, x_2, x_3 whose type's tail is isomorphic to that of τ. The tail of τ is $\underline{c}$, and the only τ_i whose tail is an occurrence of c is τ_1, so v must be x_1. Since τ_1 has two premises, x_1 must be followed by exactly two arguments. Hence M must have form

(1) $$M \equiv \lambda x_1^{a\to b\to c} x_2^{a\to b} x_3^{a} \cdot x_1^{a\to b\to c} U^a V^b.$$

Step 2. Search for suitable U^a and V^b. First U^a: its type is an atom so U^a cannot be an abstract, by 8B2(i). Thus U^a has form

$$U^a \equiv (wP_1 \dots P_r)^a \qquad (r \geq 0)$$

where w is an x_i whose type's tail is isomorphic to the tail of the type of U. This tail is an occurrence of a, so the only possibility is

$$w \equiv x_3.$$

Since the type of x_3 has no premises we have $r = 0$ and hence

(2) $$U^a \equiv x_3^a.$$

Next search for V^b. Since b is an atom, V^b cannot be an abstract and its head must be an x_i whose type's tail is an occurrence of b. The only possibility is x_2, and the type of x_2 allows only one argument, so

(3) $$V^b \equiv x_2^{a\to b} W^a$$

for some W^a.

Step 3. Search for W^a. Just as for U^a, the only possibility is

(4) $$W^a \equiv x_3^a.$$

Conclusion. Modulo $\equiv_\alpha$ there is at most one term in $Long(\tau)$, namely

$$\mathbf{S}^\tau \equiv \lambda x_1^{a\to b\to c} x_2^{a\to b} x_3^{a} \cdot x_1 x_3 (x_2 x_3).$$

It is easy to check that $\mathbf{S}^\tau$ is actually in $Long(\tau)$. Hence, by 8A10 and the fact that $\mathbf{S}^\tau$ is η-irreducible,

$$Nhabs(\tau) = \{\mathbf{S}^\tau\}.$$

By the PT algorithm it is easy to check that τ is a principal type of $\mathbf{S}^\tau$; hence

$$Nprinc(\tau) = \{\mathbf{S}^\tau\}. \qquad \square$$

8B4 Example (A type τ with $\#(\tau) = m$) For each $m \geq 2$ the following τ has exactly m normal inhabitants and all are long and non-principal:

$$\tau \equiv a \to \dots \to a \to a \qquad (m+1\ a\text{'s}).$$

In fact its normal inhabitants are the following m terms (called ***projectors*** or ***selectors***):

$$\Pi_i^m \equiv \lambda x_1^a \dots x_m^a \cdot x_i^a \qquad (1 \leq i \leq m).$$

Proof By 8B2, any $M^\tau \in Long(\tau)$ must have form

$$M^\tau \equiv \lambda x_1^a \dots x_m^a \cdot v V_1 \dots V_n$$

where $v \equiv x_i$ for some $i \leq m$. But the types of $x_1, \dots, x_m$ have no premises, so $n = 0$. Hence

$$M^\tau \equiv \lambda x_1^a \dots x_m^a \cdot x_i^a.$$

It is easy to see that every such selector is in fact in $Long(\tau)$. Also all these selectors are η-irreducible, so by 8A10,

$$Nhabs(\tau) = Long(\tau).$$

Now $m \geq 2$, so by the PT algorithm no selector is in $Nprinc(\tau)$; hence

$$Nprinc(\tau) = \emptyset. \qquad \square$$

8B5 Example (Types τ with $\#(\tau) = 0$) (i) No atomic type has inhabitants.

(ii) No type that is skeletal (i.e. in which each atom occurs at most once, cf. 7B2) has inhabitants.

Proof (i) Every type with an inhabitant has a normal one by 8A13(i). But every type with a normal inhabitant has arity $m \geq 1$ by 8B2(iii).

(ii) Let τ be skeletal and let $\tau \equiv \tau_1 \rightarrow \dots \rightarrow \tau_m \rightarrow e\, (m \geq 1)$. If τ had inhabitants it would have at least one long normal one by 8A8, and by 8B2 this inhabitant would have form

$$\lambda x_1 \dots x_m \cdot x_i M_1 \dots M_n$$

with x_i having type τ_i and the tail of τ_i being an occurrence of e. But τ is skeletal, so e cannot occur in any τ_i. Hence τ has no inhabitants. $\square$

8B5.1 *Corollary* *Intuitionist implicational logic is consistent in the sense that not all formulae are provable.*

Proof If an atomic formula e were provable it would be the type of a closed term M^e by 6B7.1, contradicting 8B5. $\square$

8B6 Example (Peirce's law, cf. 6A1.2) The type $\tau \equiv ((a \rightarrow b) \rightarrow a) \rightarrow a$ has no inhabitants.

Proof Suppose $M^\tau \in Long(\tau)$. Then by 8B2, M^τ must have form

$$M^\tau \equiv \lambda x^{(a \rightarrow b) \rightarrow a} \cdot v U_1 \dots U_n \qquad (n \geq 0).$$

And $v \equiv x$, since M^τ is closed. Hence $n = 1$, since the type of x has only one premise. Thus

$$M^\tau \equiv \lambda x^{(a \rightarrow b) \rightarrow a} \cdot x^{(a \rightarrow b) \rightarrow a} U^{a \rightarrow b}$$

for some $U^{a \rightarrow b}$. Since $a \rightarrow b$ has just one premise, $U^{a \rightarrow b}$ must have form

$$U^{a \rightarrow b} \equiv \lambda y^a \cdot (w V_1 \dots V_r)^b \qquad (r \geq 0).$$

Since M^τ is closed, w must be x or y. But w must have a type whose tail is an occurrence of b and neither x nor y has such a type, so no suitable $U^{a\to b}$ exists. Thus $Long(\tau) = \emptyset$ and hence $Nhabs(\tau) = \emptyset$ by 8A8.1. Hence $Habs(\tau) = \emptyset$ by 8A13(i). □

8B7 Exercise* Verify the information in Table 8B7a by proving that the types shown there have no other inhabitants than those displayed. The notation used in the table's last row is:

$$P_0 \equiv \lambda x \cdot x\mathbf{I},$$
$$P_n \equiv \lambda x \cdot x(\lambda y_1 \cdot x(\ldots(\lambda y_n \cdot x\mathbf{I})\ldots)) \qquad (n \geq 1),$$
$$Q_{n,i} \equiv \lambda x \cdot x(\lambda y_1 \cdot x(\ldots(\lambda y_n \cdot x(\lambda z \cdot y_i))\ldots)) \qquad (n \geq 1, 1 \leq i \leq n).$$

Table 8B7a. *Some types and their normal inhabitants*

	Type τ	$Nhabs(\tau)$	$Long(\tau)$	$Nprinc(\tau)$	Notes
1	a	None	None	None	See Ex. 8B5
2	$a\to a$	**I**	**I**	**I**	$\mathbf{I} \equiv \lambda x \cdot x$
3	$a\to b\to a$	**K**	**K**	**K**	$\mathbf{K} \equiv \lambda xy \cdot x$
4	$(a\to b)\to(c\to a)\to c\to b$	**B**	**B**	**B**	$\mathbf{B} \equiv \lambda xyz \cdot x(yz)$
5	$(a\to b\to c)\to b\to a\to c$	**C**	**C**	**C**	$\mathbf{C} \equiv \lambda xyz \cdot xzy$
6	$(a\to b\to c)\to(a\to b)\to a\to c$	**S**	**S**	**S**	$\mathbf{S} \equiv \lambda xyz \cdot xz(yz)$ see Ex. 8B3
7	$(a\to a\to b)\to a\to b$	**W**	**W**	**W**	$\mathbf{W} \equiv \lambda xy \cdot xyy$
8	$a\to\ldots\to a\to a$ $\{m + 1 a\text{'s}, m \geq 2\}$	$\Pi_1^m, \ldots, \Pi_m^m$	$\Pi_1^m, \ldots, \Pi_m^m$	None	$\Pi_i^m \equiv \lambda x_1 \ldots x_m \cdot x_i$ see Ex. 8B4
9	$(a\to a)\to a\to a$	**I**, $\bar{0}, \bar{1}, \bar{2}, \ldots$	$\bar{0}, \bar{1}, \bar{2}, \ldots$	$\bar{2}, \bar{3}, \ldots$	$\bar{n} \equiv \lambda xy \cdot x^n y$
10	$(a\to b)\to a\to b$	**I**, $\bar{1}$	$\bar{1}$	$\bar{1}$	$\bar{1} \equiv \lambda xy \cdot xy$
11	$((a\to b)\to a)\to a$	None	None	None	τ is Peirce's law see Ex. 8B6
12	$((a\to a)\to a)\to a$	P_0, P_n, $Q_{n,i}$	P_0, P_n, $Q_{n,i}$	P_n, $Q_{n,i}$	$n \geq 1, 1 \leq i \leq n$; see Ex. 8B7 for P_0, P_n, $Q_{n,i}$

8C The search algorithm

The search strategy introduced informally in the last section will be crystallised into a formal algorithm in this one. The treatment will be in full detail as a preparation for the correctness-proof at the end of the chapter, but the core strategy is very simple as the examples in the last section have shown, and the reader who prefers to stay on an informal level should omit the present section and move on to the counting algorithm in 8D.

The method of the search algorithm will be to first look for members of

Long(τ) with depth $d = 0$, then $d = 1$, etc. The search will output a sequence $\mathscr{A}(\tau,0), \mathscr{A}(\tau,1), \mathscr{A}(\tau,2), \ldots$ of finite sets of expressions that will serve as "approximations" to these members. Those in $\mathscr{A}(\tau,d)$ will look like typed β-nf's with depth $\leq d$ but may have some "holes" to be filled in by the algorithm at a later stage. These holes will be represented by new symbols called *meta-variables* and the approximations will be called *nf-schemes.* (In Example 8B3 the expression on the right-hand side of (1) was in effect a nf-scheme and "U" and "V" were its meta-variables.)

To construct $\mathscr{A}(\tau,d+1)$ the approximations in $\mathscr{A}(\tau,d)$ will be extended by replacing their meta-variables by certain chosen nf-schemes with depth 1.

8C1 Definition (Nf-schemes) We assume given an infinite sequence of expressions called ***meta-variables***, distinct from each other and from term-variables. Meta-variables will be denoted by

$$\text{“}V\text{”}, \text{“}V_1\text{”}, \text{“}V_2\text{”}, \ldots.$$

Nf-schemes are defined like terms in 1A1 except that they may contain meta-variables or term-variables or both, and must satisfy the following restrictions:

(i) each nf-scheme is a β-nf without bound-variable clashes;
(ii) meta-variables do not bind, i.e. λV is forbidden;
(iii) in a composite nf-scheme meta-variables only occur in argument positions (as defined in 9A1);
(iv) each meta-variable in a nf-scheme occurs only once.

Proper nf-schemes are those that contain at least one meta-variable.

8C1.1 *Examples* The expression $\lambda xyz\cdot(xV_1V_2)$ is a nf-scheme. So also is the atomic expression V. But the following are not nf-schemes:

$$\lambda V\cdot V, \qquad Vxy, \qquad \lambda x\cdot V.$$

8C1.2 *Notes* (i) The reader familiar with "context" notation will see that a nf-scheme with k meta-variables is essentially a context containing k different kinds of hole.

(ii) The restrictions in 8C1 are imposed simply because no wider class of expressions will be needed below.

(iii) Non-proper nf-schemes are just terms (in β-nf without bound-variable clashes).

(iv) In what follows, a ***new*** variable or meta-variable will be one that has not been used earlier in the chapter.

(v) Most of the term-notation introduced in Chapter 1 extends to nf-schemes in an obvious way, and the same holds for the definition of depth in 8A6. But a few concepts need defining afresh and the next three definitions will cover these.

8C2 Definition A ***closed*** nf-scheme is one containing no free variables. (But possibly containing meta-variables, for example $\lambda x\cdot xV$ and V are closed.)

8C3 Definition (Typed nf-schemes, $\mathbb{TNS}(\Gamma)$) In this chapter a ***type-context*** Γ is any set of assignments whose subjects are meta-variables or variables, such that no subject receives more than one type in Γ (cf. 2A5). The set $\mathbb{TNS}(\Gamma)$ of all ***typed nf-schemes relative to*** Γ is defined just like $\mathbb{TT}(\Gamma)$ in 5A1 but satisfying the restrictions in the definition of "nf-scheme" (8C1).

The typed-term notation in Chapter 5 will be used here for typed nf-schemes also.

8C4 Definition (Long typed nf-schemes) A typed nf-scheme X^τ is ***long*** iff each component of X^τ with form

$$(zY_1 \dots Y_n)^\sigma \qquad (n \geq 0)$$

that is not in a function position has atomic type. (cf. Definition 8A7.)

8C4.1 *Example* The nf-scheme (i) below is long, though in contrast the term (ii) is not:

(i) $x^{(a\to b)\to c}Y^{a\to b}$,
(ii) $x^{(a\to b)\to c}z^{a\to b}$.

The description of the search algorithm will now be given: it will begin with a precise statement of what the algorithm does (in the following theorem), followed by the algorithm itself.

8C5 Search Theorem for Long(τ) (Ben-Yelles 1979 §§3.14–3.17.) *The search algorithm in* 8C6 *below accepts as input any composite type τ and outputs a finite or infinite sequence of sets $\mathscr{A}(\tau,d)$ $(d = 0,1,2,\dots)$ such that for all $d \geq 0$,*

(i) *each member of $\mathscr{A}(\tau,d)$ is a closed long typed nf-scheme with type τ, and is either*
  (a) *a proper nf-scheme with depth d, or*
  (b) *a term with depth $d-1$;*
(ii) *$\mathscr{A}(\tau,d)$ is finite;*
(iii) *$Long(\tau,d) \subseteq \mathscr{A}(\tau,0) \cup \dots \cup \mathscr{A}(\tau,d+1)$;*
(iv) *if we call the set of all terms in $\mathscr{A}(\tau,d)$ "$\mathscr{A}_{\text{terms}}(\tau,d)$", then*

$$Long(\tau) = \bigcup_{d\geq 0} \mathscr{A}_{\text{terms}}(\tau,d)$$

8C5.1 *Proof-note* Parts (i)–(ii) will be proved by induction on d in the notes accompanying the steps of the search algorithm.

Part (iii) states that the algorithm is "complete", i.e. finds everything it is looking for; its proof is postponed to 8F1.

Part (iv) follows easily from (i)–(iii).

8C6 Search Algorithm (Ben-Yelles 1979 §§3.14–17.) ***Input***: any type τ. If τ is an atom it has no inhabitants (by 8B5). If τ is composite, proceed as follows.

Step 0. *Choose any meta-variable V and define*

$$\mathscr{A}(\tau,0) = \{V^\tau\}.$$

Note. This $\mathscr{A}(\tau,0)$ trivially satisfies 8C5(i)–(ii). (The algorithm may be seen as building approximations to an unknown term M^τ; V^τ is the weakest approximation and represents the fact that at this stage we know nothing at all about M^τ other than its type.)

Step d + 1. *Assume $\mathscr{A}(\tau,d)$ has been defined and satisfies* 8C5(i)–(ii).

***Substep* I.** *If $\mathscr{A}(\tau,d) = \emptyset$ or no member of $\mathscr{A}(\tau,d)$ contains meta-variables then stop. (In this case $\mathscr{A}(\tau,d+1)$ is undefined and the algorithm's output is just the finite sequence $\mathscr{A}(\tau,0),\ldots,\mathscr{A}(\tau,d)$.)*

***Substep* II.** *Otherwise, begin the construction of $\mathscr{A}(\tau,d+1)$ by listing the proper nf-schemes in $\mathscr{A}(\tau,d)$ and applying* IIa–IIb *below to each one.*

***Subsubstep* IIa.** *Given any proper $X^\tau \in \mathscr{A}(\tau,d)$, list the meta-variables in X^τ; say they are*

$$V_1^{\rho_1},\ldots,V_q^{\rho_q} \qquad (q \geq 1),$$

and apply IIa1–IIa2 *to each one.*

***Part* IIa1.** *Given any meta-variable V^ρ in an $X^\tau \in \mathscr{A}(\tau,d)$, say*

$$(1) \qquad \rho \equiv \sigma_1 \to \ldots \to \sigma_m \to a \qquad (m \geq 0);$$

first list all $i \leq m$ for which $Tail(\sigma_i) \cong \underline{a} \cong Tail(\rho)$. (If there are none or $m = 0$, go direct to IIa2.*) For each such i, σ_i has form*

$$(2) \qquad \sigma_i \equiv \sigma_{i,1} \to \ldots \to \sigma_{i,n_i} \to a \qquad (n_i \geq 0).$$

Define

$$(3) \qquad Y_i^\rho \equiv \lambda x_1^{\sigma_1} \ldots x_m^{\sigma_m} \cdot (x_i^{\sigma_i} V_{i,1}^{\sigma_{i,1}} \ldots V_{i,n_i}^{\sigma_{i,n_i}})^a,$$

where the x's and V's are distinct new variables and meta-variables. (Y_i^ρ is called a **suitable replacement** *for V^ρ.)*

***Part* IIa2.** *List the abstractors that cover the (unique) occurrence of V^ρ in X^τ, in the order they occur in X^τ from left to right; say they are*

$$(4) \qquad \underline{\lambda z_1^{\zeta_1}},\ldots,\underline{\lambda z_t^{\zeta_t}} \qquad (t \geq 0).$$

List all $j \leq t$ (if any) such that Tail $(\zeta_j) \cong a$. For each such j, ζ_j has form

$$(5) \qquad \zeta_j \equiv \zeta_{j,1} \to \ldots \to \zeta_{j,h_j} \to a \qquad (h_j \geq 0).$$

Define

$$(6) \qquad Z_j^\rho \equiv \lambda x_1^{\sigma_1} \ldots x_m^{\sigma_m} \cdot (z_j^{\zeta_j} V_{j,1}^{\zeta_{j,1}} \ldots V_{j,h_j}^{\zeta_{j,h_j}})^a,$$

where the x's and V's are distinct and new. (Z_j^ρ is called a **suitable replacement** *for V^ρ.)*

Notes. (i) It is easy to see that each Y_i^ρ defined in IIa1 and each Z_j^ρ defined in IIa2 is a long nf-scheme with depth ≤ 1 and the same type as V^ρ, so V^ρ can be replaced by Y_i^ρ or Z_j^ρ in X^τ without violating type-restrictions or the restrictions in the definition of long nf-scheme (8C1, 8C3–4). And the result of making such a replacement will clearly have depth $\leq d+1$.

(ii) Y_i^ρ and Z_j^ρ need not contain meta-variables. In fact Y_i^ρ is without meta-variables iff σ_i is an atom, and in this case

$$Y_i^\rho \equiv \lambda x_1^{\sigma_1} \dots x_m^{\sigma_m} \cdot x_i^{\sigma_i}.$$

Similarly Z_j^ρ is without meta-variables iff ζ_j is an atom, and in this case

$$Z_j^\rho \equiv \lambda x_1^{\sigma_1} \dots x_m^{\sigma_m} \cdot z_j^{\zeta_j}.$$

Hence if Y_i^ρ or Z_j^ρ is without meta-variables its depth is 0 and if V^ρ is replaced by it then $Depth(X^\tau)$ will not increase.

(iii) The total number of suitable replacements (Y's and Z's) for V^ρ is at most $m+t$.

> ***Subsubstep* IIb.** *When* IIa1–IIa2 *have been applied to all the meta-variables in* X^τ *the result is a list of suitable replacements for each* V_i *in* X^τ.
>
> *If one or more of* $V_1, \dots, V_q$ *has no suitable replacements, abandon* X^τ, *calling it a* ***reject****, and start applying Substep* II *to the next member of* $\mathscr{A}(\tau, d)$. *(A reject will generate no members of* $\mathscr{A}(\tau, d+1)$.)
>
> *If all of* $V_1, \dots, V_q$ *in* X^τ *have suitable replacements,* X^τ *is called* ***extendable****; in this case list all possible sequences*
>
> (7) $\langle W_1^{\rho_1}, \dots, W_q^{\rho_q} \rangle$
>
> *where* W_i *is a suitable replacement for* V_i *for* $i = 1, \dots, q$. *For each sequence* (7) *construct a new nf-scheme* $X^{*\tau}$ *from* X^τ *by simultaneously replacing* V_i *by* W_i *in* X^τ *for* $i = 1, \dots, q$. *(Call each sequence (7) a* ***suitable multi-replacement*** *and call* $X^{*\tau}$ *an* ***extension*** *of* X^τ*; if this extension is a term call it a* ***success****.)*

Notes. (i) The number of extensions of X^τ is finite since each is generated by a suitable multi-replacement and the number of these is clearly finite (for a given X^τ).

(ii) To construct an extension each meta-variable in X^τ is replaced by either a nf-scheme with depth 1 or a term with depth 0. If the latter holds for all the meta-variables in X^τ the extension has depth $\leq d$ and is a success. If the former holds for at least one meta-variable, the extension has depth $\leq d+1$ and contains meta-variables.

> ***Substep* III.** *Finally, if the set* $\mathscr{A}(\tau, d)$ *contains at least one proper nf-scheme, define* $\mathscr{A}(\tau, d+1)$ *to be the set containing all the extensions of all the extendable proper nf-schemes in* $\mathscr{A}(\tau, d)$.

Notes. (i) By the notes after IIa and IIb above it is easy to check that $\mathscr{A}(\tau, d+1)$ satisfies 8C5(i) and (ii).

(ii) By the way, $\mathscr{A}(\tau, d+1)$ does not contain $\mathscr{A}(\tau, d)$ as a subset. □

8C6.1 *Example* (cf. Example 8B3.) Applying the search algorithm to the type

$$\tau \equiv (a{\to}b{\to}c){\to}(a{\to}b){\to}a{\to}c$$

produces the following sets:

$$\begin{aligned}
\mathscr{A}(\tau,0) &= \{V^{\tau}\},\\
\mathscr{A}(\tau,1) &= \{\lambda x_1^{a\to b\to c}x_2^{a\to b}x_3^{a}\cdot x_1^{a\to b\to c}V_1^{a}V_2^{b}\},\\
\mathscr{A}(\tau,2) &= \{\lambda x_1^{a\to b\to c}x_2^{a\to b}x_3^{a}\cdot x_1^{a\to b\to c}x_3^{a}(x_2^{a\to b}V_3^{a})\},\\
\mathscr{A}(\tau,3) &= \{\lambda x_1^{a\to b\to c}x_2^{a\to b}x_3^{a}\cdot x_1^{a\to b\to c}x_3^{a}(x_2^{a\to b}x_3^{a})\}.
\end{aligned}$$

8C6.2 *Example* (cf. Example 8B4.) Applying the search algorithm to the type

$$\tau \equiv a{\to}\ldots{\to}a{\to}a$$

(with $m+1$ a's) produces the following sets:

$$\begin{aligned}
\mathscr{A}(\tau,0) &= \{V^{\tau}\},\\
\mathscr{A}(\tau,1) &= \{(\lambda x_1^{a}\ldots x_m^{a}\cdot x_1^{a}),\ldots,(\lambda x_1^{a}\ldots x_m^{a}\cdot x_m^{a})\}.
\end{aligned}$$

8C6.3 *Example* (cf. Example 8B6.) Applying the search algorithm to the type

$$\tau \equiv ((a{\to}b){\to}a){\to}a$$

produces the following sets:

$$\begin{aligned}
\mathscr{A}(\tau,0) &= \{V^{\tau}\},\\
\mathscr{A}(\tau,1) &= \{\lambda x_1^{(a\to b)\to a}\cdot x_1^{(a\to b)\to a}V_1^{a\to b}\},\\
\mathscr{A}(\tau,2) &= \emptyset.
\end{aligned}$$

8C6.4 *Exercise** List members of the sets $\mathscr{A}(\tau,0),\mathscr{A}(\tau,1),\ldots$ for all the types in Table 8B7a.

8C6.5 *Comments* (i) Besides Ben-Yelles' 1979 search algorithm there are others in Zaionc 1985 and 1988 and in Takahashi, Akama and Hirokawa 1994. Also procedures essentially equivalent to the main parts of 8C6 are used in some decision-algorithms for provability in intuitionist logic, cf. 6B7.3, and in algorithms that seek to unify pairs of typed λ-terms, for example the original one in Huet 1975 §3.

(ii) The algorithm in 8C6 can be viewed as a context-free grammar for generating a language whose expressions are exactly the inhabitants of τ. In the standard notation for context-free grammars (see for example Hopcroft and Ullman 1979 Ch. 4) the meta-variables in 8C6 would be called non-terminal variables and each suitable replacement defined in Subsubstep IIa of 8C6 would determine a production in the grammar. The set of all such productions need not be finite, however, so the original definition of "grammar" must be relaxed if this view is to be made precise. This view was taken in Huet 1975 §3, Zaionc 1985 §3 and 1988 §5, and was used and analysed in detail in Takahashi, Akama and Hirokawa 1994.

(iii) A very smooth description of a search algorithm in terms of solving sets of polynomial equations over the domain $\{0,1,2,\ldots,\infty\}$ is in Zaionc 199-.

8D The Counting algorithm

In this section the search algorithm will be extended to count and enumerate normal inhabitants. The extension will be very simple indeed to state; but the proof that it works will need some care and will be postponed to Sections 8E–F.

As noted in 8A2, it does not matter whether typed or untyped inhabitants are counted since there is a one-to-one correspondence between the two: in this section "$Long(\tau)$" and "$Nhabs(\tau)$" will denote sets of typed terms.

8D1 Definition (i) For the sets $\mathscr{A}(\tau, d)$ and $\mathscr{A}_{\text{terms}}(\tau, d)$ introduced in 8C5, define

$$\begin{aligned} \mathscr{A}(\tau, \leq d) &= \mathscr{A}(\tau, 0) \cup \ldots \cup \mathscr{A}(\tau, d), \\ \mathscr{A}_{\text{terms}}(\tau, \leq d) &= \mathscr{A}_{\text{terms}}(\tau, 0) \cup \ldots \cup \mathscr{A}_{\text{terms}}(\tau, d). \end{aligned}$$

(ii) For any τ, recall from 2A2 that $|\tau|$ is the number of atom-occurrences in τ and $\|\tau\|$ is the number of distinct atoms in τ; define

$$\mathbb{D}(\tau) = |\tau| \times \|\tau\|.$$

8D2 Stretching Lemma *If $Long(\tau)$ has a member M^{τ} with depth $d \geq \|\tau\|$ then it has members with depths greater than any given integer, and hence is infinite.*

Proof-note The proof will be given in 8F2 (cf. Ben-Yelles 1979 §§3.20–3.21). It will show that if M^{τ} is in $Long(\tau)$ and has depth $d \geq \|\tau\|$ then M^{τ} must contain two distinct components $\underline{B}$ and $\underline{B}'$ with the same type and with one inside the other. Then replacing the smaller one by the larger will change M^{τ} to a new term $M^{*\tau}$ deeper than M^{τ}, and it will be easy to check that $M^{*\tau}$ is a genuine typed term and is in $Long(\tau)$. Then a similar replacement in $M^{*\tau}$ will change it to a still deeper term, and so on.[1]

8D3 Shrinking Lemma *If $Long(\tau)$ has a member M^{τ} with depth $\geq \mathbb{D}(\tau)$ then it has a member N^{τ} with*

$$\mathbb{D}(\tau) - \|\tau\| \leq Depth(N^{\tau}) < \mathbb{D}(\tau).$$

Proof-note The proof will be given in 8F3 (cf. Ben-Yelles 1979 Thm. 3.28). Just as for the previous lemma, M^{τ} will be seen to contain two components $\underline{B}$ and $\underline{B}'$ with the same type and one inside the other; but now $M^{*\tau}$ will be constructed by replacing the larger by the smaller. A problem is that if $\underline{B}$ and $\underline{B}'$ are not chosen carefully this replacement risks deleting some abstractors and giving a non-closed $M^{*\tau}$: to prevent this, and to ensure that the depth of $M^{*\tau}$ lies in the range required, $\underline{B}$ and $\underline{B}'$ will be chosen only after a close analysis of the structure of M^{τ}.[2]

[1] This lemma is very like the pumping lemma in the theory of context-free grammars and regular languages, see for example Hopcroft and Ullman 1979 §3.1 and Comment 8C6.5(ii) above. And the next lemma will also be very like one in that theory, see Hopcroft and Ullman 1979 §3.3 Theorem 3.7, though its proof here will be more complicated due to the presence of bound variables. For a precise statement of the analogy between typed λ-calculus and the theory of context-free grammars see Takahashi et al. 1994, where a generalised concept of context-free grammar is introduced and generalizations of the classical results are proved which imply the corresponding λ-results.

[2] Ben-Yelles 1979 Thm. 3.28, whose lines the proof in 8F3 will follow, was actually slightly weaker than the above lemma. The first proof of a full-strength shrinking lemma was outlined in Hirokawa 1993c; it was different from the one to be given in 8F3.

8D3.1 *Corollary* *If* $Long(\tau)$ *has a member* M^{τ} *with depth* $\geq \mathbb{D}(\tau)$ *then it has a member* N^{τ} *with*

$$\|\tau\| \leq Depth(N^{\tau}) < \mathbb{D}(\tau).$$

Proof If $Long(\tau)$ has a member then τ is composite by 8B5. Hence $|\tau| \geq 2$, so

$$\mathbb{D}(\tau) - \|\tau\| \geq 2\|\tau\| - \|\tau\| = \|\tau\|.$$

The result then follows by the shrinking lemma. □

8D4 Theorem (Counting long normal inhabitants) (Ben-Yelles 1979 Cor. 3.33.) *When given a type* τ *the algorithm in* 8D5 *below outputs* $\#(Long(\tau))$ *and an enumeration of* $Long(\tau)$.

Proof See the notes in brackets in the following algorithm. □

8D5 Counting Algorithm for $\boldsymbol{Long(\tau)}$ *If* τ *is an atom,* $Long(\tau)$ *is empty by* 8B5. *If* τ *is composite, apply the search algorithm* (8C6) *to* τ*; this outputs a finite or infinite sequence of sets*

$$\mathscr{A}(\tau, d) \qquad (d = 0, 1, 2, \ldots).$$

Stop the search algorithm at $d = \mathbb{D}(\tau)$ *and enumerate* $\mathscr{A}_{\text{terms}}(\tau, \leq \mathbb{D}(\tau))$.

[By 8C5 this set is finite and contains all members of $Long(\tau)$ with depth $< \mathbb{D}(\tau)$.]

***Case* I**: $\mathscr{A}_{\text{terms}}(\tau, \leq \mathbb{D}(\tau)) = \emptyset$. *Then* $Long(\tau) = \emptyset$.

[By 8D3, if $Long(\tau)$ had a member with depth $\geq \mathbb{D}(\tau)$ it would have one with depth $< \mathbb{D}(\tau)$.]

***Case* II**: $\mathscr{A}_{\text{terms}}(\tau, \leq \mathbb{D}(\tau))$ *has a member with depth* $\geq \|\tau\|$. *Then by* 8D2 $Long(\tau)$ *is infinite. To enumerate* $Long(\tau)$, *apply the search algorithm to enumerate* $\mathscr{A}_{\text{terms}}(\tau, d)$ *for* $d = 0, 1, 2, \ldots$.

[By 8C5(iv) the union of these sets is $Long(\tau)$.]

***Case* III**: $\mathscr{A}_{\text{terms}}(\tau, \leq \mathbb{D}(\tau))$ *has members but they all have depth* $< \|\tau\|$. *Then* $Long(\tau) = \mathscr{A}_{\text{terms}}(\tau, \leq \mathbb{D}(\tau))$, *which is finite.*

[The only way for $Long(\tau)$ to differ from this set would be for $Long(\tau)$ to have members with depth $d \geq \mathbb{D}(\tau)$, but by 8D3.1 it would then have a member with $\|\tau\| \leq d < \mathbb{D}(\tau)$ contrary to the assumption of the present case.] □

8D5.1 *Corollary* (Counting $\beta\eta$-normal inhabitants) *The algorithm in* 8D5 *can be used to count and enumerate* $Nhabs_{\eta}(\tau)$ *for every* τ.

Proof By 8A10 the members of $Nhabs_{\eta}(\tau)$ are the η-nf's of those of $Long(\tau)$. And by 8A10(iii), $\#_{\eta}(\tau) = \#(Nhabs_{\eta}(\tau)) = \#(Long(\tau))$. □

8D5.2 *Corollary* (Emptiness test) *The algorithm in* 8D5 *can be used to decide whether a type* τ *has no inhabitants.*

Proof By 8A13(i), $Habs(\tau) = \emptyset \Leftrightarrow \#(Nhabs(\tau)) = \#(\tau) = 0$. And by 8A10(ii) and (iii), $\#(\tau) = 0 \Leftrightarrow \#(Long(\tau)) = 0$. □

8D6 Theorem (Counting all normal inhabitants) (Ben-Yelles 1979 Ch. 3.) *When given a type τ the algorithm in 8D7 below outputs $\#(\tau)$ and an enumeration of the set $Nhabs(\tau)$ of all the β-normal inhabitants of τ.*

8D7 Counting Algorithm for *Nhabs*(τ) *If τ is an atom then $Nhabs(\tau)$ is empty by* 8B5. *If τ is composite, apply Algorithm* 8D5 *to count $Long(\tau)$.*

***Case* I**: *If $Long(\tau) = \emptyset$ then $Nhabs(\tau) = \emptyset$.* [By 8A8.1.]

***Case* II**: *If $Long(\tau) \neq \emptyset$ then $Nhabs(\tau)$ is counted and enumerated by counting and enumerating $Long(\tau)$ and enumerating the η-family of each member of $Long(\tau)$.*

[By 8A10 these η-families are finite and their union is $Nhabs(\tau)$.]

Before ending this section we shall digress from the main theme to look at an interesting application of the counting algorithm to types that contain only one atom. Such types have been studied and used as tools by several workers, for example see Statman 1979a, 1979b and 1980, Dekkers 1988, and Zaionc 1987b and 1990.

8D8 Definition A type τ will be called ***monatomic*** iff $\|\tau\| = 1$, i.e. iff only one atom occurs in τ.

8D9 Theorem (Ben-Yelles 1979 §3.25.) *Let τ be a monatomic type with the form $\tau \equiv \tau_1 \to \ldots \tau_m \to a$ $(m \geq 0)$. Then*

(i) *if at least one τ_i is composite, $\#(\tau)$ is either ∞ or 0;*
(ii) *if $\tau_1 \equiv \ldots \equiv \tau_m \equiv a$ then $\#(\tau) = m$.*

Proof Part (ii) is just 8B4. To prove (i), assume $Nhabs(\tau)$ is finite and non-empty and assume τ has form

$$\tau \equiv \tau_1 \to \ldots \to \tau_m \to a$$

with $m \geq 1$ and at least one premise composite. By 8A8 $Long(\tau)$ is also finite and has a member M^τ. By 8D2, $Depth(M^\tau) < \|\tau\| = 1$, so M^τ must have form

$$M^\tau \equiv \lambda x_1^{\tau_1} \ldots x_m^{\tau_m} \cdot x_p^{\tau_p} \qquad (1 \leq p \leq m).$$

And $\tau_p \equiv a$ since M^τ is long. Choose a composite premise of τ; say it is τ_i and has form

$$\tau_i \equiv \tau_{i,1} \to \ldots \to \tau_{i,m_i} \to a \qquad (m_i \geq 1).$$

For $j = 1, \ldots, m_i$ each $\tau_{i,j}$ has form

$$\tau_{i,j} \equiv \tau_{i,j,1} \to \ldots \to \tau_{i,j,m_{i,j}} \to a \qquad (m_{i,j} \geq 0).$$

For each $j \leq m_i$ choose distinct new variables $y_1, \ldots, y_{m_{i,j}}$ and define

$$P_j^{\tau_{i,j}} \equiv \lambda y_1^{\tau_{i,j,1}} \ldots y_{m_{i,j}}{}^{\tau_{i,j,m_{i,j}}} \cdot x_p^a$$

where x_p^a is the rightmost variable in M^τ (and is therefore distinct from the y's). Then define

$$N^\tau \equiv \lambda x_1^{\tau_1} \dots x_m^{\tau_m} \cdot (x_i^{\tau_i} P_1^{\tau_{i,1}} \dots P_{m_i}{}^{\tau_{i,m_i}})^a.$$

Clearly $N^\tau \in Long(\tau)$. But $Depth(N^\tau) \geq 1$ since N^τ contains $m_i \geq 1$ arguments. Hence $Long(\tau)$ is infinite by 8D2. □

8D10 Problems The above algorithms have solved the problem of counting normal inhabitants. But the following related problems are still open.

(i) ***Counting principal normal inhabitants*** (***Nprinc***(τ), ***Nprinc***$_\eta(\tau)$). I know of no way to count these sets that covers the case when $Nhabs(\tau)$ is infinite. Hirokawa 1991a contains a structural analysis of principal deductions that may help. It is applied to give interesting results in Hirokawa 1991a–c, 1992b and 1993a–b, and these results include stating some sufficient conditions for $Nprinc(\tau)$ to have only one member.

(ii) ***Counting principal inhabitants in general*** (***Princ***(τ)). Each member of $Princ(\tau)$ must have a β-nf and that nf must have type τ, but since β-reduction does not preserve principality there is no direct connection between $Princ(\tau)$ and $Nprinc(\tau)$. By the way, if $Nprinc(\tau) = \emptyset$ but $Princ(\tau) \neq \emptyset$ then τ has the curious property of being the principal type of a non-normal form but not of a normal form. (An example of such a type is $a \to a \to a$, see 8A13(iii).) Is there any neat characterization of the types that have this property?

(iii) ***Counting inhabitants in restricted classes of terms***, for example the λI-terms, BCKλ-terms or BCIλ-terms introduced in 1D. The search algorithm would give no trouble in such a class but the crucial shrinking lemma (8D3) would need a new proof for each restricted class, and indeed might fail for some classes. An example of a result for a restricted class is the proof in Komori and Hirokawa 1993 that for BCKλ-terms $\#(\tau)$ is always finite. An example of a currently unsolved problem for a restricted class is that of finding a decision-procedure for the Hilbert-style logic $T_\to$ whose axioms are the principal types of **B**, **B**$'$, **I**, **W** (see 7D11(ii)). This is equivalent to finding an algorithm to decide whether a given type τ has any inhabitants that are applicative combinations of these four terms.

8D11 Comment (Efficiency) At first glance the algorithms in this section may seem remarkably efficient, as they terminate in only $|\tau| \times \|\tau\|$ steps. But this impression is totally misleading, as each one of these steps involves listing a set $\mathscr{A}(\tau, d)$ which, although finite, may be very large indeed. In fact any counting algorithm will decide as a special case whether $Nhabs(\tau)$ is non-empty, which is equivalent to deciding whether τ is provable in Intuitionist logic (by 6B7.2), and this decision problem is polynomial-space complete (Statman 1979a Prop. 4).

8E The structure of a nf-scheme

The earlier sections left the stretching and shrinking lemmas unproved (8D2, 8D3), as well as the "completeness" part of the search theorem for $Long(\tau)$ (8C5 (iii)). The aim of the next section will be to fill in these gaps, and the present one

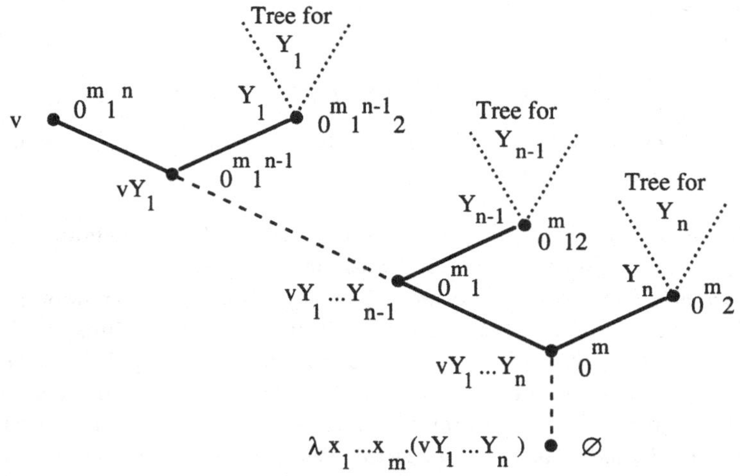

Fig. 8E1a.

will lay the foundation by analysing the structure of an arbitrary long typed nf-scheme.

A key role will be played by a slightly strengthened form of the subformula property (2B3.1). That property says in effect that the types of all the components of a closed β-nf M^τ are subtypes of τ, and this implies that all the successes produced by the search algorithm, growing deeper and deeper, have the types of their components drawn from the same fixed finite set. This limitation is the source of the bounds in the stretching and shrinking lemmas.

8E1 Notation Recall that a nf-scheme is essentially a β-nf that may contain meta-variables under certain restrictions, see Definitions 8C1 (untyped) and 8C3 (typed). The early parts of the present section will apply to both typed and untyped nf-schemes, so types will be omitted when nf-schemes are written. But later parts will apply only to typed nf-schemes and types will then be displayed.

We shall need the notation for positions, components and construction-trees introduced in 9A1–4.

In writing positions a sequence of n 0's may be written as 0^n (with $0^0 = \emptyset$), and similarly for 1's and 2's.

Recall from 8A5 that every non-atomic nf-scheme X can be expressed uniquely in the form

(1) $\quad X \equiv \lambda x_1 \dots x_m{\cdot}v Y_1 \dots Y_n \qquad (m+n \geq 1),$

where v is one of $x_1, \dots, x_m$ if X is closed. The construction-tree of such an X is shown in Fig. 8E1a. The ***head*** and ***arguments*** of X are $\underline{v}$ and $\underline{Y}_1, \dots, \underline{Y}_n$. (If X is an atom its head is X and it has no arguments.) Note that the position of $\underline{Y}_i$ is

(2) $\quad 0^m 1^{n-i} 2 \qquad (1 \leq i \leq n).$

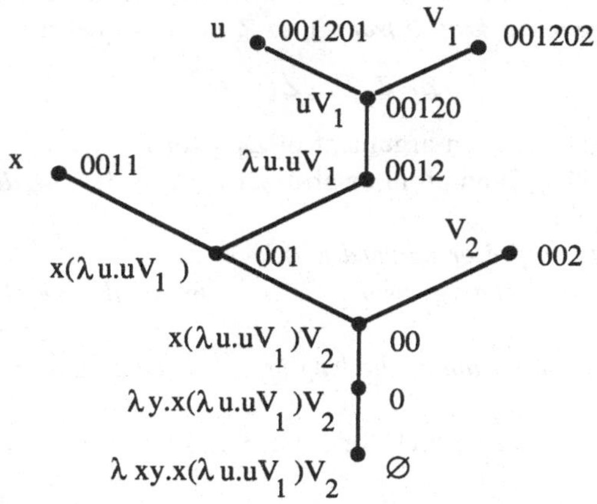

Fig. 8E2.1a. Construction-tree for $\lambda xy\cdot x(\lambda u\cdot uV_1)V_2$

8E2 Definition (Subarguments) A ***subargument*** of a typed or untyped nf-scheme X is a component that is an argument of X or an argument of a proper component of X.

8E2.1 *Lemma A component* $\underline{Y}$ *of a typed or untyped nf-scheme* X *is a subargument iff its position is not* $\emptyset$ *and the last symbol in its position is* 2.

Proof Induction on $|X|$. As an example, consider the subarguments in the tree in Fig. 8E2.1a. □

8E2.2 *Note* (i) All occurrences of meta-variables in a composite nf-scheme are subarguments (by restriction 8C1(iii) in the definition of nf-scheme).

(ii) A subargument of a subargument of X is a subargument of X.

8E3 Definition (Relative depth) The ***2-length*** of a position-string p is the number of 2's in p. The ***depth in*** X of a subargument $\underline{Z}$ of X is the 2-length of its position (i.e. the number of right-hand choices made when travelling up the tree of X from the bottom node to $\underline{Z}$, cf. Fig. 8E2.1a).

8E3.1 *Lemma Let* X *be a typed or untyped nf-scheme with* $Depth(X) \geq 1$. *(Depth is defined in* 8A6.) *Then*

(i) *$Depth(X)$ is the maximum of the depths in* X *of all subarguments of* X,

(ii) X *has at least one subargument whose depth in* X *is the same as* $Depth(X)$, *and each such subargument is an atom or abstracted atom.*

Proof By induction on $|X|$, using 8A6. □

8E4 Definition (Argument-branch) If $\underline{Z}$ is a subargument of a typed or untyped nf-scheme X, the ***argument-branch from*** $\underline{X}$ ***to*** $\underline{Z}$ is the sequence

$$\langle \underline{Z}_0, \underline{Z}_1, \dots, \underline{Z}_k \rangle \qquad (k \geq 1)$$

such that $\underline{Z}_0 \equiv \underline{X}$ and $\underline{Z}_i$ is an argument of $\underline{Z}_{i-1}$ for $i = 1, \dots, k$, and $\underline{Z}_k \equiv \underline{Z}$. It is called ***unextendable*** iff $\underline{Z}$ is an atom or abstracted atom. Its ***length*** is k (not $k+1$).

8E4.1 *Lemma For any typed or untyped nf-scheme X:*

(i) *the depth in X of a subargument* $\underline{Z}$ *is the same as the length of the argument-branch from* $\underline{X}$ *to* $\underline{Z}$*;*

(ii) *Depth(X) is the maximum of the lengths of all the argument-branches in X.*

Proof For (i) use induction on $|X|$; for (ii) use 8E3.1. □

8E5 Definition (IA, CA) Let $\underline{Z}$ be a subargument of a typed or untyped nf-scheme X; say

$$Z \equiv \lambda x_1 \dots x_m \cdot y Z_1 \dots Z_n \qquad (m \geq 0, n \geq 0).$$

The ***Initial Abstractors sequence IA(Z)*** is the (possibly empty) sequence

$$IA(Z) = \langle x_1, \dots, x_m \rangle.$$

The ***Covering Abstractors sequence CA(Z,X)*** is defined to be

$$CA(\underline{Z}, X) = \langle z_1, \dots, z_q \rangle,$$

where $\underline{\lambda z_1}, \dots, \underline{\lambda z_q}$ are the abstractors in X whose scopes contain $\underline{Z}$, written in the order they occur in X from left to right. Also define:

$$Length(IA(Z)) = m, \qquad Length(CA(\underline{Z}, X)) = q.$$

8E5.1 *Note* (i) If X has no bound-variable clashes the member of $IA(Z)$ are distinct and so are those of $CA(\underline{Z}, X)$.

(ii) $IA(Z)$ and $CA(\underline{Z}, X)$ are sequences of variables not components.

(iii) For typed nf-schemes each variable in $IA(Z)$ or $CA(\underline{Z}, X)$ is typed.

(iv) If the argument-branch from $\underline{X}$ to $\underline{Z}$ is $\langle \underline{Z}_0, \dots, \underline{Z}_k \rangle$ $(k \geq 1)$, then

$$CA(\underline{Z}, X) = IA(Z_0) * \dots * IA(Z_{k-1})$$

where "$*$" denotes concatenation of sequences. (Because the abstractors whose scopes contain $\underline{Z}$ are exactly the initial abstractors of $\underline{Z}_0, \dots, \underline{Z}_{k-1}$.)

The next definition and lemma will have meaning for typed nf-schemes only. The lemma will be the strengthened form of the subformula property mentioned at the start of the section, and will lead to a computation of upper bounds for several key sequences and sets. Part of it will use notation from 9E.

8E6 Definition (IAT) Let $\underline{Z}^\sigma$ be a subargument of a typed nf-scheme X^τ; say

$$Z^\sigma \equiv \lambda x_1^{\sigma_1} \dots x_m^{\sigma_m} \cdot y Z_1 \dots Z_n \qquad (m \geq 0, n \geq 0).$$

The ***Initial Abstractors' Types sequence*** $IAT(Z^\sigma)$ is defined to be

$$IAT(Z^\sigma) = \langle \sigma_1, \ldots, \sigma_m \rangle;$$

also define

$$Length(IAT(Z^\sigma)) = m.$$

8E7 Enhanced Subformula Lemma (cf. Ben-Yelles 1979 Lemma 3.31.) *If* $\underline{Z}^\sigma$ *is a subargument of a closed long typed nf-scheme* X^τ, *then*

(i) σ *occurs as a positive subpremise in* τ *(as defined in 9E6–8),*
(ii) *if* σ *is an atom,* $IAT(Z^\sigma) = \emptyset$,
(iii) *if* σ *is composite,* $IAT(Z^\sigma) \in NSS(\tau)$ *(defined in 9E9),*
(iv) $NSS(\sigma) \subseteq NSS(\tau)$.

Proof Since Z^σ is long, $IAT(Z^\sigma)$ coincides with the sequence of all premises of σ, so (ii) holds. Also if σ is composite we have

(1) $\quad IAT(Z^\sigma) \in NSS(\sigma)$

by the definition of $NSS(\sigma)$ in 9E9. Now (i) implies (iv) by 9E9.2(iii), and (iv) and (1) imply (iii). Hence only (i) remains to be proved.

The proof of (i) is an induction on $|X^\tau|$. To make this work we shall prove

(2) $\left\{\begin{array}{l} \text{If } X^\tau \text{ is a long member of } \mathbb{TNS}(\Gamma) \text{ (defined in 8C3) and} \\ \qquad \Gamma = \{u_1{:}\theta_1, \ldots, u_p{:}\theta_p, V_1{:}\phi_1, \ldots, V_q{:}\phi_q\} \\ \text{and } \underline{Z}^\sigma \text{ is a subargument of } X^\tau, \text{ then } \sigma \text{ occurs as a positive} \\ \text{subpremise of} \\ \qquad \theta_1 \to \ldots \to \theta_p \to \tau. \end{array}\right.$

Basis. If X^τ is an atom the conclusion of (2) holds vacuously.

Induction step. Let X^τ have form

(3) $\quad (\lambda x_1^{\tau_1} \ldots x_m^{\tau_m} \cdot (y^{(\rho_1 \to \ldots \to \rho_n \to e)} X_1^{\rho_1} \ldots X_n^{\rho_n})^e)^{(\tau_1 \to \ldots \to \tau_m \to e)}$

where $m, n \geq 0$ and $\tau \equiv \tau_1 \to \ldots \to \tau_m \to e$. Then either $y \equiv x_i$ for some $i \leq m$ or $y \equiv u_i$ for some $i \leq p$. If $y \equiv x_i$ then

(4) $\quad \tau_i \equiv \rho_1 \to \ldots \to \rho_n \to e$

and if $y \equiv u_i$ then

(5) $\quad \theta_i \equiv \rho_1 \to \ldots \to \rho_n \to e.$

In both cases each of $\rho_1, \ldots, \rho_n$ occurs as a positive subpremise of

(6) $\quad \theta_1 \to \ldots \to \theta_p \to \tau.$

Now $\underline{Z}^\sigma$ must be in an $\underline{X}_j^{\rho_j}$ for some $j \leq n$. If $\underline{Z}^\sigma \equiv \underline{X}_j^{\rho_j}$ then $\sigma \equiv \rho_j$ and the conclusion of (2) follows by the above. Next, suppose $\underline{Z}^\sigma$ is a subargument of $\underline{X}_j^{\rho_j}$. Note that

$$X_j^{\rho_j} \in \mathbb{TNS}(\{x_1{:}\tau_1, \ldots, x_m{:}\tau_m\} \cup \Gamma).$$

Hence, by the induction hypothesis, σ occurs as a positive subpremise of

$$\tau_1 \to \ldots \to \tau_m \to \theta_1 \to \ldots \to \theta_p \to \rho_j.$$

Thus σ occurs as a positive subpremise of (6), giving (2). □

8E7.1 *Corollary If X^τ is a closed long typed nf-scheme, the type of each meta-variable in X^τ either occurs as a positive subpremise of τ or is τ itself.*

Proof By 8E2.2(i) and 8E7(i). □

The main effect of 8E7 is to connect $IAT(Z^\sigma)$, which in general depends on the structure of Z^σ and hence implicitly on that of X^τ, with $NSS(\tau)$ which depends on τ and nothing else. The next corollary will use this to deduce reasonably neat bounds for $IA(\underline{Z}^\sigma)$ and $CA(\underline{Z}^\sigma, X^\tau)$.

8E7.2 *Corollary If X^τ is a closed long typed nf-scheme and $\underline{Z}^\sigma$ is a subargument of X^τ or $\underline{Z}^\sigma \equiv \underline{X}^\tau$, then*

(i) $Length(IA(Z^\sigma)) = Length(IAT(Z^\sigma)) \leq |\tau| - 1$,
(ii) $Length(CA(\underline{Z}^\sigma, X^\tau)) \leq (|\tau| - 1) \times Depth(X^\tau)$.

Further, if $\underline{\lambda v}_1^{\rho_1}, \ldots, \underline{\lambda v}_r^{\rho_r}$ are all the abstractors in X^τ (not just its initial ones), then

(iii) $\{\rho_1, \ldots, \rho_r\}$ *has* $\leq |\tau| - 1$ *distinct members.*

Proof For (i): $Length(IAT(Z^\sigma)) \leq |\tau| - 1$ by 8E7(iii) and 9E9.3(iv).

For (ii): If $\underline{Z} \equiv \underline{X}$ the left side of (ii) is 0. If $\underline{Z} \not\equiv \underline{X}$ let $\langle \underline{Z}_0, \ldots, \underline{Z}_k \rangle$ $(k \geq 1)$ be the argument-branch from $\underline{X}$ to $\underline{Z}$; then by 8E5.1(iv)

$$\begin{aligned} Length(CA(\underline{Z}, X)) &= Length(IA(Z_0)) + \cdots + Length(IA(Z_{k-1})) \\ &\leq k(|\tau| - 1) \end{aligned}$$

by (i). But $Depth(X) \geq k$ by 8E4.1(ii), so (ii) holds.

For (iii): Each ρ_i is in $IAT(X^\tau)$ or in $IAT(Y^\theta)$ for some subargument Y^θ of X^τ; and in both cases $\rho_i \in \bigcup NSS(\tau)$ (in the former case trivially, and in the latter case by 8E7(iii)). Then use 9E9.3(iii). □

8E7.3 *Exercise** Show that if τ is composite and $d \geq 1$ and $\mathscr{A}(\tau, d)$ is defined, then

(i) each $X^\tau \in \mathscr{A}(\tau, d)$ contains $\leq |\tau|^d$ meta-variables,
(ii) $\#(\mathscr{A}(\tau, d)) < (d \times |\tau|)^{(|\tau|^{d-1})} \times \#(\mathscr{A}(\tau, d-1))$,
(iii) $\#(\mathscr{A}(\tau, d)) < 1 \times 2^{|\tau|} \times 3^{(|\tau|^2)} \times \ldots \times d^{(|\tau|^{d-1})} \times |\tau|^{(1+|\tau|+|\tau|^2+\cdots+|\tau|^{d-1})}$.

8F Stretching, shrinking and completeness

This section fills in the three gaps that were left in the verification of the counting algorithm in 8C–D: the stretching and shrinking lemmas and the "completeness" part of the search theorem.

8F1 Search-Completeness Lemma *Part* (iii) *of the search theorem* 8C5 *holds; i.e. if τ is composite and $d \geq 0$, then*

$$Long(\tau, d) \subseteq \mathscr{A}(\tau, \leq d + 1).$$

Proof The lemma will be proved by induction on d but to make the induction work we must prove something slightly stronger. Recall that $Long(\tau, d)$ is the set of all long inhabitants of τ with depth $\leq d$ (8A7.2). Let $\mathbb{L}^*(\tau, d)$ be the set of all long typed closed nf-schemes X^τ such that $Depth(X^\tau) = d$ and

$$(1) \quad \begin{cases} \text{(a) } X^\tau \text{ is proper and all its meta-variables have depth } d \text{ in } X^\tau, \\ \text{(b) all subarguments with depth } d \text{ in } X^\tau \text{ are meta-variables.} \end{cases}$$

We shall prove both the inclusions

$$(2) \qquad \mathbb{L}^*(\tau, d) \subseteq \mathscr{A}(\tau, \leq d),$$

$$(3) \qquad Long(\tau, d) \subseteq \mathscr{A}(\tau, \leq d + 1),$$

where (2) is understood modulo renaming of meta-variables (i.e. (2) says that if $X^\tau \in L^*(\tau, d)$ then $\mathscr{A}(\tau, \leq d)$ contains either X^τ or a nf-scheme that differs from X^τ only by replacing its meta-variables by distinct others.)

Basis: $d = 0$. For (2): the only nf-schemes with depth 0 are meta-variables; also $\mathscr{A}(\tau, 0) = \{V^\tau\}$ by Step 0 of the search algorithm (8C6), so (2) holds modulo renaming.

For (3): let $\tau \equiv \tau_1 \to \ldots \to \tau_m \to e$ $(m \geq 1)$, and let $M^\tau \in Long(\tau, 0)$. Then M^τ is a term and has form

$$(4) \qquad \lambda y_1^{\tau_1} \ldots y_m^{\tau_m} \cdot y_i^{\tau_i} \qquad\qquad (1 \leq i \leq m, \tau_i \equiv e).$$

Now $\mathscr{A}(\tau, 0) = \{V^\tau\}$. To construct $\mathscr{A}(\tau, 1)$ apply 8C6 Step 1: Part IIa1 therein will output (4) as a suitable replacement for V^τ because the tail of τ_i is isomorphic to that of τ. Hence $\mathscr{A}(\tau, 1)$ is defined and contains M^τ.

Induction step: d to $d+1$. For (2): let $X \in \mathbb{L}^*(\tau, d+1)$. (Types will not be displayed from now on.) Then $Depth(X) = d + 1$, so by 8E3.1(ii) X has a subargument whose depth in X is $d + 1$, and so by 8E4.1 X has one whose depth in X is d. List all such subarguments (without repetitions); say they are $\underline{W}_1, \ldots, \underline{W}_r$ $(r \geq 1)$. Clearly $\underline{W}_1, \ldots, \underline{W}_r$ are disjoint components since they all have the same depth d in X; and since $Depth(X) = d + 1$ we have $Depth(W_i) \leq 1$ for each i. Also since X satisfies (1a) and (1b) relative to $d + 1$, no W_i can be a meta-variable; hence each W_i must have form

$$(5) \qquad W_i \;\equiv\; \lambda x_{i,1} \ldots x_{i,m_i} \cdot y_i V_{i,1} \ldots V_{i,n_i} \qquad\qquad (m_i, n_i \geq 0).$$

Let X' be the result of replacing each $\underline{W}_i$ in X by a distinct new meta-variable $\underline{V}_i$ with the same type as $\underline{W}_i$.

Then X' is a nf-scheme. (It satisfies restriction (iii) in Definition 8C1 because each $\underline{W}_i$ is a subargument.) And it is clearly long and closed and has depth d. Also, by its construction X' satisfies condition (1b) for membership of $\mathbb{L}^*(\tau, d)$. It also satisfies (1a), because if it contained a meta-variable-occurrence $\underline{V}$ at a depth $< d$ such a $\underline{V}$ could not be a $\underline{V}_i$ and hence would occur also in X at a depth $< d$, contrary to the assumption that X satisfies (1a) relative to $d + 1$.

Hence $X' \in \mathbb{L}^*(\tau, d)$. Therefore by the induction hypothesis there is an $X'' \in \mathscr{A}(\tau, \leq d)$ that is identical to X' except perhaps for alphabetic variation of meta-variables. Apply Step $d + 1$ of Algorithm 8C6 to each V_i in X''. Since W_i has form (5) and is part of a closed nf-scheme, namely X, it is easy to see that $\underline{W}_i$ is a suitable replacement for $\underline{V}_i$ (modulo renamings in W_i). Hence the algorithm will give X as an extension of X'', so $X \in \mathscr{A}(\tau, \leq d + 1)$, giving (2) for $d + 1$.

For (3): let $M \in Long(\tau, d+1)$. Then by 8E3.1 M has a subargument whose depth in M is $d+1$. List all such subarguments without repetitions; say they are $\underline{U}_1, \ldots, \underline{U}_r$ ($r \geq 1$). Clearly $\underline{U}_1, \ldots, \underline{U}_r$ are disjoint; and since $Depth(M) = d+1$ each U_i must have depth 0 and hence must have form

(6) $$U_i \equiv \lambda x_{i,1} \ldots x_{i,m_i}.y_i \qquad (m_i \geq 0).$$

Define M' to be the result of replacing each $\underline{U}_i$ in M by a distinct new meta-variable $\underline{V}_i$ with the same type as $\underline{U}_i$. Then M' is a genuine nf-scheme. And it is clearly long and closed and has depth $d+1$. Also M' satisfies condition (1b) for membership of $\mathbb{L}^*(\tau, d+1)$, and satisfies (1a) because all its meta-variables have been introduced by the above replacements. Hence $M' \in \mathbb{L}^*(\tau, d+1)$.

Therefore by (2) for $d+1$ there is an M'', differing from M' only by renaming meta-variables, such that

$$M'' \in \mathscr{A}(\tau, \leq d+1).$$

Apply Step $d+1$ of Algorithm 8C6 to M'': it is easy to check that $\underline{U}_i$ is a suitable replacement for $\underline{V}_i$ in M'', so the algorithm will give M as an extension of M''. Hence $M \in \mathscr{A}(\tau, \leq d+2)$, proving (3) for $d+1$. □

8F2 Detailed Stretching Lemma (cf. 8D2.) *If Long* (τ) *has a member* M^τ *with depth* $\geq ||\tau||$ *then*

(i) *there exists* $M^{*\tau} \in Long(\tau)$ *with Depth* $(M^{*\tau}) \geq Depth(M^\tau) + 1$,

(ii) *Long* (τ) *is infinite.*

Proof [Ben-Yelles 1979 §§3.20–3.21.] We shall prove (i) and then (ii) will follow by repetition. Types of typed terms will be omitted.

To prove (i), let M be a typed closed long β-nf with type τ and without bound-variable clashes. Let $d = Depth(M) \geq ||\tau|| \geq 1$. By 8E4.1, M has at least one argument-branch with length d. Choose any such branch, call it

(1) $$\langle \underline{N}_0, \ldots, \underline{N}_d \rangle,$$

where $\underline{N}_0 \equiv \underline{M}$ and $\underline{N}_{i+1}$ is an argument of N_i for $i = 0, \ldots, d-1$. Each of $N_0, \ldots, N_d$ must have form

(2) $$N_i \equiv \lambda x_{i,1} \ldots x_{i,m_i}.y_i P_{i,1} \ldots P_{i,n_i} \qquad (m_i, n_i \geq 0),$$

and for $i \leq d-1$ we have $\underline{N}_{i+1} \equiv \underline{P}_{i,k_i}$ for some $k_i \leq n_i$ (and hence $n_i \geq 1$). Since $d = Depth(M)$ the last member of (1) has no arguments, so $n_d = 0$.

For $i = 0, \ldots, d$ let $\underline{B}_i$ be the body of $\underline{N}_i$; that is

(3) $$\underline{B}_i \equiv \underline{y_i} \underline{P}_{i,1} \cdots \underline{P}_{i,n_i}.$$

Since $\underline{N}_i$ is long, the type of $\underline{B}_i$ is an atom. And this atom occurs in τ by 2B3(i). But $||\tau|| \leq d$ and there are $d+1$ components $\underline{B}_0, \ldots, \underline{B}_d$, so at least two of these must have the same type.

Choose any pair $\langle p, p+r \rangle$ such that $\underline{B}_p$ and $\underline{B}_{p+r}$ have the same type (and $r \geq 1$). Note that $\underline{B}_p$ properly contains $\underline{B}_{p+r}$ and

$$Depth(B_p) \geq r + Depth(B_{p+r}).$$

Define M^* to be the result of replacing $\underline{B}_{p+r}$ in M by a copy of $\underline{B}_p$ (after changing bound variables in this copy to avoid clashes). Then M^* has an argument-branch with length $d+r$. (Its members are

$$\underline{N}_0^*, \ldots, \underline{N}_{p+r}^*, \underline{N}_{p+1}^\circ, \ldots, \underline{N}_d^\circ,$$

where for $i = 0, \ldots, p+r$ each $\underline{N}_i^*$ has the same position in M^* as $\underline{N}_i$ had in M, and for $j = p+1, \ldots, d$ we have $N_j^\circ \equiv N_j$.) Hence by 8E4.1,

$$Depth(M^*) \geq d + r \geq d + 1.$$

To complete the proof of (i) it only remains to show that M^* is a genuine typed term. This will be done by applying Lemma 5B2.1(ii) on replacement in typed terms.

First, for $i = 0, \ldots, d$ let Γ_i be the context that assigns to the initial abstractors of N_i the types they have in M. Since M has no bound-variable clashes the variables in $\Gamma_0, \ldots, \Gamma_d$ are all distinct, so

(4) $\quad \Gamma_0 \cup \ldots \cup \Gamma_d$ is consistent.

Also every variable free in B_i is bound in one of $N_0, \ldots, N_i$ because M is closed and $\underline{B}_i$ is in $\underline{N}_i$. Hence, by the definitions of typed term (5A1) and *Con* (5A4),

(5) $\quad B_i \in \mathbb{TT}(\Gamma_0 \cup \ldots \cup \Gamma_i), \qquad Con(B_i) \subseteq \Gamma_0 \cup \ldots \cup \Gamma_i.$

To apply 5B2.1(ii) it is enough to show that the set

(6) $\quad Con(B_p) \cup Con(M) \cup \Gamma_0 \cup \ldots \cup \Gamma_{p+r}$

is consistent. (The abstractors in M whose scopes contain $\underline{B}_{p+r}$ are exactly the initial abstractors of $N_0, \ldots, N_{p+r}$.) But M is closed, so $Con(M) = \emptyset$. And by (5),

$$Con(B_p) \subseteq \Gamma_0 \cup \ldots \cup \Gamma_p \subseteq \Gamma_0 \cup \ldots \cup \Gamma_{p+r}.$$

Thus (6) is consistent by (4). □

8F3 Detailed Shrinking Lemma (cf. 8D3.) *If* $Long(\tau)$ *has a member* M^τ *with depth* $\geq \mathbb{D}(\tau)$ *then*

(i) *it has a member* $M^{*\tau}$ *with*

$$Depth(M^\tau) - ||\tau|| \leq Depth(M^{*\tau}) < Depth(M^\tau),$$

(ii) *it has a member* N^τ *with*

$$\mathbb{D}(\tau) - ||\tau|| \leq Depth(N^\tau) < \mathbb{D}(\tau).$$

Proof [cf. Ben-Yelles 1979 Thm. 3.28.] Part (ii) is proved by repeating (i) and taking the first output with depth $< \mathbb{D}(\tau)$.

Part (i) is proved as follows. (Types of typed terms will be omitted.) Let M be a member of $Long(\tau)$ without bound-variable clashes. Let $d = Depth(M) \geq \mathbb{D}(\tau)$. Incidentally $\mathbb{D}(\tau) \geq 2$ because τ is composite since atomic types have no inhabitants.

By 8E4.1, M has at least one argument-branch with length d; to reduce the depth of M we must shrink all these branches. Consider any such branch; just as in the proof of the stretching lemma 8F2 it has form

(1) $\quad \langle N_0, \ldots, N_d \rangle,$

where $\underline{N}_0 \equiv \underline{M}$ and $\underline{N}_{i+1}$ is an argument of $\underline{N}_i$ for $i = 0, \ldots, d-1$. And

(2) $\quad N_i \;\equiv\; \lambda x_{i,1} \ldots x_{i,m_i} \cdot y_i P_{i,1} \ldots P_{i,n_i} \qquad (m_i, n_i \geq 0)$

for $0 \leq i \leq d-1$. Let the type of N_i be

(3) $\quad \rho_i \;\equiv\; \rho_{i,1} \rightarrow \ldots \rightarrow \rho_{i,m_i} \rightarrow a_i.$

Then since $\underline{N}_i$ is long, the types of $x_{i,1}, x_{i,2}, \ldots$ are exactly $\rho_{i,1}, \rho_{i,2}, \ldots$; that is, using the "*IAT*" notation introduced in 8E6,

$$IAT(N_i) = \langle \rho_{i,1}, \ldots, \rho_{i,m_i} \rangle.$$

Just as in the proof of 8F2 let $\underline{B}_i$ be the body of $\underline{N}_i$ for $i = 0, \ldots, d$. Then the type of $\underline{B}_i$ is the tail of the type of $\underline{N}_i$, namely a_i.

Define a sequence of integers $d_0, d_1, \ldots$ thus: $d_0 = 0$ and d_{j+1} is the least $i > d_j$ such that $IAT(N_i)$ differs from all of

(4) $\quad IAT(N_{d_0}),\ IAT(N_{d_1}),\ \ldots,\ IAT(N_{d_j}).$

Let n be the greatest integer such that d_n is defined. The branch (1) has only d members after $\underline{N}_0$, so $n \leq d$ and $d_n \leq d$. Then

(5) $\quad 0 = d_0 < d_1 < \ldots < d_n \leq d,$

and for $0 \leq i \leq d$, $IAT(N_i)$ is identical to one of

(6) $\quad IAT(N_{d_0}),\ IAT(N_{d_1}),\ \ldots,\ IAT(N_{d_n}).$

Also the $n+1$ *IAT*'s in (6) are distinct, and by 8E7 they are either empty or members of $NSS(\tau)$. Hence by 9E9.3(ii),

(7) $\quad n + 1 \leq |\tau|.$

Now $d_0, \ldots, d_n$ partition the set $\{0, 1, \ldots, d\}$ into the following $n+1$ non-empty sets which will be called ***IAT-intervals***:

$$\begin{aligned} \mathbb{I}_j &= \{d_j, d_j + 1, \ldots, d_{j+1} - 1\} \qquad (0 \leq j \leq n-1), \\ \mathbb{I}_n &= \{d_n, d_n + 1, \ldots, d\}. \end{aligned}$$

If $\mathbb{I}_j$ contains two numbers $p, p+r$ such that $r \geq 1$ and B_p and B_{p+r} have the same type (i.e. $a_p \equiv a_{p+r}$) we shall call $\langle p, p+r \rangle$ a ***tail-repetition***. It will be called ***minimal*** iff there is no other tail-repetition $\langle p', q' \rangle$ with

$$p \leq p' < q' \leq p + r.$$

Now an $\mathbb{I}_j$ that contains no tail-repetitions must have $\leq ||\tau||$ members. Because for such an $\mathbb{I}_j$ the atoms

$$a_{d_j}, \ldots, a_{d_{j+1}-1}$$

must all be distinct, and by (3) each a_i occurs in ρ_i, which occurs in τ by 8E7, and there are only $||\tau||$ distinct atoms in τ. This argument also shows that for a minimal tail-repetition $\langle p, p+r \rangle$ we have

(8) $\quad r \leq ||\tau||.$

Now there are $n+1$ IAT-intervals in the given branch and $n+1 \leq |\tau|$ by (7), so if no interval contained a tail-repetition the branch would have $\leq |\tau| \times ||\tau||$ members. But the branch has $d+1$ members and

$$d+1 = Depth(M)+1 \geq \mathbb{D}(\tau)+1 > |\tau| \times ||\tau||.$$

Hence at least one IAT-interval contains a tail-repetition.

We start to build M^* as follows. In the given branch take the last $\mathbb{I}_j$ containing a tail-repetition, choose a minimal tail-repetition $\langle p, p+r\rangle$ in it, and change M to a new term M' by replacing B_p by B_{p+r}.

To see that M' is a genuine typed term we apply 5B2.1(ii) similarly to the proof of 8F2. Using the notation of (4) in that proof, it is enough to show that the set

$$(9) \qquad Con(B_{p+r}) \cup Con(M) \cup \Gamma_0 \cup \ldots \cup \Gamma_p$$

is consistent. But, as in the proof of 8F2, $Con(M) = \emptyset$ and $Con(B_{p+r})$ is a subset of $\Gamma_0 \cup \ldots \cup \Gamma_{p+r}$, so (9) is consistent by (4) in the proof of 8F2.

It is straightforward to prove that M' is a long β-nf with the same type as M. Also that $|M'| < |M|$.

But M' might not be closed, because the change from M to M' has removed the initial abstractors of $\underline{N}_{p+1}, \ldots, \underline{N}_{p+r}$ from M, and so some free variable-occurrences in $\underline{B}_{p+r}$ that were bound in M might now be free in M'. To close M', apply the following procedure to every such variable-occurrence.

Let $\underline{v}$ be free in the occurrence of B_{p+r} in M' that has replaced $\underline{B}_p$ in M, and let $\underline{v}$ be also free in M'. Then v does not occur in a covering abstractor of this occurrence of B_{p+r} in M'. But these covering abstractors are exactly the initial abstractors of $\underline{N}_0, \ldots, \underline{N}_p$ in M, so

$$v \notin IA(\underline{N}_0) \cup \ldots \cup IA(\underline{N}_p).$$

But M is closed, so the free $\underline{v}$ in $\underline{B}_{p+r}$ in M must be in the scope of a $\underline{\lambda v}$ in one of $IA(\underline{N}_0), \ldots, IA(\underline{N}_{p+r})$. Hence v occurs in $IA(\underline{N}_h)$ for some h with $p+1 \leq h \leq p+r$; in the notation of (2) we have

$$v \equiv x_{h,k}$$

for some $k \leq m_h$. And the type of v is $\rho_{h,k} \in IAT(\underline{N}_h)$. Now by the definition of $d_0, \ldots, d_n$, and the fact that the tail-repetition $\langle p, p+r\rangle$ we are eliminating is in an interval $\mathbb{I}_j, IAT(\underline{N}_h)$ coincides with one of

$$IAT(\underline{N}_{d_0}), \ldots, IAT(\underline{N}_{d_j});$$

say $IAT(\underline{N}_h) = IAT(\underline{N}_{d_q})$ for some $q \leq j$. Hence there is a variable

$$x_{d_q,k} \in IA(N_{d_q})$$

with the same type as v. Replace v by this variable throughout M'. The result will be a long β-nf with the same type and depth as M' and containing one less free variable.

Similarly replace every variable of $\underline{B}_{p+r}$ that is free in M' by a new one which has the same type but is bound in M'. The result will be a long β-nf M'' with the same type and depth as M' and which is closed.[1]

Now M'' has been obtained by removing a type-repetition from an argument-branch in M which originally contained d subarguments. And by (8) the number of subarguments removed is $\leq ||\tau||$. Hence

(10) $\quad d - ||\tau|| \leq Depth(M'') \leq d.$

If $Depth(M'') < d$, define $M^* \equiv M''$. If not, select a branch in M'' with length d and apply the above removal procedure to it, then continue shortening branches with length d until there are none left. (This process must terminate because each removal strictly reduces $|M|$.) Define M^* to be the first term produced by this procedure whose depth is less than d. Then

$$d - ||\tau|| \leq Depth(M^*) < d$$

as required. □

8F3.1 *Example* Let $\tau \equiv (a \to a) \to a \to a$, and let M^τ be a typed version of the Church numeral for the number four, namely

$$M^\tau \quad \equiv \quad (\lambda u^{a \to a} v^a \cdot (u(u(u(uv)))))^\tau.$$

Then

$$||\tau|| = 1, \quad |\tau| = 4, \quad \mathbb{D}(\tau) = |\tau| \times ||\tau|| = 4.$$

And $Depth(M) = 4$, so the above shrinking procedure can be applied to M. There is only one argument-branch in M containing four subarguments, and its members are

$$\underline{\lambda uv \cdot u^4 v}, \quad \underline{u^3 v}, \quad \underline{u^2 v}, \quad \underline{uv}, \quad \underline{v}.$$

(Call them $\underline{N}_0, \ldots, \underline{N}_4$ respectively.) And

$$IAT(N_0) = \langle a \to a, a \rangle$$
$$IAT(N_1) = IAT(N_2) = IAT(N_3) = IAT(N_4) = \emptyset.$$

Thus the only change in $IAT(N_i)$ comes at $i = 1$, so in the notation of the proof of 8F3 we have

$$n = 1, \quad d_0 = 0, \quad d_1 = 1, \quad \mathbb{I}_0 = \{0\}, \quad \mathbb{I}_1 = \{1, 2, 3, 4\}.$$

There are three minimal tail-repetitions in $\mathbb{I}_1$ and the last one is $\langle 3, 4 \rangle$. The proof of 8F3 removes this by replacing $\underline{uv}$ by $\underline{v}$; this changes M to

$$M^* \quad \equiv \quad \lambda uv \cdot u^3 v.$$

And $Depth(M^*) = 3 < \mathbb{D}(\tau)$.

[1] No claim is made that M'' is related to M' by α-conversion or any other semantically significant relation!

8F3.2 *Warning* As mentioned in 8D10(iii) the proof of the shrinking lemma does not necessarily apply to restricted systems of λ-terms, for example the λI-calculus. In fact there is no guarantee that if we shrink a λI-term the result will still be a λI-term, since shrinking may cut out some variables.

9

Technical details

To avoid interrupting the main lines of thought in the earlier chapters some concepts were defined there only in outline and their main properties were stated without proof. This chapter gives the full definitions and proofs. It should be read only as required to follow the arguments in the other chapters. Its sections are largely independent of each other.

9A The structure of a term

From the viewpoint of logical order this section is best read between 1A3 and 1A4.

As remarked in 1A4, a subterm of a term may have more than one occurrence. The present section introduces a precise notation to distinguish such different occurrences; it is rather clumsy and the reader should avoid using it whenever possible, but in some proofs its precision will be vital. The first step is to define a set of expressions called ***positions*** that can be assigned to different occurrences of a subterm to show where they occur.

9A1 Definition (Positions) A ***position*** $p = i_1 \dots i_m$ is any finite (perhaps empty) string of symbols such that $i_1, \dots, i_{m-1}$ are integers and i_m is either an integer or an asterisk, $*$. Its ***length*** is m, and if $m = 0$ we say $p = \emptyset$.

If $m \geq 1$ and $i_m = 1$ we call p a ***function*** position;
if $m \geq 1$ and $i_m = 2$ we call p an ***argument*** position;
if $m \geq 1$ and $i_m = 0$ we call p a ***body*** position; and
if $m \geq 1$ and $i_m = *$ we call p an ***abstractor*** position.

(Positions containing integers ≥ 3 will be used later but not in the present section.)

The ***concatenation*** pq of positions $p = i_1 \dots i_m$ and $q = j_1 \dots j_n$ is defined thus: $p\emptyset = p$, $\emptyset q = q$, and if $m, n \geq 1$ and $i_m \neq *$, define

$$pq = i_1 \dots i_m j_1 \dots j_n.$$

(pq is undefined if $m,n \geq 1$ and $i_m = *$.)

A ***refinement*** of p is any position with form pq; it is ***proper*** iff $q \neq \emptyset$.

Two positions $p = i_1 \dots i_m$ and $q = j_1 \dots j_n$ are said to ***diverge*** iff neither is a refinement of the other, i.e. iff there exists h such that

$$i_h \neq j_h, \qquad 1 \leq h \leq Min\{m, n\}.$$

9A2 Definition (Occurs, occurrence) The phrase "P ***occurs in*** M ***at position*** p" (or "M ***contains*** P ***at position*** p") is defined by induction on the length of p, thus:

(i) M occurs in M at position $\emptyset$;

(ii) if P_1P_2 occurs in M at p, then P_i occurs in M at pi for $i = 1,2$;

(iii) if $\lambda x{\cdot}Q$ occurs in M at p, then Q occurs in M at $p0$ and x occurs in M at $p*$.

An ***occurrence of*** P ***in*** M is a triple $\langle P, p, M\rangle$ such that P occurs in M at p. If $P \equiv x$ and the last symbol of p is $*$ we call $\langle x, p, M\rangle$ a ***binding occurrence of*** x or an ***occurrence of*** $\boldsymbol{\lambda x}$.

An ***abstractor*** is an occurrence of λx for some x.

A ***subterm*** of M is any term P that occurs in M.

9A2.1 *Note* It is easy to prove that at most one term can occur in M at one position. (We assume of course that a term cannot be simultaneously an application and an abstraction, or a composite term and an atom; also that

$$\begin{array}{rclcrcl} P_1P_2 & \equiv & Q_1Q_2 & \Longrightarrow & P_1 \equiv Q_1 & \& & P_2 \equiv Q_2, \\ \lambda x{\cdot}P & \equiv & \lambda y{\cdot}Q & \Longrightarrow & x \equiv y & \& & P \equiv Q.) \end{array}$$

9A2.2 *Notation* An occurrence $\langle P, p, M\rangle$ may be called simply "$\underline{P}$" when no confusion is likely. A binding occurence of x may be called either of

$$\underline{x}, \qquad \underline{\lambda x}.$$

9A3 Definition (Components) A ***component*** of a term M is any occurrence in M other than a binding occurrence of a variable, i.e. any occurrence $\langle P, p, M\rangle$ such that the last symbol in p is not $*$.

A component is called ***proper*** iff it is not $\langle M, \emptyset, M\rangle$.

9A3.1 *Note* The reason that binding occurrences of variables are denied the name "components" in the above definition is that they play a very different role from other occurrences. In a term such as $\lambda z{\cdot}xy$ we shall think of $\underline{x}$ and $\underline{y}$ as being the material from which the term is built, but think of $\underline{z}$ as being part of one of the operations which do the building.

9A4 Definition (The construction-tree of a term) We can display the structure of a term as a tree with each node carrying two labels, a position and a subterm that occurs at that position. This tree is defined for an arbitrary term M as follows.

(i) If $M \equiv x$, its tree is a single node labelled with x and the empty position, thus:

$$x \bullet \emptyset.$$

(ii) If $M \equiv PQ$, its tree is obtained by first concatenating "1" onto the left end of each position-label in the tree for P, then concatenating "2" onto the left of each position-label in the tree for Q, and then placing an extra node beneath the two modified trees, as shown below.

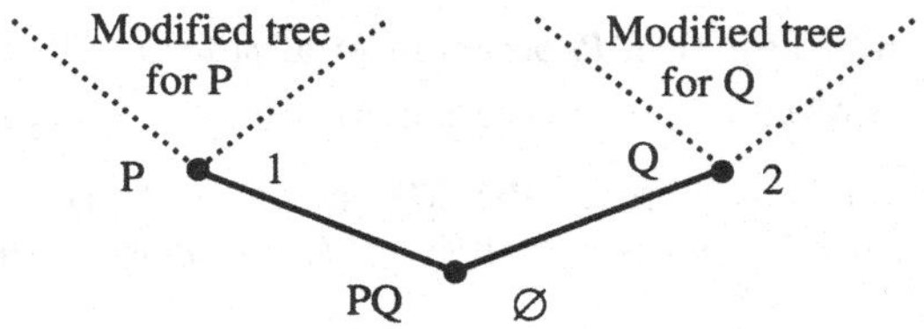

(iii) If $M \equiv \lambda x \cdot P$, its tree is obtained by first concatenating "0" onto the left end of each position-label in the tree for P, and then placing an extra node beneath the modified tree, as shown below.

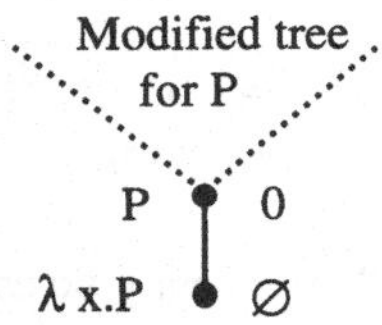

9A4.1 *Example* The construction-tree of $(\lambda x \cdot yx)(\lambda z \cdot x(yx))$ is shown in Fig. 9A4.1a.

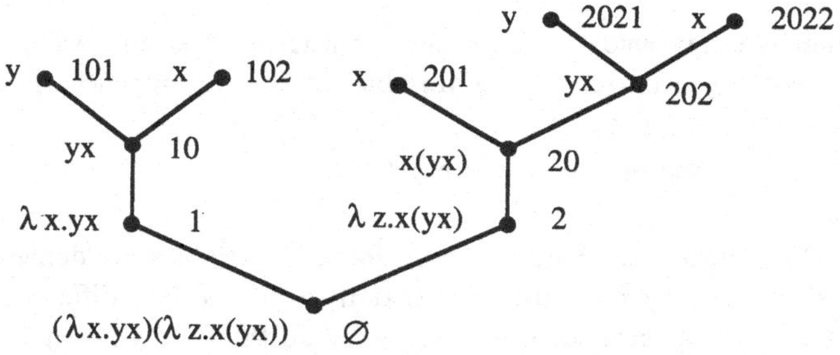

Fig. 9A4.1a. Construction-tree of $(\lambda x \cdot yx)(\lambda z \cdot x(yx))$

9A4.2 *Note* Each component has a node on the construction-tree; but binding occurrences of variables are not components and do not have their own nodes.

9A5 Definition (Relations between components) Let $\underline{P} \equiv \langle P, p, M \rangle$ and $\underline{R} \equiv \langle R, r, M \rangle$ be components of a term M:

(i) iff r is a refinement of p we may say any of

$\underline{P}$ ***contains*** $\underline{R}$, $\underline{R}$ ***is a part of*** $\underline{P}$, $\underline{R}$ ***is in*** $\underline{P}$;

(ii) iff r is a proper refinement of p we may say either of

$\underline{P}$ ***properly contains*** $\underline{R}$, $\underline{R}$ ***is a proper part of*** $\underline{P}$;

(iii) iff p and r diverge we may say either of

$\underline{P}$ ***is disjoint from*** $\underline{R}$, $\underline{P}$ ***does not overlap*** $\underline{R}$;

(iv) iff $R \equiv P$ (i.e. $\underline{R}$, $\underline{P}$ are occurrences of the same term) we may say

$\underline{R}$ ***is isomorphic to*** $\underline{P}$, $\underline{R} \cong \underline{P}$.

9A5.1 *Notes* (i) If $\underline{P}$ is not disjoint from $\underline{R}$ it is easy to see that either $\underline{P}$ is in $\underline{R}$ or $\underline{R}$ is in $\underline{P}$. Hence if $\underline{P}_1, \dots \underline{P}_n$, are components of a term M and no two are disjoint they must be linearly ordered by the relation "*is in*"; i.e. there must exist a permutation $\langle i_1, \dots, i_n \rangle$ of $\langle 1, \dots, n \rangle$ such that

$$\underline{P}_{i_1} \textit{ is in } \underline{P}_{i_2} \textit{ in } \underline{P}_{i_3} \textit{ in} \dots \textit{in } \underline{P}_{i_n}.$$

(ii) If $\underline{P}$ is a proper part of $\underline{R}$ then $P \not\equiv R$.

9A6 Definition (Replacement in a term) Let $\underline{P} \equiv \langle P, p, M \rangle$ be a component of a term M. The result of replacing $\underline{P}$ by a term T will be called

$$\{T/P\}_p M.$$

Its detailed definition proceeds by induction on the length of p, thus:

(i) if $p \equiv \emptyset$: then $P \equiv M$; define

$$\{T/M\}_\emptyset M \ \equiv \ T;$$

(ii) if $p \equiv q1$: then M contains a term PQ at position q; define

$$\{T/P\}_{q1} M \ \equiv \ \{(TQ)/(PQ)\}_q M;$$

(iii) if $p \equiv q2$: then M contains a term QP at q; define

$$\{T/P\}_{q2} M \ \equiv \ \{(QT)/(QP)\}_q M;$$

(iv) if $p \equiv q0$: then M contains a term $\lambda x{\cdot}P$ at q; define

$$\{T/P\}_{q0} M \ \equiv \ \{(\lambda x{\cdot}T)/(\lambda x{\cdot}P)\}_q M.$$

(The case $p \equiv q*$ is excluded above because then $\underline{P}$ would be a binding occurrence of a variable and not a component; $\{T/P\}_p M$ is undefined in this case.)

9A6.1 *Example* Let $M \equiv (\lambda x{\cdot}yx)(\lambda z{\cdot}x(yx))$, $\underline{P} \equiv \langle yx, 10, M \rangle$, $T \equiv xxyz$. Then

$$\{T/P\}_{10} M \ \equiv \ (\lambda x{\cdot}xxyz)(\lambda z{\cdot}x(yx)).$$

9A6.2 *Note* In substitution we change bound variables to avoid clashes but in replacement we do not.

9A6.3 *Note* Of course replacing one component of a term can disturb or destroy other components. To see what happens in two important cases, let $\underline{P} \equiv \langle P, p, M\rangle$ and $\underline{R} \equiv \langle R, r, M\rangle$ and let

$$M^* \equiv \{T/P\}_p M.$$

(i) If $\underline{P}$ is disjoint from $\underline{R}$, it is not hard to show that M^* contains an occurrence of R at position r (i.e., roughly speaking, replacing $\underline{P}$ does not change its disjoint neighbours.)

(ii) If $\underline{P}$ is in $\underline{R}$, then $p \equiv rq$ for some position q such that P occurs in R at position q, and it is not hard to show that M^* contains, at position r, the term

$$\{T/P\}_q R.$$

9B Residuals

This section summarises some properties of β-contractions needed in the proof of the weak normalisation theorem in 5C. The full theory of β-reduction is in fact quite deep (see Barendregt 1984 Chapters 3 and 11–14), but none of it is used in this book except the following few very basic ideas.

Everything in this section is valid for both the untyped terms of Chapter 1 and the typed terms of Chapter 5.

9B1 Notation Recall the definitions of ***β-redex*** and ***β-contraction*** in 1B1. (In this section "β" will usually be omitted.) A ***redex-occurrence***

$$\underline{R} \equiv \underline{(\lambda x{\cdot}M)N}$$

is a particular occurrence of a redex in a term. The notations ***function-part*** and ***argument-part*** of $\underline{R}$ will be used here for $\underline{\lambda x{\cdot}M}$ and $\underline{N}$ respectively.

Recall from 1B2 that a ***reduction*** is a finite or infinite sequence of contractions

$$\langle P_1, \underline{R}_1, Q_1\rangle, \qquad \langle P_2, \underline{R}_2, Q_2\rangle, \ldots$$

where $P_1 \equiv_\alpha P$ and $Q_i \equiv_\alpha P_{i+1}$ for $i = 1, 2, \ldots$. This definition allows a reduction to make α-conversions before or after each of its contractions, but the reader may safely ignore these and concentrate on the contractions; the next lemma will say contractions are unaffected by α-conversions in a certain precise sense.

Recall from 1B3 that the ***length*** of a reduction is the number of its contractions. (And α-conversions are not counted.)

In this section "ξ" will denote an arbitrary contraction and "$\mathbb{r}$" an arbitrary reduction.

If $\mathbb{r}_1$ is a finite reduction from a term P to a term Q and $\mathbb{r}_2$ is a reduction of $\mathbb{Q}$, the reduction consisting of $\mathbb{r}_1$ followed by $\mathbb{r}_2$ will be called

$$\mathbb{r}_1 + \mathbb{r}_2.$$

9B1.1 *Lemma* (α-invariance) *If $P \equiv_\alpha P'$ and P contains a β-redex-occurrence $\underline{R} \equiv \langle R, p, P\rangle$ whose contraction changes P to Q, then P' contains a β-redex-occurrence $\langle \underline{R}', p, P'\rangle$ whose contraction changes P' to a term $Q' \equiv_\alpha Q$.*

Proof-note Two cases must be considered: (i) P' comes from P by replacing $\lambda x \cdot M$ by $\lambda y \cdot [y/x]M$, (ii) P' comes from P by replacing $\lambda y \cdot [y/x]M$ by $\lambda x \cdot M$ (where $y \notin FV(M)$). The proof is boring but can be slightly simplified by restricting rule (α) as follows (cf. HS 86 Remark 1.21):

(α_0) *replace $\lambda x \cdot M$ by $\lambda y \cdot [y/x]M$ if y does not occur at all in M.*

(It is straightforward to prove that every re-writing by (α) can be done by a series of re-writings by (α_0).) The reverse of an (α_0)-replacement is also an (α_0)-replacement, so case (ii) above becomes redundant.

9B1.2 *Warning* The above lemma does not claim that $R' \equiv_\alpha R$. In fact the following is an example where this fails:

$$P \equiv \lambda x \cdot R, \qquad R \equiv (\lambda u \cdot ux)z, \qquad P' \equiv \lambda y \cdot [y/x]R.$$

The next definition will describe what happens to a redex-occurrence $\underline{S}$ in a term P when another redex-occurrence $\underline{R}$ in P is contracted.

9B2 Definition (Residuals) Let $\underline{R} \equiv \langle R, p, P \rangle$ and $\underline{S} \equiv \langle S, q, P \rangle$ be redex-occurrences in a term P, say

$$R \equiv (\lambda x \cdot M)N, \qquad S \equiv (\lambda y \cdot H)L.$$

Let P change to P' by contracting R. The ***residuals of $\underline{S}$ with respect to $\underline{R}$*** are certain redex-occurrences in P' defined as follows (from Curry and Feys 1958 §4B1).

***Case* 1**: $\underline{R}$ does not overlap $\underline{S}$. Then contracting $\underline{R}$ leaves $\underline{S}$ unchanged; more precisely, by 9A6.3(i), P' contains an occurrence of S at position q; we call this occurrence the residual of $\underline{S}$.

***Case* 2**: $\underline{R} \equiv \underline{S}$. Then contracting $\underline{R}$ is the same as contracting $\underline{S}$; we say $\underline{S}$ has no residual.

***Case* 3**: $\underline{R} \not\equiv \underline{S}$ and $\underline{R}$ is in $\underline{S}$. Then $\underline{R}$ must be in $\underline{H}$ or in $\underline{L}$, and contracting $\underline{R}$ will change $\underline{(\lambda y \cdot H)L}$ to a component $\underline{(\lambda y \cdot H')L}$ or $\underline{(\lambda y \cdot H)L'}$ of P'. We call this the residual of $\underline{S}$.

***Case* 4**: $\underline{R} \not\equiv \underline{S}$ and $\underline{S}$ is in $\underline{R}$. Then $\underline{S}$ must be in $\underline{M}$ or in $\underline{N}$.

***Subcase* 4a**: $\underline{S}$ is in $\underline{M}$. The contraction of $\underline{R}$ changes $\underline{(\lambda x \cdot M)N}$ to $[N/x]\underline{M}$ and changes $\underline{S}$ to a redex-occurrence $\underline{S}'$ with one of the forms

$$[N/x]\underline{S}, \qquad [N/x][z_1/y_1] \ldots [z_n/y_n]\underline{S}, \qquad \underline{S}.$$

(The second form will apply if some changes of bound variables are needed during the substitution $[N/x]\underline{M}$; the third if $\underline{S}$ is in the scope of an occurrence of λx in $\underline{M}$.) We call this $\underline{S}'$ the residual of $\underline{S}$.

***Subcase* 4b**: $\underline{S}$ is in $\underline{N}$. Let $\underline{M}$ contain $k \geq 0$ free occurrences of x. The contraction of $\underline{R}$ changes $\underline{(\lambda x \cdot M)N}$ to $[N/x]\underline{M}$ which contains k substituted occurrences of N, each containing an occurrence of S. We call these occurrences of S the residuals of $\underline{S}$.

9B2.1 *Notation* The set of all the residuals of $\underline{S}$ with respect to $\underline{R}$ will be called "$\underline{S}/\underline{R}$" (or "$\underline{S}/\xi$" if ξ is the contraction $\langle P, \underline{R}, P'\rangle$).

A redex-occurrence $\underline{S}$ will be called the ***parent*** of its residuals.

9B2.2 *Note* (i) If $\underline{S}$ is not a part of $\underline{R}$ then $\underline{S}/\underline{R}$ has exactly one member (because then Case 2 and Subcase 4b cannot happen).

(ii) Each member of $\underline{S}/\underline{R}$ is an occurrence of a term $(\lambda z{\cdot}H')L'$, where $z \equiv y$ except possibly in Case 4a if changes of bound variables are needed, and H' and L' are either H and L or terms obtained from them by substitutions.

(iii) The definition of residuals is meaningful for the typed-term system in Chapter 5 as well as for untyped terms. If P is a typed term then by (ii) each residual $\underline{(\lambda z{\cdot}H')L'}$ of $\underline{S}$ in P' has the same type as $\underline{S}$. Further, its function-part $\underline{\lambda z{\cdot}H'}$ has the same type as the function-part $\underline{\lambda y{\cdot}H}$ of $\underline{S}$. This fact is needed in the proof of the weak normalisation theorem in 5C.

9B3 Definition Let $\mathbb{r}$ be a reduction from P to Q and let $\underline{S}$ be a redex-occurrence in P. The set $\underline{S}/\mathbb{r}$ of the ***residuals of $\underline{S}$ with respect to*** $\mathbb{r}$ is a set of redex-occurrences in Q defined thus:

(i) If $\mathbb{r}$ has no contractions and no α-conversions (so $P \equiv Q$), define

$$\underline{S}/\mathbb{r} = \{\underline{S}\}.$$

(ii) If $\mathbb{r} = \mathbb{r}^\circ + \xi$ where $\mathbb{r}^\circ$ reduces P to a term Q° and ξ is a contraction reducing Q° to Q, and $\underline{S}/\mathbb{r}^\circ = \{\underline{S}_1, \ldots, \underline{S}_n\}$, define

$$\underline{S}/(\mathbb{r}^\circ + \xi) \;=\; \underline{S}_1/\xi \cup \underline{S}_2/\xi \cup \ldots \cup \underline{S}_n/\xi.$$

(iii) If $\mathbb{r}$ ends with an α-conversion $Q' \equiv_\alpha Q$ and the residuals of $\underline{S}$ in Q' are $\underline{S}_1, \ldots, \underline{S}_n$, define the residuals of $\underline{S}$ in Q to be the redex-occurrences in Q with the same positions as $\underline{S}_1, \ldots, \underline{S}_n$ in Q'. (These exist by 9B1.1.)

Finally, if $\mathbb{S} = \{\underline{S}_1, \ldots, \underline{S}_m\}$ is a set of redex-occurrences in P, define

$$\mathbb{S}/r \;=\; \underline{S}_1/\mathbb{r} \cup \ldots \cup \underline{S}_m/\mathbb{r}.$$

9B4 Definition (M.C.D.'s) Let $\mathbb{S} = \{\underline{S}_1, \ldots, \underline{S}_m\}$ be a set of redex-occurrences in a term P. A ***development*** of $\mathbb{S}$ is a finite or infinite reduction $\xi_1 + \xi_2 + \xi_3 + \ldots$ (with α-conversions allowed), such that $\xi_1 \in \mathbb{S}$ and for $n \geq 1$,

$$\xi_{n+1} \in \mathbb{S}/(\xi_1 + \cdots + \xi_n).$$

A ***complete development*** of $\mathbb{S}$ is a finite development $\xi_1 + \cdots + \xi_n$ such that

$$\mathbb{S}/(\xi_1 + \cdots + \xi_n) = \emptyset.$$

A ***minimal*** member of $\mathbb{S}$ is one that does not contain another member. A ***minimal complete development (m.c.d.)*** of $\mathbb{S}$ is a complete development $\xi_1 + \ldots + \xi_n$ such that ξ_1 is minimal in $\mathbb{S}$ and ξ_{i+1} is minimal in $\mathbb{S}/(\xi_1 + \ldots + \xi_i)$ for $i = 1, \ldots, n-1$ (and the only α-conversions are at the end of ξ_n).

If P changes to Q by an m.c.d. of some set of redex-occurrences in P we shall say

$$P \rhd_{\mathrm{mcd}} Q.$$

9B4.1 *Lemma* *Every set* $\mathbb{S}$ *of redex-occurrences in a term has an m.c.d..*

Proof Let $\mathbb{S} = \{\underline{S}_1, \ldots, \underline{S}_m\}$. Since $\mathbb{S}$ is finite it has at least one minimal member; choose one, say $\underline{S}_j$, and contract it; by 9B2.2(i) each $\underline{S}_i$ $(i \neq j)$ will have just one residual, so $\mathbb{S}/\underline{S}_j$ will have only $n-1$ members. By continuing this process we must eventually reach a term containing no residuals of $\mathbb{S}$. □

9B4.2 *Notes* (i) If $\mathbb{S}$ is empty an m.c.d. of $\mathbb{S}$ has no contractions.

(ii) A single contraction is an m.c.d. of a one-member set.

(iii) The main properties of developments are described in Barendregt 1984 §11.3. In particular it is shown there that infinite developments are impossible even in the untyped λ-calculus. Also the concept of m.c.d. is used in HS86 Appendix 1 as the basis of a proof of the Church-Rosser theorem.

9B5 Definition (Newly created redex-occurrences) If P changes to P' by contracting a redex-occurrence $\underline{R}$, and P' contains a redex-occurrence S that is not a residual of a redex-occurrence in P, we say $\underline{S}$ has been ***newly created*** by the contraction of $\underline{R}$.

9B5.1 *Discussion* The proof of the weak normalisation theorem in 5C depends on knowing how a newly created redex-occurrence can be produced, so the possible ways of doing this will be analysed here. Let $\underline{R}$ be a redex-occurrence at a position p in a term P, say

$$R \equiv ((\lambda x \cdot M)N).$$

Let P change to P' by contracting $\underline{R}$; then at position p in P' there is an occurrence of

$$[N/x]M.$$

Let $\underline{S}$ be any newly created redex-occurrence in P'; say

$$S \equiv ((\lambda z \cdot H)L).$$

Now $\underline{S}$ must overlap $\underline{[N/x]M}$, otherwise it would be the residual of a redex-occurrence in P that did not overlap $\underline{R}$. Hence either $\underline{S}$ properly contains $\underline{[N/x]M}$ or $\underline{S}$ is in $\underline{[N/x]M}$.

***Case* 1**: $\underline{S}$ properly contains $\underline{[N/x]M}$. If $\underline{[N/x]M}$ were in $\underline{H}$ or $\underline{L}$ then $\underline{S}$ would not be new; hence $\underline{[N/x]M \equiv \lambda z \cdot H}$. Thus $\underline{S} \equiv \underline{([N/x]M)L}$ and P must contain $\underline{RL}$. Now the only way to obtain $\underline{[N/x]M} \equiv \underline{\lambda z \cdot H}$ is either to have $M \equiv x$ and $N \equiv \lambda z \cdot H$ or to have $M \equiv \lambda y \cdot H'$ for some y and H'.

***Subcase* 1a**: $M \equiv x$, $N \equiv \lambda z \cdot H$. Then $R \equiv (\lambda x \cdot x)N$ and the contraction of $\underline{R}$ proceeds thus:

$$RL \equiv (\lambda x \cdot x)NL \rhd_\beta NL \equiv (\lambda z \cdot H)L \equiv S.$$

***Subcase* 1b**: $M \equiv \lambda y \cdot H'$. Then $R \equiv (\lambda x \cdot (\lambda y \cdot H'))N$ and the contraction of $\underline{R}$ proceeds thus:

$$RL \equiv (\lambda x \cdot (\lambda y \cdot H'))NL \rhd_\beta ([N/x](\lambda y \cdot H'))L \equiv S.$$

***Case* 2**: $\underline{S}$ is in $[N/x]M$. Let $\underline{x}_1,\ldots,\underline{x}_k$ be the free occurrences of x in $\underline{M}$ in P, and let $\underline{N}_1,\ldots,\underline{N}_k$ be the corresponding occurrences of N in $\underline{[N/x]M}$ in P'. If $\underline{S}$ were in an $\underline{N}_i$ or were disjoint from all of $\underline{N}_1,\ldots,\underline{N}_k$, it is easy to see that $\underline{S}$ would not be new. Hence at least one $\underline{N}_i$ must be in $\underline{S}$. If each such $\underline{N}_i$ was in $\underline{H}$ or $\underline{L}$, $\underline{S}$ would be a residual of a redex-occurrence in $\underline{M}$, so one $\underline{N}_i$ must coincide with $\underline{\lambda z \cdot H}$. This can only happen if $\underline{M}$ contains a component with form xL' for some L', and

$$N \equiv \lambda z \cdot H, \qquad \underline{S} \equiv [N/x](\underline{xL'}), \qquad L \equiv [N/x]L'.$$

Conclusion: in each of the above cases the function-part of the newly created redex $\underline{S}$ is an occurrence of N or of $[N/x]M$.

9C The structure of a TA$_\lambda$-deduction

This section should be read in parallel with the outline definition of "TA$_\lambda$-deduction" in 2A8. That outline is filled in here and some lemmas are proved for use in Chapters 5 and 8.

A TA$_\lambda$-deduction as defined below will be a slightly more elaborate object than the trees shown in the examples in Chapter 2, and each deduction-tree in that chapter should be regarded as an abbreviation for a deduction as defined below.

9C1 Definition (TA$_\lambda$-deductions) TA$_\lambda$-deductions are labelled trees defined as follows, each node carrying two labels, a TA$_\lambda$-formula and a position.

(i) An ***atomic*** deduction is a single node labelled with an axiom and the empty position, thus:

$$x{:}\tau \mapsto x{:}\tau \quad \bullet \quad \emptyset.$$

(ii) If Δ_1 and Δ_2 are deductions whose bottom nodes are labelled by the position $\emptyset$ and the formulae, respectively,

$$\Gamma_1 \mapsto P{:}(\sigma\rightarrow\tau), \quad \Gamma_2 \mapsto Q{:}\sigma,$$

and $\Gamma_1 \cup \Gamma_2$ is consistent, then a new deduction called $(\Delta_1\Delta_2)$ is constructed by first putting "1" on the left end of each position-label in Δ_1, then putting "2" on the left end of each position-label in Δ_2, and then placing an extra node beneath the two modified deductions, as shown below.

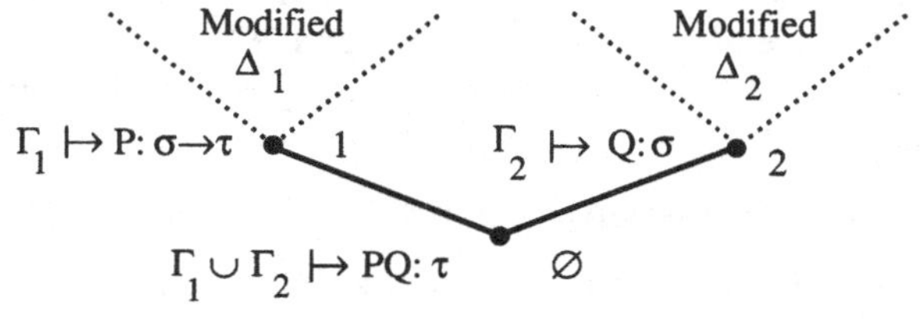

(iii) If Δ_1 is a deduction whose bottom node is labelled by the position $\emptyset$ and the formula $\Gamma \mapsto P{:}\tau$, and Γ is consistent with $x{:}\sigma$, then a new deduction called $(\lambda x \cdot \Delta_1)$

is constructed by first putting "0" on the left end of each position-label in Δ_1 and then placing an extra node beneath the modified deduction, as shown below.

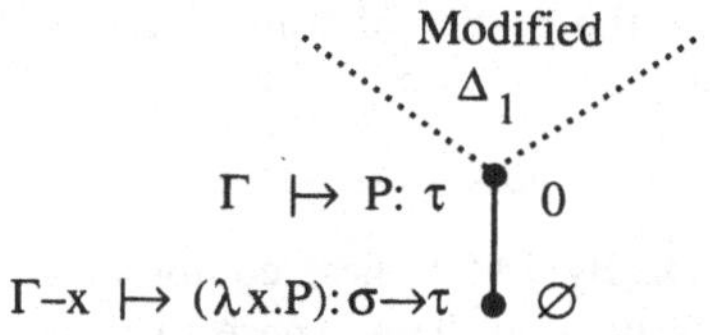

9C1.1 *Example* For examples of deductions see 2A8.2–5 and the answers to Exercises 2A8.7–8. (The deductions in those examples omit all position-labels and are displayed in the standard space-saving way using horizontal lines instead of the node-and-line way shown in the diagrams above, but this is merely a matter of representation and is not intended to conflict with the definition.)

9C1.2 *Note* If we remove contexts and types from all the TA_λ-formulae in a deduction-tree whose conclusion is $\Gamma \mapsto M{:}\tau$, it will be transformed into the construction-tree of M as defined in 9A4.

9C2 Definition The ***length***, $|\Delta|$, of a TA_λ-deduction Δ is defined thus: $|\Delta| = 1$ for atomic Δ, and for composite Δ

$$|\Delta_1\Delta_2| = |\Delta_1| + |\Delta_2|, \qquad |\lambda x{\cdot}\Delta_1| = 1 + |\Delta_1|.$$

Clearly $|\Delta| = |M|$ if the conclusion of Δ is $\Gamma \mapsto M{:}\tau$. (For $|M|$ see 1A2.)

9C3 Definition The set of all type-variables occurring in a deduction Δ will be called

$$Vars(\Delta).$$ [1]

9C4 Discussion (Replacement in a deduction) Let M contain a component $\underline{P} \equiv \langle P, p, M\rangle$ and let Δ be a TA_λ-deduction of

$$\Gamma \mapsto M{:}\tau.$$

Then from 9C1 it is easy to see that Δ contains a deduction $\Delta_{\underline{P}}$ of a formula

(1) $\quad \Gamma_{\underline{P}} \mapsto P{:}\sigma_{\underline{P}}$

for some $\Gamma_{\underline{P}}$ and $\sigma_{\underline{P}}$.

It is natural to expect that replacing P by a new term T with the same type will leave the type of M unchanged. But the types of P, T and M all depend on contexts: Γ for M, $\Gamma_{\underline{P}}$ for P, and an unspecified one for T. So our expectation is imprecise. It will be made precise and proved in the two replacement lemmas below.

[1] Warning: deductions Δ contain term-variables as well as type-variables but only the latter are included in $Vars(\Delta)$.

The first step towards precision is to clarify the relationship between $\Gamma_{\underline{P}}$ and Γ. If $\underline{P}$ is not in the body of a λ-abstract in M then clearly

(2) $\qquad \Gamma_{\underline{P}} \subseteq \Gamma$.

But now suppose $\underline{P}$ is in the bodies of some λ-abstracts in M; say there are n distinct such abstracts:

$$\underline{\lambda x_1 {\cdot} N_1}, \ldots, \underline{\lambda x_n {\cdot} N_n},$$

with $\underline{P}$ in $\underline{N_i}$ for $i = 1, \ldots, n$. By 9A5.1 these components must be linearly ordered by the relation "*is in*"; by renaming them if necessary, we can assume that

$$\underline{P} \textit{ is in } \underline{N_1} \textit{ in } \underline{\lambda x_1 {\cdot} N_1} \textit{ in } \underline{N_2} \textit{ in } \underline{\lambda x_2 {\cdot} N_2} \ldots \textit{in } \underline{N_n} \textit{ in } \underline{\lambda x_n {\cdot} N_n}.$$

By the subject-construction theorem (2B2) Δ must contain n applications of ($\rightarrow$I) below (1), and each of these has one of the following forms, depending on whether $x_i \in FV(N_i)$ or not:

(3) $$\frac{\Gamma_i, x_i{:}\xi_i \;\mapsto\; N_i{:}\eta_i}{\Gamma_i \;\mapsto\; (\lambda x_i {\cdot} N_i){:}\xi_i \rightarrow \eta_i}, \qquad \frac{\Gamma_i \;\mapsto\; N_i{:}\eta_i}{\Gamma_i \;\mapsto\; (\lambda x_i {\cdot} N_i){:}\xi_i \rightarrow \eta_i}.$$

(Here $1 \leq i \leq n$.) Hence

(4) $\qquad \Gamma_{\underline{P}} \subseteq \Gamma \cup \{x_1{:}\xi_1, \ldots, x_n{:}\xi_n\}$.

If M has no bound-variable clashes then $x_1, \ldots, x_n$ are distinct and the right-hand side of (4) is consistent. (But if M has bound-variable clashes an $x_i{:}\xi_i$ might be inconsistent with an $x_j{:}\xi_j$ ($j \neq i$) or even with a member of Γ.)

The replacement lemmas will now be stated. The first one is easy and is used in proving the subject-reduction theorem (2C1). The second is more complex to state but gives a stronger result; it is applied in 5B2.1(ii) which is used in 8F2.

9C5 First Replacement Lemma for Deductions *Let Δ be a* TA$_\lambda$*-deduction of the formula $\Gamma \mapsto M{:}\tau$ and let M contain a component $\underline{P}$ with a position p. Then Δ contains a deduction $\Delta_{\underline{P}}$ of a formula with form*

$$\Gamma_{\underline{P}} \;\mapsto\; P{:}\sigma_{\underline{P}}$$

for some $\Gamma_{\underline{P}}$ and $\sigma_{\underline{P}}$; let $\{T/P\}_p M$ be the result of replacing P at p by a term T such that

$$\Gamma_T \;\vdash_\lambda\; T{:}\sigma_{\underline{P}}$$

for some $\Gamma_T \subseteq \Gamma_{\underline{P}}$. Then

$$\Gamma \;\vdash_\lambda\; \{T/P\}_p M{:}\tau.$$

Proof Let $\Gamma_T^* \equiv \Gamma_T \restriction T$. Then $Subjects(\Gamma_T^*) \doteq FV(T)$ and by 2A11(i) there is a deduction Δ_T of

$$\Gamma_T^* \;\mapsto\; T{:}\sigma_{\underline{P}}.$$

Replace $\Delta_{\underline{P}}$ by Δ_T in Δ and modify the contexts and subjects in all the formulae below $\Delta_{\underline{P}}$ accordingly. Since $\Gamma_T \subseteq \Gamma_{\underline{P}}$ none of these modifications enlarges a context, so no inconsistencies are introduced. Therefore

$$\Gamma \vdash_\lambda \{T/P\}_p M{:}\tau. \qquad \square$$

9C6 Second Replacement Lemma for Deductions *Let $\Delta, M, \underline{P}$ be as in the first replacement lemma, and let $\{T/P\}_p M$ be the result of replacing P at p by a term T such that*

(i) $\quad \Gamma_T \vdash_\lambda T{:}\sigma_{\underline{P}}$

for some Γ_T such that

(ii) $\quad \Gamma_T \cup \Gamma \cup \{x_1{:}\xi_1, \ldots, x_n{:}\xi_n\}$ *is consistent,*

where $x_1, \ldots, x_n$ $(n \geq 0)$ are the binding variables of the λ-abstracts in M whose bodies contain $\underline{P}$, and $\xi_1, \ldots, \xi_n$ are their types in Δ (see 9C4 *for details). Then*

(iii) $\quad \Gamma \cup \Gamma_T \vdash_\lambda \{T/P\}_p M{:}\tau.$

Proof Just as in the previous lemma, by 2A11(i) we can assume $\mathit{Subjects}(\Gamma_T) = FV(T)$. Replace $\Delta_{\underline{P}}$ by Δ_T in Δ and modify the contexts and subjects in all the formulae below $\Delta_{\underline{P}}$ accordingly. No inconsistencies will be introduced, because by 9C4(4) the only variables not in Γ that could cause problems are $x_1, \ldots, x_n$. $\square$

9C6.1 *Corollary The conclusion of Lemma* 9C6 *also holds if instead of* 9C6(ii) *we assume that $\Gamma \cup \Gamma_T$ is consistent and none of $x_1, \ldots, x_n$ occurs free in T.*

Proof If $\mathit{Subjects}(\Gamma_T) = FV(T)$ the above assumption implies that Γ_T satisfies 9C6 (ii). $\square$

9D The structure of a type

This section and the next give two alternative approaches to the structure of an arbitrary type. The approach in the next section is used in Chapter 8; that in this one is more basic and is included mainly as a contrast and introduction to the other approach.

From the viewpoint of logical order the present section fits between 2A2 and 2A3.

9D1 Definition (Occurs, occurrence) Here ***positions*** are the same as in 9A1; however, positions containing $*$ are not needed in the present section. The phrase "***σ occurs in τ at position p***" is defined thus (cf. 9A2):

(i) τ occurs in τ at position $\emptyset$;
(ii) if $\sigma_1 \to \sigma_2$ occurs in τ at p, then σ_i occurs in τ at pi $(i = 1, 2)$.

A triple $\langle \sigma, p, \tau \rangle$ such that σ occurs in τ at p is called an ***occurrence*** of σ in τ, or a ***component*** of τ. A type that occurs in τ is called a ***subtype*** of τ.

9D1.1 *Notation* An occurrence $\langle \sigma, p, \tau \rangle$ may be called simply "$\underline{\sigma}$" when no confusion is likely.

Recall from 2A2 that the number of occurrences of variables in τ is called $|\tau|$ and the set of these variables is called $Vars(\tau)$. The set of all variables occurring in a finite sequence $\langle \tau_1, \ldots, \tau_n \rangle$ will be called

$$Vars(\tau_1, \ldots, \tau_n).$$

9D2 Definition (Construction-tree of a type) The ***construction-tree*** of a type τ is a labelled tree showing how τ is built up (cf. the tree of a term in 9A4). Each node has two labels, a type and a position, and the tree is defined thus:

(i) If τ is an atom, say $\tau \equiv e$, its tree has just one node:

$$e \bullet \emptyset.$$

(ii) If $\tau \equiv \rho{\to}\sigma$, its tree is built from the trees for ρ and σ by first putting "1" on the left end of each position-label in the tree for ρ, next putting "2" on the left end of each position-label in the tree for σ, and then placing an extra node beneath the two modified trees, thus:

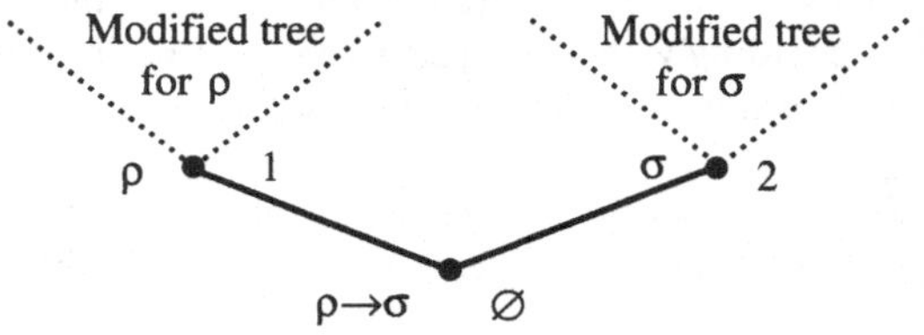

9D2.1 *Example* Let $\tau \equiv (a{\to}(b{\to}c)){\to}((a{\to}b){\to}(a{\to}c))$; its tree is as shown in Fig. 9D2.1a.

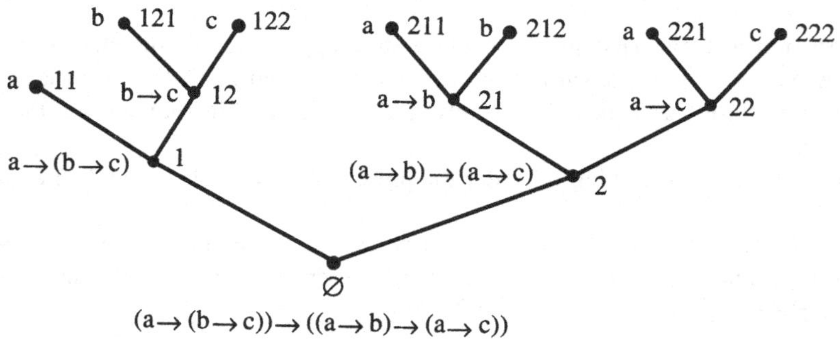

Fig. 9D2.1a.

9D3 Definition (Positive and negative occurrences) Let $\underline{\sigma} \equiv \langle \sigma, p, \tau \rangle$ be an occurrence of σ. We call $\underline{\sigma}$ ***positive*** (and say that σ ***occurs positively*** in τ) iff $p = \emptyset$ or the number of 1's in p is even. We call $\underline{\sigma}$ ***negative*** and say that σ ***occurs negatively*** in τ iff the number of 1's in p is odd.

9D3.1 *Example* The positive occurrences in the type τ shown in Example 9D2.1 are

$$\langle\tau,\emptyset,\tau\rangle,\quad \langle a,11,\tau\rangle,\quad \langle b,121,\tau\rangle,\quad \langle(a\to b)\to(a\to c),2,\tau\rangle,$$
$$\langle a,211,\tau\rangle,\quad \langle a\to c,22,\tau\rangle,\quad \langle c,222,\tau\rangle.$$

All other occurrences in this type τ are negative.

The reader familiar with the usual concept of positive and negative occurrences in propositional logic can easily check that the above definition agrees with it.

9E The condensed structure of a type

The present section analyses the structure of an arbitrary type in a more compact way than the last, and computes a bound on the number of its components of a certain kind. This bound is used in the proof of 8F3.

The starting point is a remark in 8B1 that every type τ can be expressed uniquely in the form

(1) $\tau_1\to\ldots\to\tau_m\to e$

where $m \geq 0$ and e is an atom. In this section we shall view a type as having been built up from its atoms by the operation of constructing (1) from $\tau_1,\ldots,\tau_m$ and e instead of the more usual operation of constructing $(\rho\to\sigma)$ from ρ and σ. Corresponding to this new view a new construction-tree of a type can be defined that is more condensed than the usual one and in which there is no bound on the number of branches that may start from a node. The following definitions formalize this view.

9E1 Notation Just as in 9A1, a ***position*** is any finite (perhaps empty) string $p = i_1\ldots i_m$ of integers and $*$'s such that $i_1,\ldots,i_{m-1} \neq *$. The present section will use the notation of 9A1, with the following exceptions:

if $m \geq 1$ and $i_m \neq *$, p will be called a ***premise*** position;

if $m \geq 1$ and $i_m = *$, p will be called a ***conclusion*** or ***tail*** position.

9E2 Definition (Condensed tree of a type) The ***condensed construction-tree*** of a type τ is defined by induction on $|\tau|$, thus. (Each of its nodes is labelled with a type and a position.)

(i) If τ is an atom e, its condensed tree is a single node:

$$e \bullet \emptyset.$$

(ii) If $\tau \equiv \tau_1\to\ldots\tau_m\to e$ $(n \geq 1)$, construct its condensed tree from the condensed trees of $\tau_1,\ldots,\tau_m$ by first replacing each position-label p in the tree of τ_i by

$(m+1-i)p$ (for $i = 1,\ldots,m$), and then combining the modified trees as follows:

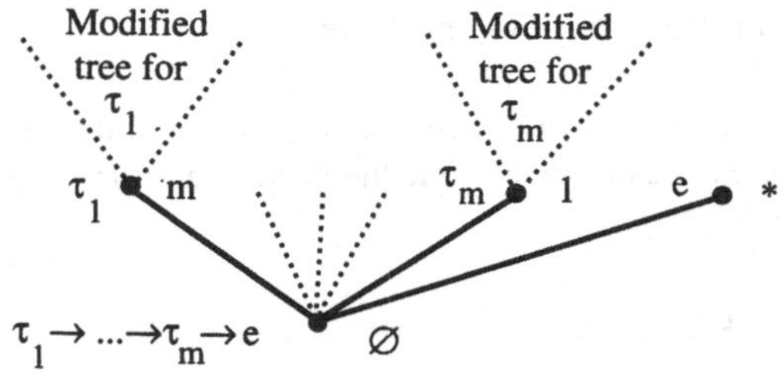

9E2.1 *Note* The use of $(m+1-i)p$ in (ii) above has the effect of assigning positions to $\tau_1,\ldots,\tau_m$ backwards, giving position 1 to τ_m, 2 to $\tau_{m-1},\ldots$, and m to τ_1. This makes it easier to relate positions in the condensed tree of $\sigma\to\tau$ to those of σ and τ, though we shall not need this facility in this book.

As an example, Fig. 9E2.1a shows the condensed tree for the type

$$\begin{aligned}\tau &\equiv (a\to(b\to c))\to((a\to b)\to(a\to c))\\ &\equiv (a\to b\to c)\to(a\to b)\to a\to c.\end{aligned}$$

9E3 Definition (S-subtypes) The ***significant subtypes*** or ***s-subtypes*** of a type τ are the types that label the nodes in the condensed tree of τ. A ***proper*** s-subtype of τ is an s-subtype $\not\equiv \tau$.

9E3.1 *Example* The s-subtypes of the type τ in Fig. 9E2.1a are

$$a, \quad b, \quad c, \quad a\to b\to c, \quad a\to b, \quad \tau.$$

Note that although $b\to c$ is a subtype of τ in the usually accepted sense (9D1) it is not an s-subtype because it does not correspond to a node on the condensed tree.

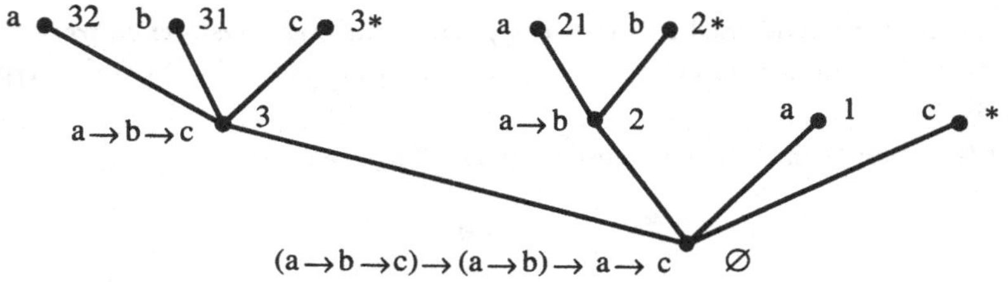

Fig. 9E2.1a.

9E4 Definition (S-components) Iff a node on the condensed tree of τ is labelled with a type σ and a position p we call the triple $\langle\sigma, p, \tau\rangle$ an ***s-component*** of τ. (Thus an s-component is a particular occurrence of an s-subtype.)

9E4.1 *Notation* S-components are distinguished from s-subtypes by underlining their names. The phrases "$\underline{\rho}$ ***contains*** $\underline{\sigma}$", "$\underline{\rho}$ ***properly contains*** $\underline{\sigma}$" etc. are defined here as in 9A5.

9E5 Definition (Premises, tail) If $\underline{\rho}$ is a composite s-component of a type τ and $\rho \equiv \rho_1 \to \ldots \to \rho_m \to a$ ($m \geq 1$), the s-components $\underline{\rho}_1, \ldots, \underline{\rho}_m$ are called the ***premises*** of $\underline{\rho}$ and $\underline{a}$ is called the ***conclusion*** or ***tail-component*** of $\underline{\rho}$, or just

$$Tail(\underline{\rho}).$$

9E5.1 *Lemma Two distinct s-components of a type τ cannot have the same tail-component.*

Proof Induction on $|\tau|$, using the fact that if $\tau \equiv \tau_1 \to \ldots \to \tau_m \to e$ the only s-components containing $\underline{e}$ are τ and $\underline{e}$, and $\underline{e}$ is not the tail of itself because atoms do not have tails (by 9E5). □

9E5.2 *Warning* The above lemma does not say that the tails of two distinct s-components $\underline{\rho}$ and $\underline{\sigma}$ cannot be occurrences of the same atom. That is, using the $\cong$-notation of (iv), the lemma forbids $Tail(\underline{\rho}) \equiv Tail(\underline{\sigma})$ but does not forbid $Tail(\underline{\rho}) \cong Tail(\underline{\sigma})$.

9E6 Definition (Subpremises, subtails) An s-component of τ is called a ***subpremise*** or ***subtail*** of τ according as it is a premise or tail of another s-component of τ. The sets of all subpremises and all subtails of τ will be called, respectively,

$$Subpremises(\tau), \qquad Subtails(\tau).$$

9E6.1 *Example* The type $\tau \equiv (a\to b\to c)\to(a\to b)\to a\to c$ in Fig. 9E2.1a has six subpremises, namely all three $\underline{a}$'s and

$$\langle a\to b\to c, 3, \tau\rangle, \quad \langle a\to b, 2, \tau\rangle, \quad \langle b, 31, \tau\rangle.$$

It has three subtails, namely

$$\langle b, 2*, \tau\rangle, \quad \langle c, 3*, \tau\rangle, \quad \langle c, *, \tau\rangle.$$

9E6.2 *Notes* (i) A proper s-component $\underline{\sigma} = \langle\sigma, p, \tau\rangle$ ($p \neq \emptyset$) is a subpremise iff p is a premise position and a subtail iff p is a tail position.

(ii) Each s-component of τ is either a subtail, an atomic subpremise, a composite subpremise, or τ itself, and cannot be more than one of these.

(iii) If τ is composite, its leftmost atom-occurrence is a subpremise and its rightmost is a subtail.

(iv) An atom has no subpremises or subtails.

9E6.3 *Lemma* *If τ is composite, then*

(i) $\#(Subtails(\tau))$	$=$	*no. of composite s-components of* τ,
(ii)	$=$	$1 +$ *no. of composite subpremises of* τ,
(iii)	$=$	$\lvert\tau\rvert -$ *no. of atomic subpremises of* τ,
(iv)	$\leq$	$\lvert\tau\rvert - 1$,
(v) $\#(Subpremises(\tau))$	$=$	$\lvert\tau\rvert - 1$,
(vi) *no. of s-components of* τ	$\leq$	$2\lvert\tau\rvert - 1$.

Proof For (i): use 9E5.1. For (ii): each composite s-component is either a subpremise or τ itself. For (iii): use 9E6.2(ii). For (iv): use 9E6.2(iii). For (v): subtract (iii) from (ii). For (vi): use 9E6.2(ii), adding (iv) to (v) and adding 1 for τ itself. □

9E7 Definition ***Order***(τ), the ***order*** of τ, is $1 +$ the length of the longest position on the condensed tree of τ. In detail: $Order(e) = 1$ for atoms e, and for composite types

$$Order\ (\tau_1 \to \ldots \to \tau_m \to e) \ = \ 1 + \mathrm{Max}\ \{Order(\tau_1), \ldots, Order(\tau_m)\}.$$

9E7.1 *Example* $Order((a \to b \to c) \to (a \to b) \to a \to c) = 3$.

9E8 Definition (Positive and negative s-components) An s-component $\underline{\sigma}$ of τ is called ***positive*** or ***negative*** according as the number of non-asterisk symbols in its position is even or odd. If $\underline{\sigma}$ is positive we say σ ***occurs positively*** in τ, otherwise σ ***occurs negatively*** in τ.

9E8.1 *Example* If $\tau \equiv (a \to b \to c) \to (a \to b) \to a \to c$, see Fig. 9E2.1a, its positive s-components are

$$\langle \tau, \emptyset, \tau \rangle, \quad \langle c, *, \tau \rangle, \quad \langle a, 32, \tau \rangle, \quad \langle b, 31, \tau \rangle, \quad \langle a, 21, \tau \rangle.$$

9E8.2 *Notes* (i) It is straightforward to show that an s-component $\underline{\sigma}$ is positive or negative according as the corresponding component in the more usual sense (9D3) is positive or negative.

(ii) A subpremise of τ is positive iff its position has even length. (Because the position of a subpremise contains no $*$'s.)

The following set plays a role in Chapter 8.

9E9 Definition **(*NSS*(τ))** (cf. Ben-Yelles 1979 Def. 3.36.) If τ is composite, $NSS(\tau)$ is the set of all finite sequences $\langle \sigma_1, \ldots, \sigma_n \rangle$ $(n \geq 1)$ such that τ contains a positive composite s-component with form

$$\sigma_1 \to \ldots \to \sigma_n \to a$$

for some atom a. Each member of $NSS(\tau)$ is called a ***negative subpremise-sequence*** (because it is a sequence of terms that have occurrences as negative subpremises in τ).

The set of all the members of the sequences in $NSS(\tau)$ will be called

$$\bigcup NSS(\tau).$$

9E9.1 *Example* If $\tau \equiv (a{\to}(b{\to}d{\to}c){\to}d){\to}(a{\to}b{\to}c){\to}d{\to}d$, we have

$$NSS(\tau) \;=\; \{\langle a{\to}(b{\to}d{\to}c){\to}d,\ a{\to}b{\to}c, d\rangle,\ \langle b,d\rangle\},$$
$$\bigcup NSS(\tau) \;=\; \{a{\to}(b{\to}d{\to}c){\to}d,\ a{\to}b{\to}c,\ d,\ b\}.$$

9E9.2 *Notes* (i) If τ is composite, say $\tau \equiv \tau_1{\to}\ldots{\to}\tau_m{\to}e$ $(m \geq 1)$, and each τ_i has form

$$\tau_i \;\equiv\; \tau_{i,1}{\to}\ldots{\to}\tau_{i,m_i}{\to}e_i \qquad (m_i \geq 0),$$

then

$$NSS(\tau) = \{\langle\tau_1,\ldots,\tau_m\rangle\} \cup \bigcup\{NSS(\tau_{i,j}) : 1 \leq j \leq m_i, 1 \leq i \leq m\}.$$

(ii) If τ is an atom, $NSS(\tau) = \emptyset$.

(iii) If ρ occurs positively in τ then $NSS(\rho) \subseteq NSS(\tau)$.

9E9.3 *Lemma If τ is composite, then*

(i) $\#(NSS(\tau)) \leq$ *no. of positive composite s-components of* τ,

(ii) $\qquad\qquad \leq |\tau| - 1$,

(iii) $\#(\bigcup NSS(\tau)) \leq |\tau| - 1$,

(iv) $\langle\sigma_1,\ldots,\sigma_n\rangle \in NSS(\tau) \implies n \leq |\tau| - 1$.

Proof For (i): each $\langle\sigma_1,\ldots,\sigma_n\rangle \in NSS(\tau)$ is obtained from a distinct positive composite s-component of τ. For (ii): use 9E6.3 (i) and (iv). For (iii): note that

$$\bigcup NSS(\tau) \subseteq Subpremises(\tau)$$

and use 9E6.3 (v). For (iv): use the definition of $NSS(\tau)$. □

9F Imitating combinatory logic in λ-calculus

This section is used in 6D and 7D. The converse PT theorems in 7A can be seen as completeness theorems for the rule (D) described in 7D1; but that rule is formulated for Hilbert-style axiom-based versions of logic not Natural Deduction versions, and in the correspondence between logic and types the Hilbert style corresponds more closely to combinatory logic than to λ-calculus. It is possible to describe this correspondence in a λ-context but to do so we must first use λ-terms to imitate a little of standard combinatory logic technique; this is done in the present section.

Recall the following closed λ-terms:

$$\mathbf{B} \equiv \lambda xyz{\cdot}x(yz),\quad \mathbf{B'} \equiv \lambda xyz{\cdot}y(xz),\quad \mathbf{C} \equiv \lambda xyz{\cdot}xzy,\quad \mathbf{I} \equiv \lambda x{\cdot}x,$$
$$\mathbf{K} \equiv \lambda xy{\cdot}x,\quad \mathbf{S} \equiv \lambda xyz{\cdot}xz(yz),\quad \mathbf{W} \equiv \lambda xy{\cdot}xyy.$$

9F1 Definition ($\mathbb{S}$-combinations) If $\mathbb{S}$ is a set of λ-terms, an ***$\mathbb{S}$-combination***, or ***applicative combination of members of*** $\mathbb{S}$, is a λ-term built from some or all of the members of $\mathbb{S}$ by application only. An ***$\mathbb{S}$-and-variables combination*** is an applicative combination of members of $\mathbb{S}$ and variables.

For subsets of $\{\mathbf{B}, \mathbf{B'}, \mathbf{C}, \mathbf{I}, \mathbf{K}, \mathbf{S}, \mathbf{W}\}$ the $\mathbb{S}$-combinations will be called **BCK**-*combinations*, **BCIW**-*combinations*, etc.

9F1.1 *Example* If $\mathbb{S} = \{\mathbf{B}, \mathbf{C}, \mathbf{K}\}$ then **CKK** and **B** are $\mathbb{S}$-combinations and $\mathbf{CK}x, xy$ and **CKK** are $\mathbb{S}$-and-variables combinations. But $\lambda x \cdot \mathbf{BC}$ is not an $\mathbb{S}$-combination or an $\mathbb{S}$-and-variables combination.

The theory called combinatory logic was originally developed from the idea that λ-abstraction can be imitated by building combinations of a very limited set of operators called *basic combinators.* (See HS 86 Ch. 2.) In many accounts of the theory just two basic combinators called **S** and **K** are assumed, with similar reduction-properties to the λ-terms **S** and **K** above. But the version below uses **B**, **C**, **K** and **W** instead; this makes it easier to discuss particular subsystems.

9F2 Definition For λ-terms P and Q, we shall say that P ***β-reduces to Q with strong type-invariance*** iff

(i) $P \rhd_\beta Q$,
(ii) $FV(P) = FV(Q)$,
(iii) *for all* Γ *and* τ, $\Gamma \vdash_\lambda P{:}\tau \iff \Gamma \vdash_\lambda Q{:}\tau$.

We shall say P ***β-converts to Q with strong type-invariance*** iff $P =_\beta Q$ and (ii) and (iii) hold.

9F3 Combinatory Completeness Theorem *There is an algorithm which accepts any λ-term M and constructs a* **BCKW**-*and-variables combination M^* which β-reduces to M with strong type-invariance.*

Proof The algorithm will construct M^* by induction on $|M|$. If M is a variable choose $M^* \equiv M$.

If $M \equiv NP$ and N^* and P^* have been constructed, choose $M^* \equiv N^*P^*$. (To see that N^*P^* satisfies 9F2 (iii), use the induction hypothesis and the subject-construction theorem, 2B2(iii).)

Now assume $M \equiv \lambda xN$ and N^* has been constructed. By the induction hypothesis,

(1) $FV(\lambda x \cdot N^*) = FV(M), \qquad \lambda x \cdot N^* \rhd_\beta M.$

Also, by the subject-construction theorem (2B2), $\Gamma \vdash_\lambda M{:}\tau$ iff $\tau \equiv \rho \to \sigma$ for some ρ and σ such that

$$\Gamma, x{:}\rho \vdash_\lambda N{:}\sigma$$

and by the induction hypothesis the latter is equivalent to

(2) $\Gamma, x{:}\rho \vdash_\lambda N^*{:}\sigma.$

We cannot simply choose $M^* \equiv \lambda xN^*$ because this is not an applicative combination. Instead, an applicative combination called "$[x] \cdot N^*$" will be constructed, such that

(3) $FV([x] \cdot N^*) = FV(N^*) - \{x\},$
(4) $[x] \cdot N^* \rhd_\beta \lambda x \cdot N^*,$
(5) $\Gamma \vdash_\lambda ([x] \cdot N^*){:}\tau \iff \tau \equiv \rho \to \sigma$ *and* $\Gamma, x{:}\rho \vdash_\lambda N^*{:}\sigma.$

Then M^* will be chosen to be $[x] \cdot N^*$ and 9F2 (i)–(iii) will follow from (1)–(5).

Before constructing $[x]\cdot N^*$, define

$$(6) \qquad I^* \equiv \mathbf{CKK}, \qquad S^* \equiv \mathbf{B(B(BW)C)(BB)}.$$

It is routine to check that I^* and S^* β-reduce to **I** and **S** with strong type-invariance.

Then $[x]\cdot N^*$ is constructed by the following algorithm (from Curry and Feys 1958 §6A3, omitting (c)).

(a) *If* $x \notin FV(N^*)$:	$[x]\cdot N^*$	$\equiv$	$\mathbf{K}N^*$;
(b) *if* $N^* \equiv x$:	$[x]\cdot N^*$	$\equiv$	I^*;
(d) *if* $N^* \equiv PQ, x \notin FV(P), x \in FV(Q)$:	$[x]\cdot N^*$	$\equiv$	$\mathbf{B}P([x]\cdot Q)$;
(e) *if* $N^* \equiv PQ, x \in FV(P), x \notin FV(Q)$:	$[x]\cdot N^*$	$\equiv$	$\mathbf{C}([x]\cdot P)Q$;
(f) *if* $N^* \equiv PQ, x \in FV(P), x \in FV(Q)$:	$[x]\cdot N^*$	$\equiv$	$S^*([x]\cdot P)([x]\cdot Q)$.

It is easy to see that $[x]\cdot N^*$ is defined for every applicative combination N^* of **B**, **C**, **K**, **W** and variables, and a routine induction on $|N^*|$ shows that (3)–(5) hold. □

9F4 Definition A set $\mathbb{S}$ of typable closed λ-terms is called a ***typable basis*** for a set $\mathbb{L}$ of λ-terms iff there is an algorithm that accepts any member of $\mathbb{L}$ and constructs an $\mathbb{S}$-and-variables combination M^* which β-reduces to M with strong type-invariance.

9F5 Partial Completeness Theorem (i) $\{\mathbf{B}, \mathbf{C}, \mathbf{I}, \mathbf{W}\}$ *is a typable basis for the set of all λI-terms (defined in* 1D1).

(ii) $\{\mathbf{B}, \mathbf{C}, \mathbf{K}\}$ *is a typable basis for the set of all BCK λ-terms* (1D2).

(iii) $\{\mathbf{B}, \mathbf{C}, \mathbf{I}\}$ *is a typable basis for the set of all BCI λ-terms* (1D3).

Proof (i) Modify the algorithm given in 9F3 by omitting (a) and replacing I^* by **I** in (b).

(ii) Modify the algorithm in 9F3 by omitting (f).

(iii) In 9F3, omit (a) and (f) and replace I^* by **I** in (b). □

Answers to starred exercises

2A8.7 Recall that (i) $\mathbf{B}' \equiv \lambda xyz.y(xz)$; (ii) $\mathbf{C} \equiv \lambda xyz\cdot xzy$; (iii) $\mathbf{S} \equiv \lambda xyz\cdot xz(yz)$; (iv) $\mathbf{W} \equiv \lambda xy\cdot xyy$; the deductions are:

$$\dfrac{\dfrac{y:b\to c \;\mapsto\; y:b\to c \qquad \dfrac{x:a\to b \;\mapsto\; x:a\to b \qquad z:a \;\mapsto\; z:a}{x:a\to b,\ z:a \;\mapsto\; xz:b}\,(\to\mathrm{E})}{x:a\to b,\ y:b\to c,\ z:a \;\mapsto\; y(xz):c}\,(\to\mathrm{E})}{\mapsto\; (\lambda xyz\cdot y(xz)):(a\to b)\to(b\to c)\to a\to c}\,(\to\mathrm{I})\ \text{ 3 times}$$

$$\dfrac{\dfrac{\dfrac{x:a\to b\to c \;\mapsto\; x:a\to b\to c \qquad z:a \;\mapsto\; z:a}{x:a\to b\to c,\ z:a \;\mapsto\; xz:b\to c}\,(\to\mathrm{E}) \qquad y:b \;\mapsto\; y:b}{x:a\to b\to c,\ y:b,\ z:a \;\mapsto\; xzy:c}\,(\to\mathrm{E})}{\mapsto\; (\lambda xyz\cdot xzy):(a\to b\to c)\to b\to a\to c}\,(\to\mathrm{I})\ \text{ 3 times}$$

$$\dfrac{\dfrac{\dfrac{x:a\to b\to c \mapsto x:a\to b\to c \quad z:a \mapsto z:a}{x:a\to b\to c,\ z:a \mapsto xz:b\to c}\,(\to\mathrm{E}) \qquad \dfrac{y:a\to b \mapsto y:a\to b \quad z:a \mapsto z:a}{y:a\to b,\ z:a \;\mapsto\; yz:b}\,(\to\mathrm{E})}{x:a\to b\to c,\ y:a\to b,\ z:a \mapsto xz(yz):c}\,(\to\mathrm{E})}{\mapsto\; (\lambda xyz\cdot xz(yz)):(a\to b\to c)\to(a\to b)\to a\to c}\,(\to\mathrm{I})\ \text{ 3 times}$$

$$\dfrac{\dfrac{\dfrac{x:a\to a\to b \;\mapsto\; x:a\to a\to b \qquad y:a \;\mapsto\; y:a}{x:a\to a\to b,\ y:a \;\mapsto\; xy:b}\,(\to\mathrm{E}) \qquad y:a \;\mapsto\; y:a}{x:a\to a\to b,\ y:a \;\mapsto\; xyy:b}\,(\to\mathrm{E})}{\mapsto\; (\lambda xy\cdot xyy):(a\to a\to b)\to a\to b}\,(\to\mathrm{I})\ \text{ twice}$$

2A8.8 The deductions are too wide to show in full here, so the context and arrow will be omitted from each formula. (This cannot be done for arbitrary deductions without ambiguity but those below are simple enough.) First note that, by deductions like 2A8.3,

$$\vdash \mathbf{I} : (a\to b)\to a\to b, \qquad \vdash \mathbf{I} : c\to c$$

(i) Let $M \equiv \lambda vxyz\cdot v(y(vxz))$ and $P \equiv M\mathbf{I}$.

$$\dfrac{\dfrac{\dfrac{v:(a\to b)\to a\to b \qquad \dfrac{y:b\to a\to b \qquad \dfrac{\dfrac{v:(a\to b)\to a\to b \quad x:a\to b}{vx:a\to b}\,(\to\mathrm{E}) \qquad z:a}{vxz:b}\,(\to\mathrm{E})}{y(vxz):a\to b}\,(\to\mathrm{E})}{v(y(vxz)):a\to b}\,(\to\mathrm{E})}{M:((a\to b)\to a\to b)\to(a\to b)\to(b\to a\to b)\to a\to a\to b}\,(\to\mathrm{I})\ \ 4\text{ times} \qquad \mathbf{I}:(a\to b)\to a\to b}{M\mathbf{I}:(a\to b)\to(b\to a\to b)\to a\to a\to b}$$

(ii) Let $Q \equiv \lambda xyz\cdot\mathbf{I}(y(\mathbf{I}xz))$.

$$\dfrac{\dfrac{\mathbf{I}:c\to c \qquad \dfrac{y:b\to c \qquad \dfrac{\dfrac{\mathbf{I}:(a\to b)\to a\to b \quad x:a\to b}{\mathbf{I}x:a\to b}\,(\to\mathrm{E}) \qquad z:a}{\mathbf{I}xz:b}\,(\to\mathrm{E})}{y(\mathbf{I}xz):b}\,(\to\mathrm{E})}{\mathbf{I}(y\mathbf{I}xz)):c}\,(\to\mathrm{E})}{(\lambda xyz\cdot\mathbf{I}(y(\mathbf{I}xz))):(a\to b)\to(b\to c)\to a\to c}\,(\to\mathrm{I})\ \ 3\text{ times}$$

2B3.2 (T. Coquand, informal correspondence 1993.) Let $\Gamma \mapsto M:\tau$ be the conclusion of Δ and Δ'. Then M has a β-nf $M*$ by WN (2D5), and by 1B9 there is a leftmost reduction ρ from M to $M*$. Such a reduction consists of the following successive parts (each of which may be empty):

(1) A reduction (called a *head reduction of order* 0) in which each step has form

$$(\lambda y\cdot P)QR_1\ldots R_k \ \rhd_1\ ([Q/y]P)R_1\ldots R_k \qquad (k \geq 0).$$

(2) A series of reductions $\rho_1,\ldots,\rho_m$ $(m \geq 0)$, where ρ_i has form

$$\lambda x_1\ldots x_i\cdot N \ \rhd\ \lambda x_1\ldots x_i\cdot N'$$

where $N \rhd N'$ by a head reduction of order 0. (We call ρ_i a *head reduction of order i*.)

(3) A reduction (called an *internal reduction*) with form

$$\lambda x_1\ldots x_m\cdot yN_1\ldots N_n \ \rhd\ \lambda x_1\ldots x_m\cdot yN_1*\ldots N_n* \ \equiv\ M*,$$

where $N_i \rhd N_i*$ by a leftmost reduction, for $i = 1,\ldots,n$.

By the proof of the Subject-reduction theorem 2C1, Δ and Δ' reduce to deductions of

$$\Gamma * \;\mapsto\; M*:\tau, \qquad \Gamma' * \;\mapsto\; M*:\tau,$$

for some $\Gamma * \subseteq \Gamma$ and $\Gamma' * \subseteq \Gamma$. (Reducing a deduction is like reducing a typed term, 5B8.) But $\Gamma * = \Gamma' * = \Gamma$, because $FV(M*) = FV(M)$ since reductions of λI-terms do not cancel, and so

$$Subjects(\Gamma *) = Subjects(\Gamma' *) = FV(M*) = FV(M) = Subjects(\Gamma).$$

Hence by 2B4, Δ and Δ' both reduce to the same deduction.

Now prove $\Delta \equiv \Delta'$ by induction on $|M*|$ with an induction on the length of the reduction ρ in both the basis and induction steps. (The case $\rho = \emptyset$ is 2B4.)

Basis: $M* \equiv y$. Then (2) and (3) are empty. For each step (1) in ρ, if the deduction for the right side of (1) is unique, then the types and deductions for $Q, P, R_1, \ldots, R_k$ are uniquely determined. (Note that Q occurs in $[Q/y]P$ because y occurs in P.) Hence the deduction for the left side is uniquely determined.

Induction step: $M* \equiv \lambda x_1 \ldots x_m . yN_1 * \ldots N_n *$, $m + n \geq 1$. For steps (1) use the above argument and for (2) and (3) use the hypothesis of the induction on $|M*|$.

3A6.1 Let $\mathbf{B} \equiv \lambda xyz.x(yz)$ and let Δ be any TA$_\lambda$-deduction of a type ξ for $\mathbf{B}$. By 2B2(iv) the last three steps in Δ must be applications of rule ($\rightarrow$I), with form

$$\cfrac{\cfrac{\cfrac{x:\alpha, y:\beta, z:\sigma \;\mapsto\; x(yz):\tau}{x:\alpha, y:\beta \;\mapsto\; \lambda z\cdot x(yz):\sigma\rightarrow\tau}}{x:\alpha \;\mapsto\; \lambda yz\cdot x(yz):\beta\rightarrow\sigma\rightarrow\tau}}{\mapsto\; \lambda xyz\cdot x(yz):\alpha\rightarrow\beta\rightarrow\sigma\rightarrow\tau}$$

for some $\alpha, \beta, \sigma, \tau$. Then by 2B2(iii) the step above these must be ($\rightarrow$E), and its premises must have form

$$x:\rho\rightarrow\tau \;\mapsto\; x:\rho\rightarrow\tau, \qquad y:\beta, z:\sigma \;\mapsto\; yz:\rho$$

for some ρ. Hence $\alpha \equiv \rho\rightarrow\tau$. Also by 2B2(iii) the step above $yz:\rho$ must be ($\rightarrow$E), with premises of form

$$y:\sigma\rightarrow\rho \;\mapsto\; y:\sigma\rightarrow\rho, \qquad z:\sigma \;\mapsto\; z:\sigma.$$

Hence $\beta \equiv \sigma\rightarrow\rho$, and the type assigned to $\mathbf{B}$ must have form

$$(\rho\rightarrow\tau)\rightarrow(\sigma\rightarrow\rho)\rightarrow\sigma\rightarrow\tau.$$

3B5.2 (i) $[a/b] \circ [b/a] \;\equiv\; [a/b, a/a]$. For example if $\tau \equiv a\rightarrow b$, we have

$$([a/b] \circ [b/a])(\tau) \;\equiv\; a\rightarrow a, \quad [a/b]([b/a](\tau)) \;\equiv\; [a/b](b\rightarrow b) \;\equiv\; a\rightarrow a.$$

(*Warning*: $[a/b] \circ [b/a] \not\equiv [a/a]$! To see this, apply $[a/a]$ to τ.)

(ii) Let $\mathsf{s} \equiv [\sigma_1/a_1, \ldots, \sigma_n/a_n]$. If $Range(\mathsf{s}) \cap Dom(\mathsf{s}) = \emptyset$, define

$$\mathsf{s}^*_\tau \;\equiv\; [\sigma_1/a_1] \circ \ldots \circ [\sigma_n/a_n]$$

If $Range(\mathsf{s}) \cap Dom(\mathsf{s}) \neq \emptyset$, choose distinct $b_1, \ldots, b_n \notin Range(\mathsf{s}) \cup Dom(\mathsf{s}) \cup Vars(\tau)$, and define $\sigma_i^* \equiv [b_i/a_i]\sigma_i$ for each $i \leq n$; then define

$$\mathsf{s}_\tau^* =_{\text{ext}} [a_1/b_1] \circ \ldots \circ [a_n/b_n] \circ [\sigma_1^*/a_1] \circ \ldots \circ [\sigma_n^*/a_n].$$

(*Warning*: The dependence of s_τ^* on τ is real; the definition of s_τ^* includes the clause "$b_1, \ldots, b_n \notin Vars(\tau)$" and this clause is more important than it looks: no claim is made that there is a composition s^* of single substitutions such that $\mathsf{s}^*(\tau) \equiv \mathsf{s}(\tau)$ for *all* τ.)

3C3.1 Let $\rho \equiv a\to(b\to c)$, $\tau \equiv (a\to b)\to a$, $v_0 \equiv ((b\to c)\to d)\to(b\to c)$. By 3C2.1, v_0 is a c.i. of ρ and τ. To show v_0 is most general, let v be any other c.i., say

$$v \equiv \mathsf{s}_1(a)\to(\mathsf{s}_1(b)\to\mathsf{s}_1(c)) \equiv (\mathsf{s}_2(a)\to\mathsf{s}_2(b))\to\mathsf{s}_2(a).$$

Then

$$\mathsf{s}_1(a) \equiv \mathsf{s}_2(a)\to\mathsf{s}_2(b), \qquad \mathsf{s}_2(a) \equiv \mathsf{s}_1(b)\to\mathsf{s}_1(c),$$

so

$$\mathsf{s}_1(a) \equiv (\mathsf{s}_1(b)\to\mathsf{s}_1(c))\to\mathsf{s}_2(b),$$

and hence v is an instance of v_0.

3D2.1 Let $\rho \equiv a\to(b\to b)$, $\tau \equiv (c\to c)\to a$, $\mathsf{u} \equiv [(b\to b)/a,\ b/c]$. First, u clearly unifies $\{\rho, \tau\}$. To prove that u is most general, let s be any other unifier, say

$$\mathsf{s} \equiv [\alpha/a,\ \beta/b,\ \gamma/c],$$

where

$$\alpha\to(\beta\to\beta) \equiv (\gamma\to\gamma)\to\alpha.$$

Then, by comparing the two sides of this identity, we have

$$\alpha \equiv \gamma\to\gamma, \quad \alpha \equiv \beta\to\beta.$$

Hence $\beta \equiv \gamma$ and

$$\mathsf{s} \equiv [(\beta\to\beta)/a,\ \beta/b,\ \beta/c] \equiv [\beta/b] \circ \mathsf{u}.$$

6B4.3 Respectively, $(\Delta_5)_\lambda$ and $(\Delta_6)_\lambda$ are

$$\dfrac{\dfrac{x{:}a \ \mapsto\ x{:}a}{x{:}a \ \mapsto\ (\lambda y\cdot x){:}\,a\to a}\,(\to\mathrm{I})_{\text{vac}}}{\mapsto\ (\lambda xy\cdot x){:}\,a\to a\to a}\,(\to\mathrm{I})_{\text{main}} \qquad \dfrac{\dfrac{x{:}a \ \mapsto\ x{:}a}{\mapsto\ (\lambda x\cdot x){:}\,a\to a}\,(\to\mathrm{I})_{\text{main}}}{\mapsto\ (\lambda yx\cdot x){:}\,a\to a\to a}\,(\to\mathrm{I})_{\text{vac}}$$

7A3.2 (M. W. Bunder) Choose $P \equiv (\lambda vxyz\cdot v(y(vxz)))\mathbf{I}$, $P' \equiv (\lambda vxyz.vy(x(vz)))\mathbf{I}$. Then $P =_\beta P'$, and by an easy computation

$$\begin{aligned} PT(P) &\equiv (a\to b)\to(b\to a\to b)\to a\to a\to b, \\ PT(P') &\equiv ((c\to d)\to c)\to(c\to d)\to(c\to d)\to d. \end{aligned}$$

These two types have no common substitution-instance, because if such an instance were obtained by substitutions $[\alpha/a, \beta/b]$ and $[\gamma/c, \delta/d]$ we would get

$$\alpha \equiv \gamma{\to}\delta, \qquad \alpha{\to}\beta \equiv \delta,$$

which would imply the impossible identity $\alpha \equiv \gamma{\to}\alpha{\to}\beta$.

7C7.2 (i) Let $M \equiv \mathbf{I}$ and $\tau \equiv (b{\to}b){\to}b{\to}b$. Define $\tau^\circ \equiv (a{\to}b){\to}c{\to}d$; then τ° is skeletal and changes to τ when we make the identifications $[b/a], [b/c], [b/d]$. The algorithm begins by applying the proof of 7C2, which begins by applying the proof of 7C1 to build a term whose PT is $\tau^\circ{\to}\tau^\circ$; and the procedure in that proof gives

$$I_{\tau^\circ} \equiv \lambda xy\cdot(\lambda uv\cdot\mathbf{I}(u(\mathbf{I}v)))(x((\lambda uv\cdot\mathbf{I}(u(\mathbf{I}v)))y)).$$

Then, following the proof of 7C2, the algorithm defines

$$M^+ \equiv I_{\tau^\circ}M \equiv I_{\tau^\circ}\mathbf{I}.$$

It then applies the PT algorithm to compute $\tau^+ \equiv PT(M^+)$; in fact in this case $\tau^+ \equiv \tau^\circ$ and the identifications $\mathfrak{s}_1, \dots, \mathfrak{s}_k$ in 7C7 are $[b/a], [b/c], [b/d]$ (and $k = 3$). The next step is to apply the proof of 7C5 to build three terms N_1, N_2, N_3 in turn, such that

$$\begin{aligned} PT(N_1) &\equiv [b/d]\tau^+ &&\equiv (a{\to}b){\to}c{\to}b,\\ PT(N_2) &\equiv [b/c][b/d]\tau^+ &&\equiv (a{\to}b){\to}b{\to}b,\\ PT(N_3) &\equiv [b/a][b/c][b/d]\tau^+ &&\equiv (b{\to}b){\to}b{\to}b. \end{aligned}$$

To do this, the algorithm first applies 7C4 to obtain three terms R_1, R_2, R_3 such that

$$\begin{aligned} PT(R_1) &\equiv (d{\to}f){\to}(g{\to}b){\to}((a{\to}b){\to}c{\to}d){\to}((a{\to}g){\to}c{\to}f),\\ PT(R_2) &\equiv (f{\to}c){\to}(g{\to}b_1){\to}((a{\to}b_1){\to}c{\to}b_2){\to}((a{\to}g){\to}f{\to}b_2),\\ PT(R_3) &\equiv (a{\to}f){\to}(g{\to}b_1){\to}((a{\to}b_1){\to}b_2{\to}b_3){\to}((f{\to}g){\to}b_2{\to}b_3). \end{aligned}$$

Then the algorithm defines

$$N_1 \equiv (\lambda x\cdot R_1xx)\mathbf{I}(I_{\tau^\circ}\mathbf{I}), \quad N_2 \equiv (\lambda x\cdot R_2xx)\mathbf{I}N_1, \quad N_3 \equiv (\lambda x\cdot R_3xx)\mathbf{I}N_2.$$

Finally it defines $M^* \equiv N_3$. (By the way, the algorithm is not claimed to be efficient! There exists a much shorter M^* than the one above, namely $M^* \equiv \lambda xy\cdot x(xy)$.)

(ii) Let $M \equiv \mathbf{K}$, $\tau \equiv b{\to}b{\to}b$. Define $\tau^\circ \equiv a{\to}b{\to}c$; then τ° has the 1-property and changes to τ under the identifications $[b/a], [b/c]$. The algorithm begins by applying the proof of 7C1 to build a term whose PT is $\tau^\circ{\to}\tau^\circ$; this term is

$$I_{\tau^\circ} \equiv \lambda xy\cdot(\lambda uv\cdot\mathbf{I}(u(\mathbf{I}v)))(x(\mathbf{I}y)).$$

Then, following the proof of 7C2, the algorithm defines

$$M^+ \equiv I_{\tau^\circ}M \equiv I_{\tau^\circ}\mathbf{K}$$

and computes $\tau^+ \equiv PT(M^+)$; in this case $\tau^+ \equiv a{\to}b{\to}a$ and for the identifications $\mathfrak{s}_1, \dots, \mathfrak{s}_k$ in 7C7 we have $k = 1$ and $\mathfrak{s}_1 \equiv [b/a]$. The next step is to apply 7C5's proof to build N such that

$$PT(N) \equiv [b/a]\tau^+ \equiv b{\to}b{\to}b.$$

To do this, the algorithm first applies 7C4 to obtain a term R such that

$$PT(R) \equiv (f \to a_1) \to (g \to b) \to (a_1 \to b \to a_2) \to (f \to g \to a_2),$$

and then defines $N \equiv (\lambda x \cdot Rxx)\mathbf{I}(I_{\tau} \circ \mathbf{K})$.

8A12.1 The eight regions contain the following terms in order from left to right.

Top row:	$\lambda xy \cdot xy$,	$\lambda xyz \cdot x(xyyy)z$,	$\lambda xyzu \cdot x(xyyy)zu$,	$\lambda xyzu \cdot xyzu$;
bottom row:	$\lambda x \cdot x$,	$\lambda xyz \cdot xz(xyyy)$,	$\lambda xyzu \cdot xu(xyyy)z$,	$\lambda xyzu \cdot uxyz$.

8B7 For items 1, 6, 8, 11 in Table 8B7a see 8B3–8B6. For the rest, see the answer to 8C6.4. (In item 12, $P_0 \notin Nprinc(\tau)$ since the PT of P_0 is $((a \to a) \to b) \to b$ by the PT algorithm, 3E1.)

8C6.4 For rows 6, 8 and 11 of Table 8B7a see Examples 8C6.1–3. The other rows are dealt with below. (For ease of reading, types are omitted and $x^d M$ is used for $x(x(\ldots(xM)\ldots))$ with d x's.)

1. $\mathscr{A}(\tau,0) = \{V\}$, $\mathscr{A}(\tau,1) = \emptyset$.
2. $\mathscr{A}(\tau,0) = \{V\}$, $\mathscr{A}(\tau,1) = \{\lambda x_1 \cdot x_1\}$.
3. $\mathscr{A}(\tau,0) = \{V\}$, $\mathscr{A}(\tau,1) = \{\lambda x_1 x_2 \cdot x_1\}$.
4. $\mathscr{A}(\tau,0) = \{V\}$, $\mathscr{A}(\tau,1) = \{\lambda x_1 x_2 x_3 \cdot x_1 V_1\}$, $\mathscr{A}(\tau,2) = \{\lambda x_1 x_2 x_3 \cdot x_1(x_2 V_2)\}$, $\mathscr{A}(\tau,3) = \{\lambda x_1 x_2 x_3 \cdot x_1(x_2 x_3)\}$.
5. $\mathscr{A}(\tau,0) = \{V\}$, $\mathscr{A}(\tau,1) = \{\lambda x_1 x_2 x_3 \cdot x_1 V_1 V_2\}$, $\mathscr{A}(\tau,2) = \{\lambda x_1 x_2 x_3 \cdot x_1 x_3 x_2\}$.
7. $\mathscr{A}(\tau,0) = \{V\}$, $\mathscr{A}(\tau,1) = \{\lambda x_1 x_2 \cdot x_1 V_1 V_2\}$, $\mathscr{A}(\tau,2) = \{\lambda x_1 x_2 \cdot x_1 x_2 x_2\}$.
9. $\mathscr{A}(\tau,0) = \{V\}$, $\mathscr{A}(\tau,1) = \{\lambda x_1 x_2 \cdot x_1 V_1,\ \lambda x_1 x_2 \cdot x_2\}$
   $\mathscr{A}(\tau,d) = \{\lambda x_1 x_2 \cdot x_1^d V_d,\ \lambda x_1 x_2 \cdot x_1^{d-1} x_2\}$ for all $d \geq 2$.
10. $\mathscr{A}(\tau,0) = \{V\}$, $\mathscr{A}(\tau,1) = \{\lambda x_1 x_2 \cdot x_1 V_1\}$, $\mathscr{A}(\tau,2) = \{\lambda x_1 x_2 \cdot x_1 x_2\}$.
12. $\mathscr{A}(\tau,0) = \{V\}$, $\mathscr{A}(\tau,1) = \{\lambda x \cdot x V_1\}$
    $\mathscr{A}(\tau,2) = \{\lambda x \cdot x(\lambda y_1 \cdot x V_2),\ \lambda x \cdot x(\lambda y_1 \cdot y_1)\}$
    $\mathscr{A}(\tau,3) = \{\lambda x \cdot x(\lambda y_1 \cdot y_1)\},\ \lambda x \cdot x(\lambda y_1 \cdot x(\lambda y_2 \cdot x V_3))$
    $\lambda x \cdot x(\lambda y_1 \cdot x(\lambda y_2 \cdot y_1)),\ \lambda x \cdot x(\lambda y_1 \cdot x(\lambda y_2 \cdot y_2))\}$
    $\mathscr{A}(\tau,d) = \{\lambda x \cdot x(\lambda y_1 \cdot x(\ldots(\lambda y_{d-1} \cdot x V_d)\ldots)),$
    $\lambda x \cdot x(\lambda y_1 \cdot x(\ldots(\lambda y_{d-2} \cdot x(\lambda y_{d-1} \cdot y_1))\ldots)),\ \ldots$
    $\lambda x \cdot x(\lambda y_1 \cdot x(\ldots(\lambda y_{d-2} \cdot x(\lambda y_{d-1} \cdot y_{d-1}))\ldots))\}$ for all $d \geq 4$.

8E7.3 For (iii), use (ii) and the fact that $\#(\mathscr{A}(\tau,0)) = 1$ (since $\mathscr{A}(\tau,0) = \{V^\tau\}$ by Step 0 of Algorithm 8C6).

For (i), use induction on d. The basis is trivial since $\mathscr{A}(\tau,0) = \{V^\tau\}$.

For the induction step (d to $d+1$), let $X^\tau \in \mathscr{A}(\tau,d)$ contain q metavariables where $1 \leq q \leq |\tau|^d$, and let V^ρ be one of these.

Consider Part IIa1 of Step $d+1$ of Algorithm 8C6: using the notation of IIa1, note that each suitable replacement Y_i^ρ generated by IIa1 for V^ρ contains $\leq n_i$ metavariables, where n_i is the arity of σ_i. But σ_i occurs in ρ which occurs in τ by 8E7.1, so

$$n_i \leq |\sigma_i| - 1 \leq |\tau| - 1 < |\tau|.$$

Next consider Part IIa2 in 8C6. Using the notation of IIa2, note that each suitable replacement Z_j generated by IIa2 for V^ρ contains $\leq h$ metavariables, where h_j is the arity of ζ_j. But ζ_j occurs in τ by 2B3(i), so

$$h_j \leq |\zeta_j| - 1 \leq |\tau| - 1 < |\tau|.$$

Thus each metavariable in X^τ is replaced by $< |\tau|$ new ones, so the total number of metavariables in the resulting extension of X^τ is $< q|\tau|$. Hence (i) holds.

To prove (ii), look at the above induction step in more detail. When IIa1 in 8C6 is applied to V^ρ the number of suitable replacements it generates is $\leq m$, where m is the arity of ρ. We have

$$m \leq |\rho| - 1 \leq |\tau| - 1.$$

When IIa2 in 8C6 is applied to V^ρ the number of suitable replacements it generates is $\leq t$, and by 8E7.2(ii),

$$t \leq (|\tau| - 1)Depth(X^\tau).$$

Thus the total number of suitable replacements for V^ρ is less than or equal to

$$|\tau| - 1 + (|\tau| - 1)d, < |\tau|(d + 1).$$

But there are q metavariables in X^τ, so when we apply IIa2 the total number of resulting extensions of X^τ is less than $(|\tau|(d + 1))^q$. Hence

$$\#(\mathscr{A}(\tau, d + 1)) < (|\tau|(d + 1))^q \times \#(\mathscr{A}(\tau, d)).$$

Then (ii) follows by (i).

Bibliography

References to unpublished manuscripts have been avoided as far as possible, as they are likely to be unavailable to most readers. A few have been included for historical and other reasons, however.

AHO, A. V., SETHI, R., ULLMAN, J. D. [1986] **Compilers**, Addison-Wesley Co., USA 1986.

ANDERSON, A. R., BELNAP, N. D. [1975] **Entailment, Vol. I**, Princeton University Press, USA 1975.

ANDERSON, A. R., BELNAP, N. D., DUNN, J. M. [1992] **Entailment, Vol. II**, Princeton University Press, USA 1992.

ANDREWS, P. B. [1965] **A transfinite type theory with type variables**, North-Holland Co., Netherlands 1965.

ANDREWS, P. B. [1971] *Resolution in type theory*, **J. Symbolic Logic** 36 (1971), 414–432.

ANDREWS, P. B. [1986] **An Introduction to Mathematical Logic and Type Theory; to Truth through Proof**, Academic Press, USA and UK 1986.

AVRON, A. [1988] *The semantics and proof theory of linear logic*, **Theoretical Computer Science** 57 (1988), 161–184.

AVRON, A. [1992] *Axiomatic systems, deduction and implication*, **J. Logic and Computation** 2 (1992), 51–98.

BAADER, F., SIEKMANN, J. H. [1994] *Unification theory*, in **Handbook of Logic in Artificial Intelligence, Vol. 2: Deduction Methodologies**, ed. D. M. Gabbay, C. J. Hogger, J. A. Robinson, Oxford University Press, UK 1994, pp. 41–126.

BARENDREGT, H. P. [1984] **The Lambda Calculus**, North-Holland Co., Netherlands, 2nd. edition 1984.

BARENDREGT, H. P. [1992] *Lambda calculi with types*, in **Handbook of Logic in Computer Science, Vol. 2**, ed. S. Abramsky et al., Clarendon Press, UK 1992, pp. 117–309.

BARENDREGT, H. P., COPPO, M., DEZANI, M. [1983] *A filter lambda model and the completeness of type assignment*, **J. Symbolic Logic** 48 (1983), 931–940.

BEN-YELLES, C.-B. [1979] **Type-assignment in the lambda-calculus; syntax and semantics**, thesis 1979, Mathematics Dept., University of Wales Swansea, Swansea SA2 8PP, UK.

BLOK, W. J., PIGOZZI, D. [1989] **Algebraizable Logics**, Memoirs of the American Mathematical Society No. 396 (1989), Amer. Math. Soc., Providence, R.I. 02901, USA.

de BRUIJN, N. G. [1980] *A survey of the project AUTOMATH*, in **To H. B. Curry**, ed. J. P. Seldin, J. R. Hindley, Academic Press, UK 1980, pp. 579–606.

BUNDER, M. W. [1982] *Deduction theorems for weak implicational logics*, **Studia Logica** 41 (1982), 95–108.

BUNDER, M. W. [1986] Review no. 03004, in **Zentralblatt für Mathematik** 574 (1986), 10–11, of Bunder, M. W. and Meyer, R. K. *A result for combinators, BCK logics and BCK algebras*, **Logique et Analyse** 28 (1985), 33–40.

BUNDER, M. W. [1991] *Corrections to some results for BCK logics and algebras*, **Logique et Analyse** 31 (1991), 115–122.

BUNDER, M. W. [1996] *Standardization of proofs in propositional logic*, in **Logic and Reality** (Proceedings of the 1989 conference in Christchurch, N. Z. in memory of A. N. Prior), ed. J. Copeland, Oxford University Press, UK, 1996.

BUNDER, M. W. [1993] *Theorems in classical logic are substitution instances of theorems in condensed BCI logic*, in **Substructural logics**, ed. P. Schroeder-Heister, K. Dosen, Clarendon Press, UK 1993, pp. 43–62.

CHURCH, A. [1940] *A formulation of the simple theory of types*, **J. Symbolic Logic** 5 (1940), 56–68.

CHURCH, A. [1941] **The Calculi of Lambda Conversion**, Princeton University Press, 1941. Reprinted by University Microfilms, Inc., Ann Arbor, Michigan, USA 1963.

CHURCH, A. [1951] *The weak theory of implication*, in **Kontrolliertes Denken, Untersuchungen zum Logikkalkül und zur Logik der Einzelwissenschaften (Festgabe zum 60. Geburtstag von Prof. W. Britzelmayr)**, ed. A. Menne, A. Wilhelmy, H. Angstl; publisher Kommissionsverlag Karl Alber, München 1951 (Sonderdruck); pp. 22–37.

CHURCH, A. [1976] *Schröder's anticipation of the simple theory of types*, **Erkenntnis** 10 (1976), 407–411. (Presented at the 5th Internat. Congress for the Unity of Science, 1939, and intended for publication in **J. Unified Science (Erkenntnis)** Vol. 9 which did not appear.)

CONSTABLE, R. L. [1991] *Type theory as a foundation for computer science*, in **Theoretical Aspects of Computer Software**, ed. by T. Ito, A. R. Meyer, **Lecture Notes in Computer Science**, Springer-Verlag, Germany, No. 526 (1991), 226–243.

COPPO, M. [1984] *Completeness of type-assignment in continuous lambda models*, **Theoretical Computer Science** 29 (1984), 309–324.

COPPO, M., DEZANI, M. [1978] *A new type-assignment for lambda terms*, **Archiv für Mathematische Logik** 19 (1978), 139–156.

CROSSLEY, J. N., SHEPHERDSON, J. C. [1993] *Extracting programs from proofs by an extension of the Curry-Howard process*, in **Logical Methods**, ed. J. N. Crossley, J. B. Remuel, R. A. Shore, M. E. Sweedler, Birkhäuser, Boston, Mass., USA 1993, pp. 222–288.

CURRY, H. B. [1934] *Functionality in combinatory logic*, **Proc. National Academy of Sciences of the USA** 20 (1934), 584–590.

CURRY, H. B. [1942] *The combinatory foundations of mathematical logic*, **J. Symbolic Logic** 7 (1942), 49–64.

CURRY, H. B. [1966] *Technique for evaluating principal functional character*, Notes dated March 17th. 1966, in Curry archive, Pennsylvania State University, Univ. Park, PA 16802, USA

CURRY, H. B. [1969] *Modified basic functionality in combinatory logic*, **Dialectica** 23 (1969), 83–92.

CURRY, H. B., FEYS, R. [1958] **Combinatory Logic**, Vol. I, North-Holland Co., Netherlands 1958.

CURRY, H. B., HINDLEY, J. R., SELDIN, J. P. [1972] **Combinatory Logic**, Vol. II, North-Holland Co., Netherlands 1972.

van DALEN, D. [1980] **Logic and Structure**, Springer-Verlag, Germany, 1980.

DAMAS, L. [1984] **Type Assignment in Programming Languages**, Ph.D. thesis, Computer Science Dept., University of Edinburgh, King's Buildings, Mayfield Rd., Edinburgh, UK 1984.

DAMAS, L., MILNER, R. [1982] *Principal type-schemes for functional programming languages*, in **Proc. Ninth Annual A.C.M. Symposium on the Principles of Programming Languages (P.O.P.L.), 1982**, Assoc. for Computing Machinery, New York, USA 1982, pp. 207–212.

DEKKERS, W. [1988] *Reducibility of types in typed lambda calculus*, **Information and Computation** 77 (1988), 131–137.

DILLER, J. [1968] *Zur Berechenbarkeit primitiv-rekursiver Funktionale endlicher Typen*, in **Contributions to Mathematical Logic**, ed. H.A. Schmidt et al., North-Holland Co., Netherlands 1968, pp. 109–120.

DOSEN, K. [1992a] *Modal translations in substructural logics*, **J. Philosophical Logic** 21 (1992), 283–336.

DOSEN, K. [1992b] *The first axiomatization of relevant logic*, **J. Philosophical Logic** 21 (1992), 339–356.

DRAGALIN, A. G. [1968] *The computation of primitive recursive terms of finite type, and primitive recursive realization*, **Zapiski Naucnyh Seminarov Leningradskogo Otdelenija Matematiceskogo Instituta im V.I. Steklova Akademii Nauk S.S.S.R. (L.O.M.I.)** 8 (1968), 32–45.

DWORK, C., KANELLAKIS, P. C., MITCHELL, J. C. [1984] *On the sequential nature of unification*, **J. Logic Programming** 1 (1984), 35–50.

DYCKHOFF, R. [1992] *Contraction-free sequent calculi for intuitionistic logic*, **J. Symbolic Logic** 57 (1992), 795–807.

FITCH, F. B. [1936] *A system of formal logic without an analogue to the Curry W operator*, **J. Symbolic Logic** 1 (1936), 92–100.

FORTUNE, S., LEIVANT, D., O'DONNELL, M. [1983] *The expressiveness of simple and second-order type structures*, **J. Assoc. for Computing Machinery** 30 (1980) 151–185.

GALLIER, J. H. [1990] *On Girard's "Candidats de déductibilité"*, in Odifreddi 1990, pp. 123–203.

GALLIER, J. H. [1993] *Constructive logics. Part 1: a tutorial on proof systems and typed λ-calculi*, **Theoretical Computer Science** 110 (1993), 249–339.

GANDY, R. O. [1977] *The simple theory of types*, in **Logic Colloquium** 76, ed. R. O. Gandy, M. Hyland, North-Holland Co., Netherlands 1977, pp. 173–181.

GANDY, R. O. [1980a] *An early proof of normalization by A. M. Turing*, in **To H. B. Curry**, ed. J. R. Hindley, J. P. Seldin, Academic Press, UK 1980, pp. 453–455.

GANDY, R. O. [1980b] *Proofs of strong normalization*, in **To H. B. Curry**, ed. J. R. Hindley, J. P. Seldin, Academic Press, UK. 1980, pp. 457–477.

GENTZEN, G. [1935] *Untersuchungen über das logische Schliessen*, **Math. Zeitschrift** 39 (1935), 176–210, 405–431. English transl. as *Investigations into logical deduction* in **The Collected Papers of Gerhard Gentzen**, ed. M. E. Szabo, North-Holland Co., Netherlands 1969.

GIANNINI, P., HONSELL, F., RONCHI DELLA ROCCA, S. [1993] *Type inference: some results, some problems*, **Fundamenta Informaticae** 19 (1993), 87–125.

GIRARD, J. -Y. [1987] *Linear logic*, **Theoretical Computer Science** 50 (1987), 1–101.

GIRARD, J. -Y., LAFONT, Y., TAYLOR, P. [1989] **Proofs and Types**, Cambridge University Press, UK 1989.

GLADSTONE, M. D. [1965] *Some ways of constructing a propositional calculus of any required degree of unsolvability*, **Trans. American Math. Soc.** 118 (1965), 192–210.

GRZEGORCZYK, A. [1953] **Some Classes of Recursive Functions**, Rozprawy Matematyczne, Panstwowe Wydawnictwo Naukowe, Warszawa, Poland 1953.

HAMILTON, A. [1988] **Logic for Mathematicians**, Cambridge University Press, UK 1978, revised edition 1988.

HANATANI, Y. [1966] *Calculabilité des fonctionnels recursives primitives de type fini sur les nombres naturels*, **Ann. Japan Assoc. for the Philosophy of Science** 3 (1966), 19–30. Revised version: *Calculability of the primitive recursive functionals of finite type over the natural numbers*, in **Proof Theory Symposium, Kiel 1974**, ed. by J. Diller, G. H. Müller, **Lecture Notes in Mathematics** 500 (1975), Springer-Verlag, Germany, pp. 152–163.

HANKIN, C. [1994] *Lambda Calculi*, Clarendon Press, Oxford, UK 1994.

HENKIN, L. [1950] *Completeness in the theory of types*, **J. Symbolic Logic** 15 (1950), 81–91.

HERBRAND, J. [1930] *Recherches sur la théorie de la démonstration*, **Trav. Soc. Sci. Lett. Varsovie, Classe III Sci. Math. Phys.**, No. 33 (1930), English transl. in **Jacques Herbrand Logical Writings**, ed. W.D. Goldfarb, Harvard University Press, USA 1971, pp. 44–202.

HEYTING, A. [1955] **Intuitionism, an Introduction**, North-Holland Co., Netherlands 1955 (3rd edition 1971).

HINATA, S. [1967] *Calculability of primitive recursive functionals of finite type*, **Sci. Report Tokyo Kyoiku Daigaku**, Section A, 9 (226) (1967), 42–59.

HINDLEY, J. R. [1969] *The principal type-scheme of an object in combinatory logic*, **Trans. American Math. Soc.** 146 (1969), 29–60.

HINDLEY, J. R. [1983a] *The completeness theorem for typing λ-terms*, **Theoretical Computer Science** 22 (1983), 1–17.

HINDLEY, J. R. [1983b] *Curry's type-rules are complete with respect to the F-semantics too*, **Theoretical Computer Science** 22 (1983), 127–133.

HINDLEY, J. R. [1989] *BCK-combinators and linear λ-terms have types*, **Theoretical Computer Science** 64 (1989), 97–106.

HINDLEY, J. R. [1992] *Types with intersection, an introduction*, **Formal Aspects of Computing** 4 (1992), 470–486.

HINDLEY, J. R. [1993] *BCK and BCI logics, condensed detachment and the 2-property*, **Notre Dame J. Formal Logic** 34 (1993), 231–250.

HINDLEY, J. R., MEREDITH, D. [1990] *Principal type-schemes and condensed detachment*, **J. Symbolic Logic** 55 (1990), 90–105.

HINDLEY, J. R., SELDIN, J. P. [1986] [HS 86] **Introduction to Combinators and λ-calculus**, Cambridge University Press, UK 1986.

HIROKAWA, S. [1991a] *Principal type assignment to lambda terms*, **International Journal of the Foundations of Computer Science** 2 (1991), 149–162.

HIROKAWA, S. [1991b] *Principal type-schemes of BCI-lambda-terms*, in **Theoretical Aspects of Computer Software**, ed. by T. Ito, A. R. Meyer, **Lecture Notes in Computer Science**, Springer-Verlag, Germany, No. 526 (1991), 633–650.

HIROKAWA, S. [1991c] *BCK-formulas having unique proofs*, in **Category Theory and Computer Science**, ed. by D. H. Pitt et al., **Lecture Notes in Computer Science**, Springer-Verlag, Germany, No. 530 (1991), 106–120.

HIROKAWA, S. [1992a] *The converse principal type-scheme theorem in lambda calculus*, **Studia Logica** 51 (1992), 83–95.

HIROKAWA, S. [1992b] *Balanced formulas, BCK-minimal formulas and their proofs*, in **Logical Foundations of Computer Science – Tver '92**, ed. by A. Nerode, M. Taitslin, **Lecture Notes in Computer Science**, Springer-Verlag, Germany, No. 620 (1992), 198–208.

HIROKAWA, S. [1993a] *Principal types of BCK-lambda-terms*, **Theoretical Computer Science** 107 (1993), 253–276.

HIROKAWA, S. [1993b] *The relevance graph of a BCK-formula*, **J. Logic and Computation** 3 (1993), 269–285.

HIROKAWA, S. [1993c] *The number of proofs for an implicational formula*, **J. Symbolic Logic** 58 (1993), 1117 (abstract only; fuller MS informally circulated 1991).

HOPCROFT, J. E., ULLMAN, J. D., [1979] **Introduction to Automata Theory, Languages, and Computation**, Addison-Wesley, USA 1979.

HOWARD, W. [1969] *The formulae-as-types notion of construction*, MS 1969, publ. in **To H. B. Curry**, ed. J. R. Hindley, J. P. Seldin, Academic Press, UK 1980, pp. 479–490.

HOWARD, W. [1970] *Assignment of ordinals to terms for primitive recursive functionals of finite type*, in **Intuitionism and Proof Theory (Proc. Buffalo Conference 1968)**, ed. A. Kino, J. Myhill, R. Vesley, North-Holland Co., Netherlands, 1970, pp. 443–458.

HUDELMAIER, J. [1993] *An* O(*n*log*n*)*-space decision procedure for intuitionistic propositional logic*, **J. Logic and Computation** 3 (1993), 63–75.

HUET, G. [1975] *A unification algorithm for typed λ-calculus*, **Theoretical Computer Science** 1 (1975), 27–57.

ISEKI, K., TANAKA, S. [1978] *An introduction to the theory of BCK-algebras*, **Mathematica Japonica** 23 (1978), 1–26.

JASKOWSKI, S. [1963] *Über Tautologien, in welchen keine Variable mehr als zweimal vorkommt*, **Zeitschrift für Mathematische Logik** 9 (1963), 219–228.

KALMAN, I. A. [1982] *The two-property and condensed detachment*, **Studia Logica** 41 (1982), 173–179.

KALMAN, J. A. [1983] *Condensed detachment as a rule of inference*, **Studia Logica** 42 (1983), 443–451.

KANELLAKIS, P., MAIRSON, H., MITCHELL, J. C. [1991] *Unification and ML-type reconstruction*, in **Computational Logic, Essays in Honour of Alan Robinson**, ed. J. -L. Lassez, G. Plotkin, M.I.T. Press, Cambridge, Mass., USA 1991, pp. 444–478.

KANELLAKIS, P., MITCHELL, J. C. [1989] *Polymorphic unification and ML typing*, in **Proceedings of the 16th Annual A.C.M. Symposium on the Principles of Programming Languages (P.O.P.L), 1989**, Assoc. for Computing Machinery, New York, USA, 1989 pp. 105–113.

KFOURY, A. J., TIURYN, J., URZYCZYN, P. [1990] *ML typability is DEXPTIME-complete*, **Lecture Notes in Computer Science** 431 (1990), Springer-Verlag, Germany, pp. 206–220.

KNIGHT, K. [1989] *Unification: a multidisciplinary survey*, **A.C.M. Computing Surveys** 21 (1989), 93–124.

KOMORI, Y. [1987] *BCK algebras and lambda calculus*, in **Proc. 10th Symposium on Semigroups, Sakado 1986**, publisher Josai University, Sakado, Saitama, Japan, 1987, pp. 5–11.

KOMORI, Y. [1989] *Illative combinatory logic based on BCK-logic*, **Mathematica Japonica** 34 (1989), 585–596.

KOMORI, Y., HIROKAWA, S. [1993] *The number of proofs for a BCK-formula*, **J. Symbolic Logic** 58 (1993), 626–628.

KRIVINE, J. -L. [1990] **Lambda-calcul, types et modèles**, Masson, France, 1990. English transl. **Lambda-Calculus, Types and Models**, Ellis-Horwood, USA 1993.

LAMBEK, J., SCOTT, P. J. [1986] **Introduction to Higher-order Categorical Logic**, Cambridge University Press, UK, 1986.

LÄUCHLI, H. [1965] *Intuitionistic propositional calculus and definably non-empty terms* (abstract), **J. Symbolic Logic** 30 (1965), 263.

LEIVANT, D. [1979] *Assumption classes in natural deduction*, **Zeitschrift für Mathematische Logik** 25 (1979), 1–4.

LEMMON, E. J., MEREDITH, C. A., MEREDITH, D., PRIOR, A. N., THOMAS, I. [1957] *Calculi of pure strict implication*, mimeographed 1957, publ. in **Philosophical logic**, ed. Davis, Hockney, Wilson, D. Reidel Co., Netherlands 1969, pp. 215–250.

LUKASIEWICZ, J. [1939] *Der Äquivalenzenkalkul*, **Collectanea Logica** 1 (1939), 145–169. English transl. as *The equivalential calculus*, in **Jan Lukasiewicz Selected Works**, ed. L. Borkowski, North-Holland Co., Netherlands 1970, pp. 250–277.

MAIRSON, H. [1990] *Deciding ML typability is complete for deterministic exponential time*, in **Proceedings of the 17th Annual A.C.M. Symposium on the Principles of Programming Languages (P.O.P.L.), 1990**, Assoc. for Computing Machinery, New York, USA 1990, pp. 382–401.

MARTELLI, A., MONTANARI, U. [1982] *An efficient unification algorithm*, **A.C.M. Transactions on Programming Languages and Systems** 4 (1982), 258–282.

MARTIN-LÖF, P. [1975] *An intuitionistic theory of types: predicative part*, in **Logic Colloquium '73**, ed. H. E. Rose et al., North-Holland Co., Netherlands 1975, pp. 73–118.

MASLOV, S. [1964] *An inverse method of establishing deducibilities in the classical predicate calculus*, **Soviet Mathematics** 5 (1964), 1420–1424. (English transl. of **Doklady Akad. Nauk S.S.S.R.** 159 (1964), 17–20.)

MEGILL, N. D., BUNDER, M. W. [1996] *Weaker D-complete logics*, **Journal of the Interest Group on Propositional Logics** 4 (1996), 215–225.

MEREDITH, C. A., PRIOR, A. N. [1963] *Notes on the axiomatics of the propositional calculus*, **Notre Dame J. Formal Logic** 4 (1963), 171–187.

MEREDITH, D. [1977] *In memoriam Carew Arthur Meredith*, **Notre Dame J. Formal Logic** 18 (1977), 513–516.

MEYER, R. K., BUNDER, M. W. [1988] *Condensed detachment and combinators*, Tech. Report TR-ARP-8/88 (1988), Research School of the Social Sciences, Australian National University, Canberra, Australia.

MILNER, R. [1978] *A theory of type polymorphism in programming*, **J. Computer and System Sciences** 17 (1978), 348–375.

MINTS, G. [1979] *A primitive recursive bound of strong normalization for predicate calculus*, **Zapiski Naucnyh Seminarov Leningradskogo Otdelenija Matematiceskogo Instituta im V. I. Steklova Akademii Nauk S.S.S.R. (L.O.M.I.)** 88 (1979), 131–135 (in Russian with English summary).

MINTS, G., TAMMET, T. [1991] *Condensed detachment is complete for relevance logic: a computer-aided proof*, **J. Automated Reasoning** 7 (1991), 587–596.

MITCHELL, J. C. [1988] *Polymorphic type inference and containment*, **Information and Computation** 76 (1988), 211–249.

MITCHELL, J. C. [1990] *Type systems for programming languages*, in **Handbook of Theoretical Computer Science Vol. B, Formal Models and Semantics**, ed. J. van Leeuwen, Elsevier, Netherlands 1990, pp. 365–458.

MITCHELL, J. C. [1996] **Foundations for Programming Languages**, M.I.T. Press, USA 1996.

MITSCHKE, G. [1979] *The standardization theorem for the λ-calculus*, **Zeitschrift für Mathematische Logik** 25 (1979), 29–31.

MOH, S.-K. [1950] *The deduction theorems and two new logical systems*, **Methodos** 2 (1950), 56–75.

MORRIS, J. H. [1968] **Lambda-calculus Models of Programming Languages**, Ph.D. thesis, Massachusetts Institute of Technology, Cambridge, Mass., USA 1968.

NEDERPELT, R. P. [1973] **Strong Normalization in a Typed Lambda-calculus with Lambda-structured Types**, Ph.D. thesis, Tech. Hogeschool, Eindhoven, Netherlands 1973.

NERODE, A., ODIFREDDI, P., [199-] **Lambda Calculi and Constructive Logics**, Cornell University Press, USA, to appear 1997.

ODIFREDDI, P. [1990] (editor) **Logic and Computer Science**, Academic Press, USA 1990 (Series *APIC Studies in Data Processing* No. 31).

PATERSON, M., WEGMAN, M. [1978] *Linear Unification*, **J. Computer and System Sciences** 16 (1978), 158–167.

PLOTKIN, G. D. [1994] *A semantics for static type-inference*, **Information and Computation** 109 (1994), 256–299.

PRAWITZ, D. [1960] *An improved proof procedure*, **Theoria** 26 (1960), 102–139.

PRAWITZ, D. [1965] **Natural Deduction**, Almqvist and Wiksell, Sweden 1965.

PRIOR, A. N. [1955] **Formal Logic**, Clarendon Press, UK 1955 (2nd. edition. 1962).

RÉVÉSZ, G. [1988] **Lambda Calculus, Combinators and Functional Programming**, Cambridge University Press, UK 1988.

REYNOLDS, J. [1985] *Three approaches to type structure*, in **Mathematical Foundations of Software Development, Vol. 1 (CAAP '85)**, ed. by H. Ehrig et al., **Lecture Notes in Computer Science**, Springer-Verlag, Germany, No. 185 (1985), 97–138.

REZUS, A. [1981] **Lambda-conversion and logic**, Ph.D. thesis, Universiteit Utrecht, Math. Inst., Budapestlaan 6, de Uithof, Utrecht, Netherlands.

ROBINSON, J. A. [1965] *A machine-oriented logic based on the resolution principle*, **J. Assoc. for Computing Machinery** 12 (1965), 23–41.

ROBINSON, J. A. [1966] Review of Prawitz 1960, **J. Symbolic Logic** 31 (1966), 126–127.

ROBINSON, J. A. [1979] **Logic: Form and Function. The Mechanization of Deductive Reasoning**, Edinburgh University Press, UK 1979.

RUSSELL, B. [1903] **Principles of Mathematics**, Allen and Unwin, UK 1903. (1992 edition: Routledge and Kegan Paul, UK.)

SALLÉ, P. [1978] *Une extension de la théorie des types*, in **Automata, Languages and Programming**, ed. by G. Ausiello, C. Böhm, **Lecture Notes in Computer Science**, Springer-Verlag, Germany, No. 62 (1978), 398–410.

SANCHIS, L. E. [1967] *Functionals defined by recursion*, **Notre Dame J. Formal Logic** 8 (1967), 161–174.

SCEDROV, A. [1990] *A guide to polymorphic types*, in Odifreddi 1990, pp. 387–420.

SCHWICHTENBERG, H. [1991] *An upper bound for reduction sequences in typed lambda-calculus*, **Archiv für Math. Logik** 30 (1991), 405–408.

SELDIN, J. P. [1968] **Studies in Illative Combinatory Logic**, Ph.D. thesis, University of Amsterdam, Netherlands 1968.

SELDIN, J. P. [1977] *A sequent calculus for type assignment*, **J. Symbolic Logic** 42 (1977), 11–28.

SELDIN, J. P. [1978] *A sequent calculus formulation of type assignment with equality rules for the λβ-calculus*, **J. Symbolic Logic** 43 (1978), 643–649.

STATMAN, R. [1979a] *Intuitionistic propositional logic is polynomial-space complete*, **Theoretical Computer Science** 9 (1979), 67–72.

STATMAN, R. [1979b] *The typed λ-calculus is not elementary recursive*, **Theoretical Computer Science** 9 (1979), 73–81.

STATMAN, R. [1980] *On the existence of closed terms in the typed λ-calculus*; Part 1 in **To H.B. Curry**, ed. J.R. Hindley and J.P. Seldin, Academic Press, UK 1980, pp. 511–534; Part 2 in **Theoretical Computer Science** 15 (1981), 329–338.

STOUGHTON, A. [1988] *Substitution revisited*, **Theoretical Computer Science** 59 (1988), 317–325.

TAIT, W. W. [1965] *Infinitely long terms of transfinite type*, in **Formal Systems and Recursive Functions**, ed. J. N. Crossley, M. A. Dummett, North-Holland Co., Netherlands 1965, pp. 176–185.

TAIT, W. W. [1967] *Intensional interpretations of functionals of finite type*, **J. Symbolic Logic** 32 (1967), 198–212.

TAKAHASHI, M. H. [1991] **Theory of Computation, Computability and Lambda-calculus**, Kindai Kagaku Sha, Tokyo, Japan 1991 (in Japanese).

TAKAHASHI, M. H., AKAMA, Y., HIROKAWA, S. [1994] *Normal proofs and their grammar*, in **Theoretical Aspects of Computer Software (TACS '94)**, ed. by M. Hagiya, J. C. Mitchell, **Lecture Notes in Computer Science**, Springer-Verlag, Germany, No. 789 (1994), 465–493.

TIURYN, J. [1990] *Type inference problems: a survey*, in **Mathematical Foundations of Computer Science 1990**, ed. by B. Rovan, **Lecture Notes in Computer Science**, Springer-Verlag, Germany, No. 452 (1990), 105–120.

TROELSTRA, A. S. [1973] (editor) **Metamathematical Investigation of Intuitionistic Arithmetic and Analysis, Lecture Notes in Mathematics**, Springer-Verlag, Germany, No. 344 (1973).

TROELSTRA, A. S., van DALEN, D. [1988] **Constructivism in Mathematics, an Introduction**, Vols. 1 & 2, North-Holland Co., Netherlands 1988.

TURING, A. M. [1942] Notes published in Gandy 1980a.

TYSZKIEWICZ, J. [1988] **Complexity of Type Inference in Finitely Typed Lambda Calculus**, Master's thesis, University of Warsaw, Poland 1988.

URQUHART, A. [1984] *The undecidability of entailment and relevant implication*, **J. Symbolic Logic** 49 (1984), 1059–1073.

URQUHART, A. [1995] *The complexity of propositional proofs*, **Bull. Symbolic Logic** 1 (1995), 425–467.

DE VRIJER, R. [1987] *Exactly estimating functionals and strong normalization*, **Proc. Koninklijke Nederlandse Akademie van Wetenschappen**, Series A, 90 (1987), 479–493.

WAND, M. [1987] *A simple algorithm and proof for type inference*, **Fundamenta Informaticae** 10 (1987), 115–122.

ZAIONC, M. [1985] *The set of unifiers in typed λ-calculus as regular expression*, in **Rewriting Techniques and Applications**, ed. by J.-P. Jouannaud, **Lecture Notes in Computer Science**, Springer-Verlag, Germany, No. 202 (1985), pp. 430–440.

ZAIONC, M. [1987a] *The regular expression descriptions of unifier set in the typed λ-calculus*, **Fundamenta Informaticae** 10 (1987), 309–322.

ZAIONC, M. [1987b] *Word operations definable in the typed λ-calculus*, **Theoretical Computer Science** 52 (1987), 1–14.

ZAIONC, M. [1988] *Mechanical procedure for proof construction via closed terms in typed λ-calculus*, **J. Automated Reasoning 4** (1988), 173–190.

ZAIONC, M. [1990] *A characterization of lambda definable tree operations*, **Information and Computation** 89 (1990), 35–46.

ZAIONC, M. [199-] *Fixpoint technique for counting terms in typed λ-calculus*, **Fundamenta Informaticae** (to appear).

ZUCKER, J. [1974] *The correspondence between cut-elimination and normalization*, **Annals of Mathematical Logic** 7 (1974): *Part I*, pp. 1–112; *Part II*, pp. 113–155.

Table of principal types

This table gives a (not necessarily unique) principal inhabitant of each of some types. It gives a β-nf where possible, but if there is no normal principal inhabitant it gives a non-normal one. It includes most of the PT informatio.ı in Tables 3E2a and 8B7a.

Type	A principal inhabitant	
$a\to a$	$\lambda x\cdot x \equiv \mathbf{I}$	
$a\to b\to a$	$\lambda xy\cdot x \equiv \mathbf{K}$	
$a\to a\to a$	$(\lambda xyz\cdot\mathbf{K}(xy)(xz))\mathbf{I}$	$[Nprinc = \emptyset]$
$(a\to b)\to a\to b$	$\lambda xy\cdot xy$	
$(a\to b)\to a\to a$	$\lambda xy\cdot\mathbf{K}y(xy)$	$[Nprinc = \emptyset]$
$(a\to a)\to a\to a$	$\lambda xy\cdot x(xy)$	[and $\lambda xy\cdot x^n y$, $n \geq 2$]
$a\to(a\to b)\to a$	$\lambda xy\cdot\mathbf{K}x(yx)$	$[Nprinc = \emptyset]$
$a\to a\to b\to b$	$(\lambda xyz\cdot\mathbf{K}(xy)(xz))(\mathbf{K}I)$	$[Nprinc = \emptyset]$
$((a\to a)\to a)\to a$	$\lambda x\cdot x(\lambda y\cdot x\mathbf{I})$[for others see 8B7a(12)]	
$(a\to a\to b)\to a\to b$	$\lambda xy\cdot xyy \equiv \mathbf{W}$	
$(a\to a\to a)\to a\to a$	$\lambda xy\cdot x(xyy)y$	
$(a\to b)\to a\to a\to b$	$\lambda xyz\cdot\mathbf{K}(xy)(xz)$	$[Nprinc = \emptyset]$
$(a\to b\to c)\to b\to a\to c$	$\lambda xyz\cdot xzy \equiv \mathbf{C}$	
$(a_1\to\ldots\to a_n\to b\to c)\to b\to a_1\to\ldots\to a_n\to c$	$\lambda uvw_1\ldots w_n\cdot uw_1\ldots w_n v$	
$(a\to b)\to(c\to a)\to c\to b$	$\lambda xyz\cdot x(yz) \equiv \mathbf{B}$	
$(a\to b)\to(b\to c)\to a\to c$	$\lambda xyz\cdot y(xz) \equiv \mathbf{B}'$	
$(a\to b\to c)\to(a\to b)\to a\to c$	$\lambda xyz\cdot xz(yz) \equiv \mathbf{S}$	
$(a\to b\to b\to c)\to a\to b\to c$	$\lambda xyz\cdot xyzz$	
$(a\to b)\to(c\to d\to a)\to c\to d\to b$	$\lambda uvwx\cdot u(vwx)$	
$(a\to b)\to(c\to b\to d)\to c\to a\to d$	$\lambda uvwx\cdot vw(ux)$	
$(a\to b)\to(c_1\to\ldots c_n\to b\to d)\to c_1\to\ldots c_n\to a\to d$	$\lambda uvw_1\ldots w_n x\cdot vw_1\ldots w_n(ux)$	
$((a\to b)\to c\to a)\to(a\to b)\to c\to b$	$\lambda uvw\cdot v(uvw)$	
$(a\to a')\to(b\to b')\to(a'\to b)\to a\to b'$	$\lambda uvwx\cdot v(w(ux))$	
$(a\to b)\to(c\to d)\to c\to(d\to a)\to b$	$\lambda uvwx\cdot u(x(vw))$	
$(a\to b\to c)\to a\to(d\to b)\to d\to c$	$\lambda uvwx\cdot uv(wx)$	

Table of principal types – *continued*

Type	A principal inhabitant
$(a\to b\to c)\to a\to(c\to d)\to b\to d$	$\lambda uvwx\cdot w(uvx)$
$(a\to b\to c)\to(d\to a)\to b\to d\to c$	$\lambda uvwx\cdot u(vx)w$
$(((a\to b)\to a\to c)\to d)\to(b\to c)\to d$	$\lambda uv\cdot u(\lambda xy\cdot v(xy))$
$(((a\to b)\to c\to b)\to d)\to(c\to a)\to d$	$\lambda uv\cdot u(\lambda xy\cdot x(vy))$
$(a\to b\to c)\to(d\to a)\to(d\to b)\to d\to c$	$\lambda uvwx\cdot u(vx)(wx)$
$(a\to a')\to(b\to c\to c')\to b\to(c'\to a)\to c\to a'$	$\lambda uvwxy\cdot u(x(vwy))$
$(a\to a')\to(b\to c\to c')\to b\to(a'\to c)\to a\to c'$	$\lambda uvwxy\cdot vw(x(uy))$
$(a\to c\to c')\to(b\to c'\to c'')\to a\to b\to c\to c''$	$\lambda uvwxy\cdot vx(uwy)$
$a_1\to\ldots\to a_n\to(a_1\to\ldots\to a_n\to b)\to b$	$\lambda u_1\ldots u_n v\cdot vu_1\ldots u_n$
$(a\to b_1\to\ldots b_n\to c\to d)\to c\to b_1\ldots b_n\to a\to d$	$\lambda uvw_1\ldots w_n x\cdot uxw_1\ldots w_n v$
$(a\to b)\to((c_1\to\ldots\to c_n\to a\to d)\to e)\to$ $(c_1\to\ldots\to c_n\to b\to d)\to e$	$\lambda uvw\cdot v(\lambda x_1\ldots x_n y\cdot wx_1\ldots x_n(uy))$
$(a\to b\to c)\to((d_1\to\ldots\to d_n\to a\to e)\to f)\to$ $b\to(d_1\to\ldots\to d_n\to c\to e)\to f$	$\lambda uvwx\cdot v(\lambda y_1\ldots y_n z\cdot xy_1\ldots y_n(uzw))$

Index